A CONSERVATIVE COUP

D1395094

A Conservative Coup

the Fall of Margaret Thatcher

second edition

Alan Watkins

Duckworth

Second edition 1992
Second impression 1991
First published in 1991 by
Gerald Duckworth & Co. Ltd.
The Old Piano Factory
48 Hoxton Square, London N1 6PB

A catalogue record for this book is available
from the British Library

ISBN 0 7156 2435 0

Photoset in North Wales by
Derek Doyle & Associates, Mold, Clwyd
Printed in Great Britain by
Redwood Press Limited, Melksham

Contents

to
MAURICE COWLING

Acknowledgments

My chief debts are to Barbara Rieck and Dee Eniffer, both of the *Observer*. Mrs Rieck typed the manuscript impeccably and pressed me to make progress, asking when I would have another chapter ready. Miss Eniffer made appointments for me to see numerous MPs and others from the end of 1990 until the middle of 1991. This often turned out to be a complicated business. With saintlike patience she dealt with misunderstandings and cancellations. Without her and Mrs Rieck's help I should not have been able to complete the book when I did, or perhaps at all.

After deciding to write about the fall of Mrs Thatcher, I looked up the list of Conservative MPs in *Vacher's Parliamentary Companion* and marked the names of those to whom I could write on Christian-name terms. To my surprise, there turned out to be over a hundred of them. I was overwhelmed by the generosity of the response. Other authors may choose to name the people who talked to them. I think it preferable to mention those who refused to talk to me.

Of those whose views I was anxious to hear, only three declined to assist in my inquiries: Cranley Onslow, the Chairman of the 1922 Committee; Sir Peter Morrison, then Mrs Thatcher's Parliamentary Private Secretary; and Tim Renton, the Chief Whip at the time. The first two refusals did not altogether surprise me. Mr Renton's, however, I minded slightly. I regarded – still regard – him as a friend or anyway as a good acquaintance. But he explained, with the diffident charm for which he is renowned, that a Whip found himself in a special position (akin, it seemed, to that of a doctor or a priest) and that accordingly he did not feel justified in revealing the secrets of his office. Yet from my point of view all was not quite lost, for other members of the Whips Office proved markedly less reticent.

Two Members, however, I should like to thank individually. Michael Howard kindly lent me the photograph of the committee of the Cambridge Union which is reproduced below. And Sir Philip Goodhart gave me a videotape of the televised parliamentary scenes relating to the fall of Mrs Thatcher, from her 'No. No. No.' through Sir Geoffrey Howe's resignation speech to her own triumphant appearance at the dispatch box. Sir Philip had caused the tape to be put together for the benefit of his grandchildren but generously gave me a copy too.

The increased televising of political events (those of November 1990 were particularly well-covered) and the availability of video-recordings have made the writing of books such as this at once easier and more difficult. They have made it more difficult because it often happens that what is recorded in the newspapers or even in *Hansard* (perhaps especially in *Hansard*) is not exactly what the man or the woman said at the time. They have made it easier because what politicians say at the time, into microphones or at cameras, often represents their true feelings more accurately than what they choose to say to interviewers later on, when prudential second thoughts may have asserted themselves or chronology may have been telescoped.

Time and again I have been struck by the way in which honest, intelligent and experienced politicians (journalists too for that matter) place a sequence of events in the wrong order, or contract or expand a period of time. For example: many now believe that Sir Geoffrey's resignation speech followed his resignation at the end of the previous week. They have forgotten that twelve days passed between the two events.

My colleagues have been as generous as the politicians. For their help I would thank particularly Peter Dobbie and Alice Miles of the *Mail on Sunday*, Robert Harris of the *Sunday Times*, Peter Jenkins of the *Independent*, Frank Johnson of the *Sunday Telegraph*, Donald Macintyre of the *Independent on Sunday*, Andrew Marr of the *Economist*, James Naughtie of the BBC and Michael Prescott. Of course, I am solely responsible for any mistakes.

While I was writing this book, several others came out concerning roughly the same subject; though some of them dealt more comprehensively with the life of John Major than I have felt it necessary to do. They are listed in the bibliography at the back. Where I have quoted anything from them, a footnote reference is supplied. But I have neither looked for confirmation of what I have written nor sought out contradictions or discrepancies between my version and theirs. Differences exist – as much about the interpretation of events as about the events themselves – but I took the view that they were for others to resolve. I decided to write my account from my own knowledge and, no doubt, prejudices.

I should also like to thank Jeffrey Care and his colleagues at the *Observer* library, Tony Mancini, of the same paper's picture library, and the library staff of the Press Association. My agent, Giles Gordon, was as helpful as ever, while my editor at Duckworth, Deborah Blake, saw the book through the press meticulously.

April-September 1991   Alan Watkins

Second Edition

I am grateful to Peter Bottomley, Brendan Bruce, Anthony Howard, Professor George Jones, Sir Robert Rhodes James and Geoffrey Wheatcroft for suggestions, corrections or both.

April 1992   A.W.

Introduction to the Second Edition

The post-war epoch has seen the final transformation of Cabinet government into prime ministerial government.... With the coming of prime ministerial government, the Cabinet, in obedience to the law that Bagehot discovered, joins the other dignified elements in the constitution.

R.H.S. Crossman, Introduction to Walter Bagehot,
The English Constitution, 1963

It's a funny old world.

Margaret Thatcher, on being removed from office
by her Cabinet colleagues, 1990

There is a school of Conservative history which teaches that all was for the best. Hidden away in its academies there are machines of retrospective self-justification. Whatever was, was right. Thus: Harold Macmillan may have made his mistakes but he was right for his time. He was the leader whom the country and the party needed in the 1950s. Likewise, more evidently still, was Margaret Thatcher the Prime Minister for the 1980s.

Within this general theory of historical benevolence even Edward Heath can be accommodated. After all, he unexpectedly won the election of 1970, so exploding Harold Wilson's widely believed claim of the time that Labour had replaced the Conservatives as 'the natural party of government'. And he had prepared the way for Mrs Thatcher with his Selsdon Park programme of 1970, from which admittedly he later diverged when he was in government, but which first made respectable the ideas that she was to put into practice after 1979.[1]

The theory breaks down, perhaps, over the choice of Lord

---

[1] The Conservative Party's 1970 Manifesto had derived from a weekend gathering of senior figures held at the Selsdon Park Hotel, Croydon, Surrey. Harold Wilson mistakenly believed that through it Edward Heath had delivered himself into his hands.

Home rather than R.A. Butler to succeed Macmillan. For if Home came within only a few seats of winning that election outright, as he did, how much better would Butler have done? Still, Home led to Heath, who in turn led to Mrs Thatcher.

Into this general theory of Conservative leaders, John Major initially fitted quite well. For, just as Mrs Thatcher was the natural leader for the 1980s, so was Mr Major the natural leader for the 1990s. The events of November 1990 may have been terrible: but they had been necessary. And, through the operations of a benign providence, they had produced the right leader once again.

There were, it is true, doubters. There always are. The self-justifying school of Conservative history does not hold universal dominion. There were many Conservative MPs who believed that Michael Heseltine would be likelier to defeat Neil Kinnock in the election which had to come at the latest in early July 1992. There were others who bubbled with indignation at the way Mrs Thatcher had been treated. Some of them also thought that she could have won the election and that Mr Major would not. Persons holding these views were more strongly represented among Conservative journalists than among Conservative MPs. This was not surprising. They had less to lose. In particular, they did not have seats to lose: influence in their own newspapers, maybe, even positions of pomp and power, in the last resort perhaps jobs. But the right to place the letters 'MP' after their names was not at risk. As things turned out, the press divided.

Sir David English, knighted on the recommendation of Mrs Thatcher, was unsentimental about his former patroness. Maggie (as in 'Battling Maggie', the standby of the Tory tabloids throughout the 1980s) was to be honoured but quietly forgotten. In future the *Daily Mail* was to support Mr Major and to embrace our glorious new future in Europe with equal degrees of conviction. The *Daily Express* and the *Sun* concealed their greater regrets for the past with attacks on Mr Kinnock, in which the *Mail* also joined enthusiastically. It was in the *Telegraph* papers that the tension was greatest. Whereas the new proprietor of the group Conrad Black wished broadly to give support to Mr Major and his party, several of the group's most distinguished writers – Charles Moore in the *Daily Telegraph*, Frank Johnson and, another Thatcher knight, Sir Peregrine Worsthorne in the *Sunday Telegraph* – still looked wistfully to the Queen over the water. So did Mr Black's other new acquisition, the *Spectator*, particularly its political correspondent, Simon Heffer.

Mr Major justifies his election

For a year after his accession these doubts, though hurtful to the sensitive Mr Major, and irritating to his new party chairman Chris Patten, were of academic interest merely. The new Prime Minister could have gone to the country and probably won in December 1990. He could have done the same, with an equal or greater chance of success, immediately after the Gulf War. He did not do so because he considered that it would have been 'wrong' to hold an election so soon. And he wished to have a replacement for the poll tax in position.[2] But some of his backbenchers were becoming restive. The recession showed no sign of abating.[3] The favourite date became 7 November 1991, which would allow the votes to be gathered in before the winter storms began and enable the Prime Minister to announce the election at the close of his speech to the party conference.

The party chairman counselled caution, at any rate to begin with. So, throughout, did the Chancellor, Norman Lamont. Mr Lamont had been one of Mr Major's few original appointments.[4] He had been with him at the Treasury and his campaign manager in 1990.[5] Many observers thought Mr Major had made a mistake and should have appointed instead John MacGregor, who, like Labour's John Smith, conveyed an impression of Scottish probity as Mr Lamont regrettably did not, even though he was a Scotsman too, or anyway an Orcadian.

There is no doubt that Mr Major took a risk in delaying the

[2] *Election Call*, BBC1 and Radio 4, 8 April 1992.

[3] For the underlying causes of the recession, see below, Ch. 5.

[4] Kenneth Clarke and William Waldegrave had both been appointed by Mrs Thatcher three weeks before her fall.

[5] See below, Ch. 8.

election until 1992. Even as late as midday on 9 April 1992 there were seasoned Conservatives who maintained that, having come so far, he would have done better to wait until 7 May or even into July. In the event, he justified his election in 1990 by success, the single criterion employed by the Conservative Party in judging its leaders. He did what he was chosen to do. He won an election which, most of his party thought 16 months before, Mrs Thatcher would have lost.

Several reviewers of the original edition, otherwise friendly enough, have objected to the word 'coup', whether in the title of the book (which was my own choice) or in the text itself.[6] But if what happened in the early evening of Wednesday 21 November 1990 was not a coup conducted by a majority of Mrs Thatcher's Cabinet, what was it? How else could it properly be described? As a fond farewell, hardly; as a tearful leave-taking, perhaps.[7] But the sentimental and in some respects genuinely affecting accompaniments to Mrs Thatcher's departure should not conceal from us the true nature of the event. I make no apology for describing it as a coup. As Bishop Butler wrote:

> Everything is what it is, and not another thing ... Things and actions are what they are, and the consequences of them will be what they will be: why then should we desire to be deceived?[8]

Of course, the coup was not a discrete event, without causes or antecedents. I never said it was. Indeed, six of the nine chapters that follow attempt to identify and to analyse those factors as they operated in 1987–90. Perhaps I should have gone back to earlier times. It were infinite to judge causes, or the causes of causes. There are limits. But I nowhere suggest that Mrs Thatcher's fall was an isolated happening: quite the reverse. What I did suggest in the original edition was that the coup had been preceded by a plot involving John Wakeham, Kenneth Clarke and John Gummer. The suggestion was contained solely

---

[6] See for example Joe Rogaly, *Financial Times*, 21 November 1991; Hugo Young, *Tablet*, 7 December 1991.

[7] See below, p. 18.

[8] Joseph Butler, *Fifteen Sermons*, ed. W.R. Matthews (1964), 23, 118.

in a crosshead, 'The initial plot', which I have now replaced with 'Mr Wakeham's plan'.[9]

The Great Tory Lies Machine

The plan was to bring Mrs Thatcher back from Paris, where she was to spend the Tuesday night, with her dignity unimpaired, as still undisputed Leader of the Conservative Party and Prime Minister of the country. She would then be persuaded to go quietly, the three participants having correctly anticipated that she would not win the first ballot against Mr Heseltine outright. As reported in the *Sunday Express*, Mr Gummer called me 'a worthy successor to Agatha Christie' and added that the book was 'based on a wholly invented story'.[10] It is not I think defamatory to compare anyone to Miss Christie, but it is certainly so to assert that a political writer invents stories. Mr Gummer and, more to the purpose, the *Sunday Express* are fortunate that I am not of a litigious disposition. Mr Wakeham was at the time in the Far East but let it be known through 'a close colleague' – in fact an ambitious young MP anxious to ingratiate himself further with Mr Wakeham – that I was 'a socialist commentator of a Welsh romantic disposition' whose account of these events was accordingly 'tendentious and inaccurate'.[11]

I ought to point out here that, contrary to the assertion of some reviewers, these stories were not engineered by Messrs Duckworth as some kind of advance publicity for the book, which came out on 21 November 1991. The week before, on the same day as these stories appeared, a long extract had been published in the *Observer*. The outlines of the so-called plot had been drawn many weeks before that, chiefly following my casual conversations with Conservative politicians and fellow-journalists.[12] The Whips took alarm and wondered what to do.[13] The consequence was that friendly newspapers were briefed. It is not wholly comfortable to be on the receiving end of the Great Tory

[9] See below, p. 4. [10] *Sunday Express*, 17 November 1991.

[11] *Sunday Telegraph*, 17 November 1991.

[12] See 'Black Dog,' *Mail on Sunday*, 6 October 1991; 'New Grub Street,' *Sunday Times*, 20 October 1991; Chris Buckland, *Daily Express*, 15 November 1991.

[13] Private information.

Lies Machine. But any small discomfort which I may have felt I was able to bear with fortitude and equanimity on account of the gratifying amount of publicity which ensued. Moreover, whatever the news-columns may have reported, neither the leader-writer (in fact Mr Moore) of the *Daily Telegraph* nor Gordon Greig in the *Daily Mail* was disposed to accept the official Conservative version of events.[14] They inclined rather towards my own account.

Mr Clarke's memorandum

The truth is that the meeting did occur, though in Mr Wakeham's rather than in Mr Gummer's room. On Thursday 15 November 1990, four days before the meeting with Mr Clarke and Mr Gummer, Mr Wakeham was heard to say that, if Mrs Thatcher did not win outright on the first ballot, she would have to resign.[15] My account of the meeting was based on a contemporary written record which I am not at liberty to quote. I am, however, able to reproduce an explanation of the event which Mr Clarke, writing from the House of Commons, circulated to Mrs Thatcher, Mr Wakeham and others, on a kind of 'To whom it may concern' basis, though the precise phrase was not used by him:

> The meeting between John Wakeham, John Gummer and me was not prearranged and did not involve anything that could be described as a 'plot'. It was a discussion between three supporters of Mrs Thatcher who were concerned about the possible result of the first ballot and who wished to ensure her return from Paris in a position to consider the next steps.
>
> The advice that John Wakeham gave to the Prime Minister that she ought to see members of the Cabinet was the best friendly and disinterested advice that he could have given in the circumstances.
>
> I believe that John Wakeham behaved honourably throughout the whole proceeding as a good friend of Margaret Thatcher and in the best interests of the Party.[16]

14 *Daily Telegraph* and *Daily Mail*, 18 November 1991.
15 Private information.
16 Private information.

The Tuesday morning meeting

On the morning of the next day, Tuesday 20 November 1990, a meeting took place in the Prime Minister's room in the House, though Mrs Thatcher was away. Those present included Mr Wakeham, Norman Tebbit – who had at this stage assumed command of Mrs Thatcher's campaign – Kenneth Baker and Peter Morrison.[17] Mr Tebbit insisted that, if Mrs Thatcher did not immediately announce that she would enter a second ballot, the omission would damage her in any such election. He was very certain of this, and Mr Wakeham quietly acquiesced.

Earlier, however, a meeting had been held at Conservative Central Office which had included Kenneth Baker, Gordon Reece and Tim Bell. Here it had been agreed that Mrs Thatcher should not make any move until she had slept on the result of the first ballot. On Tuesday Mr Baker tried to repeat the argument for delay, or apparent delay: but the others would not listen. So he desisted; while the discussion proceeded to an assessment of a paper which Peter Morrison had circulated giving three possible outcomes and the statements by Mrs Thatcher appropriate to each.

Thus Mr Tebbit wanted Mrs Thatcher to declare her candidature at once and thought she could win a second ballot. Mr Baker did not want Mrs Thatcher to make an immediate announcement but nevertheless believed that she should enter and would win the contest. While Mr Wakeham wanted – or had been persuaded to agree to – her Paris declaration, mainly because he wished her to be seen to be returning to this country with her dignity unimpaired. But really he did not think that she ought to contest the second election at all.

The best advice undoubtedly came from Mr Baker. Whether he clearly foresaw it or not, the declaration on the steps of the Paris Embassy did more than anything else to turn parliamentary opinion against Mrs Thatcher.[18] Mr Baker turned out to be right, Mr Tebbit wrong. In the 1990–2 period it became the political fashion to denigrate Mr Baker. In April 1992 he left Mr Major's Cabinet for the back benches. But he

[17] For others attending, see below, p. 191.
[18] See below, pp. 3–4.

insists, probably correctly, that he could have won Mrs Thatcher's second campaign for her, despite (perhaps because of) the doctrinal antipathy which existed between them. Mr Tebbit could probably have won it too, notwithstanding his initial misjudgment, in which Mr Wakeham had concurred, about the likely effect of the Paris declaration. Mr Wakeham was the worst choice as campaign manager because he did not believe in the cause which he was meant to be promoting. As Hugo Young has written:

> Wakeham's subsequent performance must be seen … against the background of his being 'bounced' by Norman Tebbit, speaking on television, into the role of second ballot manager without ever agreeing to it.[19]

This does not mean that Mr Wakeham either behaved dishonourably or plotted Mrs Thatcher's downfall. What it does mean is that he found himself in a bit of a muddle, as most of us do at various stages in our lives. The parade of Cabinet Ministers, together with a few others, which was organised by him was no doubt well-intentioned. But there is equally no doubt that it was this nervous procession which encompassed Mrs Thatcher's destruc tion. Shortly before half-past-seven on that evening Mr Baker confided to a colleague that she would now probably withdraw.

John Biffen has suggested that these and other, larger questions 'will be better answered when the Thatcher and Lawson memoirs are available'.[20] I hope that this turns out to be so. But my expectations are not high. Most books by recent Conservative politicians have been a disgrace to their publishers and little short of a fraud on the public. But Brendan Bruce, Alan Clark, Kenneth Clarke and Sir Robert Rhodes James have all kept diaries of these events or written down their accounts shortly afterwards. Almost certainly others have done likewise. Part of the trouble is that, in modern politics, the participants communicate by telephone rather than by letter. But I have no doubt that there is more to come out about the fall of Mrs Thatcher. My only claim is to have made a start.

---

[19] Young, art. cit. Cf. below, p. 6.
[20] John Biffen, 'Mrs T's Manic Mistake', *Observer*, 8 December 1991.

1

The Fall of a Prime Minister

> After all the investigations that have been made into this
> intricate affair, ... it still remains enveloped in all that kind of
> mystery which ever accompanies events produced more from a
> concurrence of awkward circumstances, than from fixed design.
>
> Thomas Paine, *Rights of Man*

> We shall astonish them with our ingratitude.
>
> Felix Schwarzenberg, Prime Minister of
> the Austrian Empire, 1849

Shortly after half past five on Tuesday 20 November 1990 a
trickle of people had begun to flow into the Committee Corridor
of the House of Commons. By six the trickle had turned into a
flood. Journalists and broadcasters who were rarely seen in
Westminster – did they all have proper passes? – crowded into
the broad, high passageway which extends from the Clerk of the
Services Committee at the north end to the Lords of Appeal in
Ordinary at the south (for by this stage the Commons have
turned into the Lords). The corridor contains portraits which are
shinily illuminated but rarely looked at: for example, Charles
Pepys, first Earl of Cottenham, by C.R. Leslie, and Sir D. Wilkes,
by Thos Phillips. Tony Benn stood on one of the benches which
line the corridor, as if about to address the multitude; while
Dennis Skinner stood on another, as if presenting a rival
attraction. By half past six the crush was uncomfortable.

The result of the ballot

Then, all of a sudden, everyone became quiet. Someone was reading somthing out. A whisper slipped through the crowd like an eel: 'Second ballot, second ballot.' People started to make for telephones. It was no place for the elderly or the frail.

Inside the big committee room the Conservative MPs were still assembled, growing hotter and worse-tempered by the minute. Anthony Beaumont-Dark, who sat for Selly Oak and represented the Birmingham commercial classes with a fine independence of which Joe Chamberlain would have been proud, said: 'The press have got the results. It's absolutely disgusting.' Other cries went up: 'Where's Cranley? I want his head.' This was a reference to Cranley Onslow, the Chairman of the 1922 Committee, who had read out the results in a different committee room. After they had been read out by a public-spirited Member, someone said: 'God Almighty, she's finished.' The results were:

Margaret Thatcher	204
Michael Heseltine	152
Abstentions	16

Mrs Thatcher had gained the absolute majority (187 or over) which was required by the rules but fallen four short of the 15 per cent 'surcharge' of those entitled to vote (56) which was also required. There would accordingly have to be a second ballot where a simple majority would suffice. Under the rules, this ballot was an entirely separate election. Either or both of the candidates could withdraw, and new ones could be nominated.

Ian Twinn, the Member for Edmonton, had been charged with conveying the result to John Whittingdale, the Prime Minister's Political Secretary. He, rather than Bernard Ingham, was involved because this was held to be a party rather than a prime ministerial matter; though, as we shall see, this unwonted deference to constitutional scrupulosity did not prevent Sir Bernard from intervening at a later stage. But it was Tim Renton, the Chief Whip, who first telephoned Peter Morrison, Mrs Thatcher's Parliamentary Private Secretary. He was in

Paris with her confidant Charles Powell and her other Foreign Secretary, Douglas Hurd. Sir Peter (as he was later to become) was a large, heavily-built man, prone to sweating, with a red face and that kind of tight, curly hair which seems to be found only in products of English public schools. He looked like a dissipated version of Simon Raven. He later explained what he did:

> I had a 'for', an 'against' and an 'abstain' and I just wrote down the figures which were read out to me by somebody over on this side of the Channel [Sir Peter was by that time back in Britain] and I passed them straightaway to her. And I said, as I passed them to her: 'I'm afraid, Prime Minister, that these figures are rather disappointing.'[1]

Down the steps

Mrs Thatcher did not hesitate. Within minutes she was bouncing down the steps of the Paris Embassy with Sir Bernard in close attendance. The BBC's man on the spot was John Sergeant, whose seriousness of demeanour belied his original occupation of actor, comedian and cabaret artist. Mr Sergeant said:

> Prime Minister, Mrs Thatcher, it's here, this is the microphone.

Mrs Thatcher knew where the microphone was and seemed to think that Mr Sergeant was preventing her from reaching it. Roughly pushing the poor chap aside, she said:

> I'm naturally very pleased that I got more than half the parliamentary party and disappointed that it's not quite enough to win on the first ballot so I confirm it is my intention to let my name go forward for the second ballot.[2]

If there is a single remembered image of the fall of Mrs Thatcher, it is of her bustling down the steps of the Paris Embassy; giving a fair imitation, when confronted by John

---

[1] Transcript, *The Thatcher Factor Special*, Brook Productions, Channel 4, 1990, 107.
[2] Ibid.

Sergeant, of a rugby forward, perhaps of her host, the Ambassador Sir Ewen Fergusson, in his own international days; and saying conceitedly that she intented to fight on, come what might. But the words were not intended to sound reminiscent of Mr Toad. On the contrary: they had been thought about carefully by John Wakeham and others before her departure for Paris.[3] As Mr Wakeham was later to observe laconically: 'She picked up the right piece of paper.' She was intended to sound steadfast and determined rather than boastful and vainglorious. That she failed to do this was, as it had been so often for her in the past, a triumph of manner over material.

Mr Wakeham's plan

Many hours before this, John Wakeham, Kenneth Clarke and John Gummer had met in Mr Wakeham's room in the House of Commons. This was not the meeting at which the forms of words (of which one was to be used) had been agreed. Of those present, only Mr Wakeham had attended that. This was a different gathering. All three agreed that Mrs Thatcher, in the words of one of the participants, 'was not going to make it': that is, to win outright on the first ballot. They further agreed that she could not, in these circumstances, proceed to a second ballot without damaging the authority of the government and splitting the party.

If Michael Heseltine, Nigel Lawson and Geoffrey Howe were the Ministers (by this time, of course, ex-Ministers) who were chiefly responsible for bringing Mrs Thatcher to her current condition – and their role will be examined in the succeeding pages – then John Wakeham was the Minister who exercised the greatest overall influence during the crucial 39 hours. This was the period between the result of the first ballot on the Tuesday and Mrs Thatcher's announcement at the Cabinet meeting on the Thursday that she intended to resign. With Norman Tebbit gone, Nicholas Ridley resigned and Cecil Parkinson not the man he was, Mr Wakeham was her best friend in the Cabinet.

[3] See below, p. 191.

He was a Carthusian accountant who was one of the few members of the Cabinet to carry on smoking, in his case Havana cigars (though not during meetings of the Cabinet). His wife had been killed in the Brighton bombing outrage of 1984. He had subsequently remarried. He himself had suffered appalling injuries to his legs. He had learnt to walk again with the help of a services rehabilitation unit. In 1986 he had organised the Bournemouth conference which inaugurated the Conservative revival, leading to the victory of 1987: but the election itself had not proved a triumph for him, not, at any rate in his mistress's eyes. After a somewhat hesitant, apologetic performance on *Election Call* – certainly a performance which Mrs Thatcher judged lacking in appropriate zeal on her behalf – she vowed to get rid of him, but was prevailed upon to desist.

He now found himself Secretary of State for Energy, having succeeded the declining Mr Parkinson in this post, and having himself been a successful though wary Leader of the House. His activities over the privatisation of electricity on the Wednesday morning were to play an important part in the unfolding of events. His true political position was as a left-of-centre, consensus Conservative – he was never 'one of us'. It was odd, in a way, that Mrs Thatcher had decided to rely on him to the extent she did.

He, for his part, had decided, with Mr Clarke and Mr Gummer, that if she failed to win on the first ballot – as all three suspected she would fail to win – then she would, in the interests of the party, have to be persuaded to go quietly. Mr Wakeham reposed great faith in the powers of persuasion and the good sense of Denis and Carol Thatcher.

There are several puzzles here. Mr Wakeham holding the views he did as to Mrs Thatcher's future, why did he support and indeed push the stronger wording of her holding declaration at Paris? Kenneth Baker, after all, had wanted a reference to 'consultations' merely. Why did Mr Wakeham not follow the more conciliatory line suggested by Mr Baker? Paradoxically perhaps, he was to prove more steadfast for Mrs Thatcher than any other Minister, with the possible exception of Mr Parkinson, more so certainly than Mr Wakeham.

One answer is that he did not expect Mrs Thatcher's declaration to produce the effect it did. She had, after all, as he said, picked up the right piece of paper. Another answer is that he thought that, if the wording of the Paris declaration had been weaker, 'the rats would have got in', as he put it to James Naughtie on *The World This Weekend*.[4] By this what Mr Wakeham truly meant was, not that Mrs Thatcher would have weakened her real position, but that she would have *appeared* to weaken her position. She would have returned from Paris a lame duck Prime Minister. Mr Wakeham's preoccupation, in the event of Mrs Thatcher's failing to secure an outright majority (which he suspected she would not, though she might) was to secure her return from Paris with her dignity unimpaired. The Thatcher family and the men in suits could then set to work, without the necessity of her seeing the colleagues.[5]

The other puzzle is why Mr Wakeham, holding his views, agreed to become Mrs Thatcher's campaign manager in the second ballot. He was surely placed, or he placed himself, in a false position. Inevitably he was more of an undertaker than a campaign manager. But there is still some doubt about whether he was really appointed campaign manager at all – or, at any rate, about the formality of his appointment. Certainly Mr Wakeham told Mr Clarke on the Wednesday that the announcement had surprised him, as no one had asked him to do the job. However, he told somebody else that he had been asked to do it from Paris.

Mr Hurd has a hard time

There Mr Hurd was being given a hard time by Mrs Thatcher. He learnt of the result separately and more or less simultaneously. From an upstairs room he observed with

[4] Transcript, *The World This Weekend*, BBC Radio 4, 25 November 1990.

[5] The original phrase was 'the men in suits'. It was used, for example, by the present writer in the *Observer*, 6 May 1990. During and before the 39 hours it became transformed into 'the men in grey suits', which stuck. As Lord Whitelaw observed on television, it was an inaccurate phrase, because on the day in question, 21 November, his interviewer could see that he was wearing a blue suit. And, indeed, the typical Conservative grandee tends to wear a dark blue or black suit, with chalk- or pin-stripes, what may be called a White's Club suit. The original phrase 'the men in suits' is the more

wonderment her progression down the steps, Bernard Ingham at hand, towards the unsuspecting John Sergeant. Afterwards he said: 'I'll back you.' To which Mrs Thatcher replied: 'It would be a great help if you went out and said so.' This Mr Hurd did, saying to press and cameras:

> The Prime Minister continues to have my full support and I am sorry this destructive, unnecessary contest should be prolonged in this way.

This was an implied rebuke to Mr Heseltine, who said outside his Belgravia home that he was:

> overwhelmed with gratitude to my parliamentary colleagues who in such large measure have given me their support.

But Mr Hurd was not at all happy with the way things appeared to be going. He had not been at Westminster to help draft Mr Wakeham's and Sir Peter Morrison's response.[6] Had he been available, it is doubtful whether he would have been involved. He was a supporter of consultations. He felt that the, from Mrs Thatcher's point of view, catastrophic result of the first ballot had changed matters completely and that little more could be done till they all got back to London. It was hard to think straight in Paris; the more so since President Mitterrand, with typical thoughtlessness, or Gallic precision, had not been prepared to make the slightest deviation from the British contingent's programme. So to the ballet and to the dinner Mrs Thatcher duly went, to be consoled by Chancellor Kohl, who took her aside, saying that he felt it to be his duty to cheer her up for the rest of the evening.

Sir Charles Powell was disinclined to rest. Privately, he thought that, as he was later to put it, 'the game was up', a phrase used also by Peter Lilley and Norman Lamont. Nevertheless, Sir Charles placed pressure on Mr Hurd – Mr

accurate.

[6] Others also were involved. See below, p. 191.

Hurd certainly thought that pressure was being placed on him –
to support Mrs Thatcher more forcefully and more publicly.
Particular importance was attached to having his signature as
Mrs Thatcher's proposer for the second ballot (Mr Major, her
prospective seconder, was still on his bed of pain in
Huntingdon). The Whips gained the clear impression from Sir
Charles that Mr Hurd had already signed, in Paris. In fact he
did not sign till half past five on the Wednesday.

The Tory loss of nerve

Meanwhile, there was such a scurrying and a conspiring as had
not been witnessed at Westminster since the war (for the
equivalent moves after the resignation of Harold Macmillan in
1963 had taken place in and around the Imperial Hotel,
Blackpool). Those loyal to Mrs Thatcher tended afterwards to
blame all kinds of people for what they described as the Tory
Party's collective loss of nerve.

One of those blamed was Robert Hayward, Member for Kings-
wood, who spoke with a West country accent and was a rugby
referee. He was the Conservative Party's self-appointed parliamentary psephologist, who knew where people's loyalties lay. He
sniffed the air, produced his pocket calculator, put his finger to the
wind and pronounced Mrs Thatcher dead. He was later to play a
leading part, in much the same role, in Mr Major's campaign.

The other was Alan Clark, a very different character. He was
the son of Kenneth, Lord Clark, lived in a castle in Kent and was
a millionaire. He looked younger than his 62 years and could
behave in an even more foolishly juvenile fashion. Yet he was a
distinguished military historian. His political views were, for a
Conservative, unorthodox: pro-Russian, pro-German (he was a
great admirer of the Wehrmacht) and anti-American. He
possessed many friends and admirers in the expensive press.
His dismissal was always predicted before any reshuffle. Mr
Clark's views were extreme about Mrs Thatcher's prospects as
well. When a friend, a few days afterwards, accused him of
exaggerating the rush from Mrs Thatcher, he replied, in roughly
these words:

You weren't there, old boy, and you're talking absolute balls. Her support was turning away so fast that by the end she'd have been lucky to have 90 f—— votes.

Mr Clark's 90 votes were to play a prominent part in his conversation over the next few days. However, Cecil Parkinson said:

He never goes near the place, and when he does he only talks to about four people.

One of Mr Clark's characteristics, perhaps his leading characteristic, was that he could not bear to be left out of things if he thought there was some political skulduggery afoot. So it was that he found himself on the Wednesday evening advising Mrs Thatcher to fight gloriously on, even though she would in his opinion lose – and even though he was not himself a member of the Cabinet.[7] So it was also that he found himself, with perhaps more justification, at Tristan Garel-Jones's house, 12 Catherine Place, Westminster, on the Tuesday evening. It seemed the natural place to go to.

The Garel-Jones meeting

Mr Garel-Jones was a Welshman, originally from Llangennech, near Llanelli in Carmarthenshire, whose family had emigrated to Madrid when he was a child to found a successful English-language school. He had been with Charles Powell at King's, Canterbury, and remained on friendly terms, which certainly did not impede his or his friends' progress in the administration. These friends included the Pattens, John and Chris, and William Waldegrave. All three were present on that late Tuesday evening. Not present was Richard Needham, who, exiled to Ulster, had been overhead calling Mrs Thatcher an 'old cow' on his car radio and had lived to tell the tale – had, indeed, made his peace with her when she visited Northern Ireland

[7] The circumstances in which Francis Maude proffered his advice were somewhat different: see below, p. 18.

immediately before her departure for France. (It is sometimes
forgotten that Mrs Thatcher made this trip also, to which she
attached some importance, before the first ballot.)

The others there, in addition to Alan Clark, the Pattens and
William Waldegrave, were Malcolm Rifkind, Norman Lamont,
Tony Newton, Douglas Hogg, Richard Ryder and Tim Yeo. Mr
Ryder arrived shortly before midnight, having had dinner with
his wife. Several of those present were still sitting around in
their overcoats. Mr Garel-Jones had promised coffee, but none
seemed to be forthcoming. They sipped mineral water ('to keep
clear heads') and nibbled nuts. Though a majority ended up
voting, some campaigning vigorously, for Mr Hurd, the nucleus
of Mr Major's campaign were also present: Mr Lamont and Mr
Ryder (if only briefly), together with Mr Newton and Mr Clark.
Mr Clark suggested they should all rally round Tom King as
leader. This was not a joke. Mr Clark had long urged the unsung
merits of the Defence Secretary. But it was treated as one. 'Oh,
for God's sake stop wasting our time, Alan,' they said.

Mr Lamont denies that he asked what would be so very wrong
with Mr Heseltine, that his elevation to leader would not be the
end of the world. It was reported then and subsequently that he
said this,[8] but Mr Lamont claims he did not. However, he was
convinced at the time that Mrs Thatcher would not beat Mr
Heseltine in the second ballot and that Mr Major would. He was
much influenced by the calculations of Robert Hayward that
30-40 people who had voted for Mrs Thatcher would now switch
to Mr Heseltine. Michael Jopling (Mrs Thatcher's phantom
campaigner in the first ballot) had compiled a similar list, as had
young William Hague, who was to campaign for Mr Major in the
second ballot. Mr Lilley, who was not present at the meeting,
shared Mr Lamont's view: that, as Mr Lilley put it, 'the game
was up'.

Oddly enough, Mr Garel-Jones did not share this view. Or, if
he did, his process of reasoning was different. He did not believe
that Mr Heseltine would undoubtedly defeat Mrs Thatcher in
the second ballot. To this extent, he was out of kilter with the

[8] See e.g. 'The Fall of Thatcher', *Economist*, 9 March 1991.

spirit of the meeting. But what would it profit a woman to win a vote, and split a party? That was Mr Garel-Jones's question. The damage was already done. It had been done by Mr Heseltine in the first ballot. In 1989, after Sir Anthony Meyer's challenge (then misguidedly regarded as a comic event), Mr Garel-Jones had warned Mrs Thatcher:

> There are a hundred assassins lurking in the bushes, Prime Minister. Those people will come back and kill you.[9]

So it had turned out. Mrs Thatcher might defeat Mr Heseltine 187-185, so satisfying the rules of the competition. But what good would that do to anyone? What good would it do to Mrs Thatcher? The assassins would only be back again in the spring.

As we have seen, this was a view which Mr Gummer, Mr Wakeham and Mr Clarke had already formed in anticipation of the result of the first ballot. And yet on Tuesday evening Mr Clarke embarked on a round of television appearances – the last on *Newsnight* between half past ten and midnight – giving a typically robust defence of Mrs Thatcher's result and her decision, for such it seemed to be, to contest the second ballot. This was why he was absent from the meeting at Mr Garel-Jones's house. Five Ministers had searched for but been unable to find him. He had been shuttling between outside cameras on Palace Green (which on occasions like this is turned into a kind of fairground) and television studios. He was pursuing the plan agreed with Mr Wakeham to get the Prime Minister back from Paris 'with dignity' and with no signs of erosion of support at home. This was disingenuous. No doubt Mr Clarke's motives were good, as were Mr Wakeham's. But they would have saved a great deal of trouble on the next day, the Wednesday, if they had made their true position clearer from the start.

Mr MacGregor does a survey

On the Wednesday morning Mr Wakeham was busy with

[9] Quoted *Observer*, 30 June 1991.

electricity privatisation. He asked John MacGregor, the recently appointed Leader of the House, to undertake a survey of Cabinet Ministers' opinions. It is clear that Mr Wakeham would have performed this task himself if he had not been occupied with other matters. It is equally clear that he asked Mr MacGregor to do the job rather than Mr Renton, the Chief Whip, because, in his opinion, Mrs Thatcher would not have accepted any findings produced by Mr Renton owing to her distrust of him. What was not clear was whether Mr Wakeham was carrying out the survey – or asking Mr MacGregor to carry it out on his behalf – as Mrs Thatcher's campaign manager or as the impresario of her fall. Was he the cheer-leader or the undertaker?

Either way, it was odd that it was Mr MacGregor who was being asked to do the job. True, he was disinterested: no one thought he was going to be made leader of the party. He was also, for those who attached importance to ancient offices, Lord President of the Council. But in former days the task of polling the Cabinet had fallen to Peers, in particular to the Lord Chancellor. In 1957 it had been undertaken by Lords Salisbury and Kilmuir; in 1963, by Lord Dilhorne. Admittedly the circumstances were different in one respect. The Prime Minister (Eden in 1957, Macmillan in 1963) had already announced his departure, or had it announced on his behalf. The question was who was to succeed him. In 1990 the question was whether the Prime Minister should resign. Nevertheless, James Mackay was the most intelligent member of the Cabinet. It was not wholly clear that he was even a Conservative. He was admirably qualified to question his colleagues.

This is not to say that Mr MacGregor made a bad job of it. He was criticised nonetheless. He was very keen on ascertaining the opinions of junior Ministers in the departments concerned. Very well then, said the Cabinet Ministers: why not ask them direct? Why expect us to answer on their behalf?

Mr MacGregor was also accused of wrongly including Mr Hurd and Mr Major in the seven Ministers who favoured Mrs Thatcher's carrying on. The figure was supposed to be 12-7 against. Mr MacGregor did not include the two Peers, Lords Belstead and Mackay, or Mrs Thatcher herself. He claims that he did not include Mr Hurd and Mr Major either. He did include the Welsh Secretary, Mr Hunt, who was away in Tokyo and confined himself to sending a message of encouragement and good cheer to the Prime Minister. Even so, the figure cannot have been as high as seven. Mr Baker and Mr Parkinson were the only Ministers who consistently urged the Prime Minister to go forward. Mr Brooke said that he had been too busy in Northern Ireland to give the matter proper consideration. Mr Waddington showed sympathy. Mr Wakeham was included by Mr MacGregor as one of the Prime Minister's supporters.

Mr Clarke told Mr MacGregor in strong terms that he believed the Prime Minister should step down. He told him that he would not support her any more, because he believed that a further contest between her and Mr Heseltine would split the party disastrously. He said his opinion was that Mr Hurd and Mr Major should be released by her and allowed to stand. He asked Mr MacGregor whether he was the only one who was expressing that view. Mr MacGregor replied that he was not. Mr Clarke later spoke to Mr Gummer, who shared his view. They assumed that the men in grey suits were going to persuade Mrs Thatcher to step down when they saw her shortly after her return from Paris.

This was the accepted political wisdom at around mid-day on the Wednesday. Peter Jenkins of the *Independent* told his friends that he had been reliably informed that the Prime Minister was shortly to resign. Ian Aitken of the *Guardian* declined a dinner invitation because he thought he would be busy writing about Mrs Thatcher's resignation. Earlier in the day Mr Renton, the Chief Whip, had breakfast with Lord Whitelaw, who, as he informed the television cameras, happened to be wearing a blue suit. He told Mr Renton that he thought Mrs Thatcher ought not to go on.

Mr Renton was making his own investigations. Or perhaps that is too strong a way of putting it. Mrs Thatcher's supporters on the back benches, notably Sir George Gardiner, certainly considered that Mr Renton was claiming too much about the state of backbench opinion without ever having done a proper trawl. In fact Mr Renton and his colleagues in the Whips Office

never claimed to have undertaken a comprehensive survey. How
could they have done, in the limited time available? What they
did was to allow – to encourage – people to come to them. And
what they discovered was that the haemorrhage (the Whips'
favourite word on this occasion) of Mrs Thatcher's vote was
25-30: lower than Mr Hayward's estimate of 30-40, but
significant nonetheless. If Mrs Thatcher lost only 20 votes from
her original figure and did not gain any additions from the 16
abstainers, she was effectively done for.

The greybeards' failure

In these circumstances, it was perhaps surprising that Mr
Renton was as encouraging as he was when, with the other men
in suits – or, as Mr Hurd called them, the greybeards – he met
Mrs Thatcher at half past one on Wednesday. Really they were
not a specially venerable collection. They included, besides Mr
Renton, Mr Onslow, Mr MacGregor, Mr Wakeham, Mr Tebbit,
Mr Baker and Mr Moore. They met in the Cabinet Room and had
mineral water and cheese and ham sandwiches. This was the
most abstemiously conducted crisis in British political history.
Mr Renton told Mrs Thatcher that the likely backbench vote was
'too close to call', a sporting phrase from the United States
which, as we have seen, hardly reflected the reality, or anyway
the reality as reflected in the Whips' survey. Mr Onslow's advice,
on behalf of the 1922 Committee, was even more ambiguous.
The truth was that the Executive of the Committee was split
between supporters and opponents of Mrs Thatcher; and Mr
Onslow's advice perhaps inevitably reflected this division. But it
was a bit of a muddle. It was, first, that Mrs Thatcher had the
best chance, from all other candidates, of defeating Mr Heseltine
but, second, that there should be a wider choice of candidates.
This made sense only on the assumption that Mrs Thatcher and
Mr Heseltine should be joined in the second ballot by A.N. Other
and perhaps even by S.O. Else as well; and Mr Major and Mr
Hurd would not fill these positions if Mrs Thatcher continued to
stand.

Mr MacGregor declined to proffer any advice. This was

another adverse criticism that was made of him. He was, it appears, inhibited by the noise and the people, in particular by Cranley Onslow. Afterwards Mr MacGregor defended himself. What he had been told, he said, was confidential: he was certainly not going to blurt it all out over a sandwich lunch.

Mr Baker and Mr Tebbit were less equivocal. They told Mrs Thatcher that, with a properly organised campaign, she could win. Mr MacGregor told Mr Wakeham, however, of his findings of that morning. This was one of the origins of the crucial event of the 39 hours: the parade of Cabinet Ministers of the Wednesday evening.

The Ministers had told Mr MacGregor; Mr MacGregor had, for reasons that seemed good to him, felt unable to tell the Prime Minister; accordingly the Ministers would have to tell the Prime Minister themselves. Similarly, Mr Wakeham asked Mr Garel-Jones and Mr Ryder, towards the middle of the day, to campaign on behalf of the Prime Minister. They refused; additionally, Mr Garel-Jones produced to Mr Wakeham a list of eight Ministers who believed that the Prime Minister ought to stand down. Mr Wakeham said that this was very interesting but that they ought to tell the Prime Minister themselves. He said the same to Ministers who approached him direct. 'Don't tell me but tell her': that was Mr Wakeham's message.

The fatal procession

Mr Wakeham's theory, as he was to adumbrate it afterwards, was that under the British constitution a Prime Minister had to enjoy the support of two bodies of people: the party's backbenchers, and the Cabinet. The backbenchers were provided for by the party's electoral system. The Cabinet was not; and accordingly a new system had to be devised for ascertaining its opinion; just as a new system had been created for establishing the views of the backbenchers after 1963. This new system was to consist in a series of individual interviews with the Prime Minister. On *The World This Weekend* of 25 November he put the same proposition in less theoretical terms: if Mrs Thatcher was to go on, she needed the calm, rational support of her Cabinet.

Did Mr Wakeham ask the question expecting the answer Yes or the answer No? Peter Morrison saw it as an exercise, as he put it, to 'gee up' Ministers and confirm them in their support. Indeed, in the early afternoon Sir Peter telephoned Kenneth Clarke, thanked him for campaigning for Mrs Thatcher on the previous night and asked him whether he would campaign further on her behalf. Mr Clarke said he would not, and would probably not support her if she stood in the second ballot. A senior civil servant who was in close touch with events thought that at the beginning of the Ministers' parade Mr Wakeham believed that Mrs Thatcher ought to go on but that by seven o'clock he had changed his mind. It was, as he put it, an exercise that went wrong. But a journalist who interviewed Mr Wakeham in great detail shortly afterwards formed the view that:

> it was evident that he had taken on the task of sending the Cabinet in to see her with a very heavy heart, not only because he knew what the outcome would be but because he had realised how much of a dreadful shock she was about to receive. Having been drafted in on the Wednesday to oversee Round 2 on her behalf it's my understanding ... that he concluded almost on the instant that she was dead. The Cabinet wheeze was a contraption to deliver the fatal message.[10]

Understandably, Mrs Thatcher did not want to see a procession of Ministers at all, not so much because she was apprehensive of them, or feared a discouraging message from their lips, as because she did not have the time. She had to deliver a statement to the House that afternoon on her Paris meeting; then she had to prepare a speech on a motion of censure unwisely put down by the Labour Party. Motions of censure nearly always are unwise, unless you are sure of winning the vote. She said all this to Mr Wakeham. He replied that nevertheless she must see the Cabinet individually. Very well then, she replied: see them she would, after seeing the Queen that evening.

[10] Private information.

At this time, mid-afternoon on Wednesday, Mrs Thatcher's instincts were to fight on. As Mr Hurd was later to put it, the greybeards had failed to deliver the message. So it was that, when she was leaving No. 10 for the House, Bernard Ingham said that there would be 'people out there. What are you going to say?' What she said to the assembled press was 'I fight on, I fight to win', which was later the subject of one of Sir Bernard's briefer press releases, infelicitous comma and all.

Kenneth Clarke and Chris Patten were, minutes later, listening to her statement to the House. They nodded to each other, indicating that they wanted a discussion. Behind the Speaker's Chair, they discovered that they agreed that Mrs Thatcher should withdraw. They were joined by Norman Lamont, whose views were equally strong.

From mid-afternoon till something after eight that evening the Cabinet Corridor, behind the Speaker's Chair, was turned into a Turkish bazaar. Ministers gathered in Mr Wakeham's room, Mr Gummer's room and Mr Patten's room, moving from one to another. They had already been told by Mr Wakeham or on his behalf – some directly, others by telephone – that they were to have five-minute interviews with the Prime Minister, beginning shortly after six, following her return from the Palace. The Ministers agreed with one another that they were going to give Mrs Thatcher their candid opinions and in talking in this way tended to reinforce one another's courage. Mr Wakeham asked several of his colleagues to be completely frank in the expression of their views but added to some that they should if possible avoid 'unnecessary brutality'.

In retrospect, it can be seen that the conditions were ideal for rebellion. If the Prime Minister had summoned her colleagues one by one into the Cabinet Room in Downing Street – if, moreover, they had been ushered in, and then out, with no chance to foregather before and after the interview – who can tell what the result would have been? Who can tell what the result would have been if Mrs Thatcher had simply summoned a meeting of the full Cabinet between six and seven, and asked for their backing? True, the two most forceful advocates of Mrs Thatcher's standing down, Mr Clarke and Mr Patten, both wanted a meeting of the full Cabinet, at 11 that night. They wanted it after they had seen her separately. If she was to stand, they wanted the full Cabinet to be consulted. A Cabinet meeting earlier in the evening, the Prime Minister taking the initiative, might have produced a different result.

The first Minister to see her was Mr Parkinson. It was in the nature of a personal visit, outside the scheduled appointments. He told Mrs Thatcher that she could win and should carry on. Afterwards he had a party piece, his version of what she should have told faint-hearted Ministers whom she had preferred, notably Peter Lilley:

> Now look here, Lilley, you miserable little worm, you are in this Cabinet because I put you there, and for no other reason. So I expect your support, and if I don't get it you will be out of my Cabinet when I reshuffle it after all this nonsense is over.

It is doubtful whether Mr Parkinson advised Mrs Thatcher in quite these terms or, if he had, whether she would have taken his advice or, if she had done so, whether it would have worked on Mr Lilley, Mr Howard, Mr Gummer, Mr Maude and Mr Lamont – all those Ministers who were in their forties, whom she had preferred as ideologically sound and whose defections hurt her most of all. Mr Maude was the second Minister to see her. He had come to see Peter Morrison. Sir Peter was present during most of the interviews. Outside were John Wakeham and Andrew Turnbull, a true civil servant, the Principal Private Secretary to the Prime Minister. Mr Maude was ushered in as a good friend. He told her tearfully that she was not going to win. In fact the political crisis of November 1990 was distinguished as much by lachrymosity as by general sobriety. Francis Maude, John Gummer, Tony Newton, David Waddington, John Wakeham: all shed tears when the events were happening, when they were recalling them afterwards or, usually, on both occasions.

Kenneth Clarke, however, was no blubber. As he was to boast later, his embarrassment threshold was high. Mrs Thatcher's mood, he remembered, was still calm and confident when he met her after Mr Maude's departure, at about 6.15. Their conversation was friendly. She was trying to cheer him up;

talking about what could be achieved by a better-organised campaign. Mr Clarke, however, had made up his mind. He was not to be moved. He refused to be cheered up, describing the proposed campaign as a 'charge of the Light Brigade'. He accused Mrs Thatcher of handing the leadership to Mr Heseltine, who would, in his opinion, win easily. He advised her to release Mr Hurd and Mr Major from their promises not to run, so as to give the party a choice. He quoted Alan Clark on her imminent defeat; though he did not give her Mr Clark's estimate of 90 votes. Mrs Thatcher was visibly stunned.

Alan Clark saw her later on. His ability to put his foot in the door would have ensured a glittering career in the heroic days of Fleet Street. He told her that she would lose disastrously but that it was her duty to go down fighting, producing a classical reference in support.

Chris Patten saw her at about 6.45, immediately after the much-moved John Gummer. Mr Wakeham had told him that he must be frank but sensitive to what had happened. Peter Morrison was in the room but Andrew Turnbull was outside. Mr Patten said that she would not beat Mr Heseltine, and must stand down. If, however, she intended to carry on, the whole Cabinet needed to discuss the matter. Mr Patten remembered that the occasion was 'not cosy' but that Mrs Thatcher did not make it 'impossibly difficult'. The spectacle of someone who had always been so powerful in her present condition was a 'bit of a tear-jerker'. Alan Clark, who was obsessed by the possibility of Mr Heseltine's victory, at one time suggested that Mr Patten should stand as a means of splitting his vote.

Mr Baker was staunch. Some of his colleagues accused him of sycophancy, though not to his face. Mr Baker maintained that 'you ought not to be able to put a cigarette-paper' between the chairman of the party and the leader. Others said that it was equally the duty of the chairman to give the leader frank even if unwelcome advice. But what if the chairman honestly believed that the leader, with proper – in Mr Baker's phrase, 'forward-looking' – campaigning, could win the second ballot? The evidence is that Mr Baker was not being sycophantic but really did believe this. In any case, it is both inconsistent and ungenerous of the friends of Mrs Thatcher to deny any credit to Mr Baker but to heap blame on Mr Lamont and his friends.

Mr Brooke appeared in full evening dress, on his way to some function, and said to Mr Wakeham that he had been told in his Oxford days that this was the correct wear when any serious decision was required of one. In the event he was far from decisive, as was Mr King.

It does not need the benefit of retrospection to see that at least two questions were being asked of Ministers. This could be perceived at the time. They were 'Do you support me?' and 'Do you think I can win?' Kenneth Clarke, Chris Patten and Malcolm Rifkind answered 'No' to both. Alan Clark said 'Yes' to the first and 'No' to the second; adding, however, that the Prime Minister should go forward decisively and lose gloriously. This was eccentric but honest and typical of Mr Clark. The majority of Ministers answered the questions as Alan Clark had done but, unlike him, concluded that, because she would (in their estimation) lose, therefore she ought not to stand.

Several of them – Mr Howard, Mr Waldegrave, Mr Lamont – added that, should she decide to stand, of course they would support her. Whether their protestations were in all cases wholly genuine may be doubted. It was a question expecting the answer No. When, for example, Neil Hamilton (a supporter of Mrs Thatcher's) saw Norman Lamont in the Library Corridor at about six that evening, he told him that he believed Mrs Thatcher intended to contest the second ballot; whereupon, according to Mr Hamilton, Mr Lamont went on his way wearing a most worried expression.

Mr Wakeham maintained on *The World This Weekend* that this question – whether Mrs Thatcher would win the second ballot – was one which members of the Cabinet were uniquely well-qualified to answer, because they were, above all other things, parliamentary animals, well-schooled in the House of Commons and its ways. Such a proposition does not bear a moment's serious examination. Once again, Mr Wakeham was muddying the waters; and, once again, from the best of motives, in this case a reluctance to hurt Mrs Thatcher's feelings. Cabinet Ministers possess no special *expertise* in the ways of the House of

Commons. How can they have, since they are speedily removed from the place by their officials as soon as they become Ministers? Ministers who continue to maintain an interest, such as Stanley Baldwin (sitting hour after hour on the front bench, sniffing the pages of *Dod's Parliamentary Companion*), find themselves accused of indolence. The only question which a Prime Minister can legitimately ask of Cabinet colleagues is 'Do you support me?'. As Chris Patten was to observe afterwards, this was too cruel a question to ask, or to answer; much better to wrap it up.

The drafting of Mr Hurd and Mr Major

Mr Patten and Mr Clarke continued to press for a Cabinet meeting at 11 that night. Mr Baker was evasive. Mr Wakeham advocated leaving it till the morning. Mr Patten and Mr Clarke said they would raise Mrs Thatcher's position at Thursday morning's Cabinet unless it had been resolved overnight. They both said to Mr Wakeham and to Alastair Goodlad, the Deputy Chief Whip (who had turned up to keep an eye on things), that they would resign if Mrs Thatcher did not bow out.

Mr Goodlad – a ginger man, a more intelligent version of Arthur Box-Bender in the *Sword of Honour* trilogy – went with Mr Clarke to fetch Mr Hurd out of a dinner that was being held in Dining Room A. Mr Clarke, Mr Patten and Mr Goodlad now wanted the Prime Minister to withdraw, and Mr Hurd and Mr Major to stand against each other. Mr Hurd and Mr Major now wanted soundings to be taken on which of them had the better chance against Mr Heseltine. Mr Goodlad and Mr Clarke explained to Mr Hurd that time did not permit of such an exercise. Mr Hurd then agreed, if necessary, to stand against Mr Major. The suggestion had first come from the phantom campaigner, Michael Jopling.

Mr Goodlad and Mr Clarke then telephoned Mr Major in Huntingdon. Mr Major explained that Mrs Thatcher's nomination papers were being sent to him to sign (even though the No. 10 Press Office was mendaciously claiming that they had already been signed by him and Mr Hurd). Mr Clarke urged him not to sign. Mr Major replied that he had promised and was bound. However, he was persuaded that both he and Mr Hurd ought to run if Mrs Thatcher withdrew.

At 11 o'clock the idea of the Cabinet meeting proposed by Mr Patten and Mr Clarke was abandoned. Mr Wakeham told Mr Clarke, and Mr Wakeham or Sir Peter Morrison told other Ministers, that Mrs Thatcher was going to sleep on it and had more or less decided to stand down.

The last ditch

That Wednesday evening was full of meetings, some of which had been arranged well in advance of the week's events. One of those directed specifically to the second ballot was of the 92 Group. This regarded itself as consisting of right-inclined Conservatives who were not necessarily economic liberals. It was so called because one of its founders, Patrick Wall, had lived in a Chelsea house numbered '92'. The name had nothing to do with the year 1992 or with the number of members. The group's chairman was Sir George Gardiner, the Member for Reigate, a former journalist who looked like a 'Spy' cartoon hurriedly redrawn by Aubrey Beardsley. He was a supporter of Mrs Thatcher and wrote for the *Sunday Express*.

That evening at about seven the group was meeting to consolidate support for Mrs Thatcher against Mr Heseltine. News reached the gathering of about 60 via David Maclean, the Member for Penrith and a junior Minister, that all was not well with the Prime Minister. She was coming under 'tremendous pressure' from her Cabinet. Tim Renton, a prominent figure in the group's demonology, was urging withdrawal. After some discussion, a decision was made to send a deputation to the Prime Minister.

Sir George, Mr Maclean, Michael Portillo and Christopher Chope (also junior Ministers, and Members for Southgate and Itchen respectively) arrived at the Prime Minister's Commons room shortly after eight. Mr Tebbit was there too. At five he had shepherded an uncomfortable-looking Mrs Thatcher through the tearoom. It is not true, as has been alleged, that Sir Peter

Morrison tried to bar the deputation's way and was promptly knocked down. He said merely that time was short, as, indeed, it was, for Mrs Thatcher had still to complete her speech for the next day. It was, it seems – or this was Sir George's impression – Mr Renton who tried to impede the delegation's progress. In this he was unsuccessful. 'We've come to bully you, Margaret,' Sir George announced, which was not perhaps the most tactful introduction after the experience which the Prime Minister had just been through.

Mrs Thatcher said: 'Well, what's all this, George, I hear about our supporters deserting in droves?' Sir George thought her use of the phrase 'deserting in droves' was significant. It was not her natural way of speaking and could have come only from a member or members of her Cabinet. He replied that Mr Heseltine could be beaten and that the Whips had not done a proper trawl. 'Thank you, thank you,' said Mrs Thatcher. Mr Tebbit told Sir George afterwards that she had indeed been glad to see Sir George and his friends, even though the visit may have had no effect on the course of events.

Another meeting was of the No Turning Back Group, a more overtly Thatcherite outfit than the '92'. It was holding a dinner at the Institute of Economic Affairs in Lord North Street. Peter Lilley was the only senior Minister present. He courageously repeated his view (which he had formed immediately after the result of the first ballot) that the game was up. He said that Mrs Thatcher should not contest the second ballot and that this was the advice he had given her. He was attacked for faint-heartedness by many of those present, notably by Neil Hamilton, Member for Tatton and a Whip.

Mr Hamilton went to 10 Downing Street with Michael Forsyth, Member for Stirling and a junior Minister. Mr Portillo was already there. So was Mr Gummer, who kept knocking down every argument in favour of Mrs Thatcher's fighting. He said she would not win. In Mr Hamilton's eyes, Mrs Thatcher presented the most pathetic spectacle he had ever seen in his life. But her mind was made up: she was not going to carry on.

In the House the One Nation Group was also holding a dinner. This was a survival of the group which had originally included

Iain Macleod, and also Enoch Powell. It was perhaps the most important Conservative group since 1945. By November 1990 it had fallen on hard times. There were only 12 people at the dinner. One of them was Timothy Raison, Member for Aylesbury and a former Minister, the epitome of welfarist Conservatism. He was deputed to carry a message to No. 10 urging Mrs Thatcher not to contest the second ballot. He did not meet her but her Political Secretary, John Whittingdale. He had rarely felt more relieved in his life. In the first ballot he had abstained; in the second he was to vote for Mr Hurd. It was odd that, of all three candidates in the second ballot, it was Mr Major who in his views came closest to the original One Nation Group.

Earlier that evening, John Whittingdale had asked Jeffrey Archer to drive to Huntingdon to procure John Major's signature on the Prime Minister's nomination papers. Mr Archer said he could not go because he had a speaking engagement in Norwood but would send his chauffeur, Bob, instead. Mr Major signed (as he had informed Mr Clarke that he was bound to do). At about 11.30 Mr Archer returned from Norwood to his flat, where there was a message for him to telephone Mr Major. Mr Archer did so and formed the impression that he had just spoken to Mrs Thatcher, who had told him that she was not going to stand. At around midnight Bob arrived at Mr Archer's flat with the nomination papers in a brown envelope.

Mr Whittingdale told Mr Archer on the telephone that it would be perfectly all right if he brought it round to Downing Street between seven and eight in the morning. Mr Archer said he would, and went to bed with the papers on the side table. But he could not sleep, telephoned Mr Whittingdale and asked whether he might deliver the envelope that night. Mr Whittingdale said he could. Mrs Thatcher was being helped with her speech by, among others, Michael Fallon, Member for Darlington and a junior Minister. Mr Archer did not speak to her but handed the papers to Peter Morrison in the next room at about half past one on the Thursday morning. Sir Peter thanked Mr Archer and tossed them aside without even opening the envelope. It was the sign that it was all over. It was subsequently learnt that the Whips had advised against a plan emanating from No. 10 to rush in the nomination papers, because they feared that Mr Patten and Mr Clarke would resign overnight if this happened.

Five hours later, Michael Portillo and Michael Forsyth were again on the doorstep, this time accompanied by Michael Brown, Member for Brigg, and Edward Leigh, Member for Gainsborough. The last two were in a tearful condition. Charles Powell refused them admission because it was too early and Mrs Thatcher was working on her speech, but told them they could come back later, which they did. Mr Tebbit, though he had been at No. 10 for most of the previous evening, was not among these last-ditchers. When asked on the Thursday morning whether he would stand, he replied that he was supporting John Major.

Tears in the Cabinet

At about half past seven Andrew Turnbull was instructed by Mrs Thatcher to put various steps in train. In particular an appointment had to be arranged with the Queen, for Mrs Thatcher to tell her that she intended to resign as Prime Minister as soon as the Conservative Party had chosen a new leader.

That day's Cabinet had long been fixed for nine on account of Lady Home's memorial service, which was to be held later that morning at St Margaret's, Westminster. Mr Major was not present. Those who were looked down at their blotting pads, embarrassed, like schoolchildren about to see one of their number being punished. Tony Newton, John Wakeham and David Waddington were in tears. Why, Cecil Parkinson wondered afterwards, should Mr Wakeham be crying, when he had precipitated the very events which they were witnessing? That, at any rate, was Mr Parkinson's opinion.

Mrs Thatcher was crying as well. She began to read a statement and broke down. She tried again and broke down a second time. 'For Christ's sake you read it, James,' Mr Parkinson said to the Lord Chancellor. Mrs Thatcher said: 'I can read it myself,' which she proceeded to do. Lord Mackay then paid a graceful tribute of his own on behalf of his colleagues.

Douglas Hurd said that, having spent the last couple of days with her, he thought her calm and bravery when all this was going on had been remarkable. Mrs Thatcher said that she could deal with business but not with sympathy, a theme which was to recur in the next few days. 'It's a funny old world,' she said, having said the same the evening before. After a short break for coffee, Mrs Thatcher dispatched an armoured brigade to the Gulf.

Just after half past nine the public announcement of Mrs Thatcher's intention to resign was made. The Cabinet was still sitting at this point. After it broke up, Mr Baker said outside:

> This is a typically brave and selfless decision by the Prime Minister.[11]

Mr Wakeham was asked about her mood:

> Well, her mood is, like always, she does her duty, she's – of course she's sad, of course she's sad.[12]

Triumph in the House

At half past twelve she went to the Palace and returned at one. She worked on her speech. Just after three Mr Heseltine entered the Chamber to Labour cheers. Mrs Thatcher then came in. Some Conservatives rose and waved their order papers. Labour Members responded by shouting 'Judas'. Mr Heath then arrived and was cheered by Labour. Mrs Thatcher answered questions at a quarter past three, and coped well with compassion from the Opposition. At ten to five she rose to reply to the motion of censure:

> The Opposition's real reason is the leadership election for the Conservative Party, which is a democratic election according to rules which have been public knowledge for many years – one member, one vote. That is a far cry from the way in which the

[11] Transcript, *The Thatcher Factor Special*, 110.
[12] Ibid. 111.

Labour Party does these things.[13]

This was true enough, though the system had been in operation only since 1981, and Neil Kinnock was its first beneficiary.[14] But it was Mrs Thatcher's day:

> *Margaret Thatcher*: Europe is strongest when it grows through willing co-operation and practical measures, not compulsion or bureaucratic dreams.
>
> *Alan Beith*: Will the Prime Minister tell us whether she intends to continue her personal fight against a single currency and an independent central bank when she leaves office?
>
> *Dennis Skinner*: No, she's going to be the governor (*Laughter*).
>
> *Mrs Thatcher*: What a good idea. I hadn't thought of that. But if I were, there'd be no European central bank, accountable to no one, least of all to national Parliaments. Because the point of that kind of Europe with a central bank is no democracy, taking powers away from every single Parliament, and having a single currency, a monetary policy and interest rates which takes all political power away from us. As my right honourable friend [Nigel Lawson] said in his first speech after the proposal for a single currency, a single currency is about the politics of Europe. It is about a federal Europe by the back door. So I'll consider the honourable gentleman's [Mr Skinner's] proposal. Now where were we? I'm enjoying this. I'm enjoying this.
>
> *Michael Carttiss*: Cancel it. You can wipe the floor with these people.[15]

Afterwards some Labour Members said uncharitably that they could have relied on Mr Skinner to present Mrs Thatcher with the greatest parliamentary triumph of her career. Was Mr Carttiss, the Conservative Member for Great Yarmouth, correct? He will play no further part in this narrative. But certainly Mrs Thatcher's performance exacerbated feelings of guilt and helped to ensure the victory of her favourite, Mr Major.

It had been the most remarkable period in the peacetime politics of the twentieth century. Foreign politicians could not

---

understand what had happened or why, in particular how Mrs Thatcher had won 204 votes to Mr Major's 185, and still lost. For once, the BBC World Service made what civil servants like to call an error of judgment and treated the fall of Mrs Thatcher as a domestic political occurrence, of parochial interest merely. Many factors had contributed to the fall of the Prime Minister: the Conservatives' own electoral system; poor opinion poll figures; bad by-election results; the resignation of Nigel Lawson and Sir Geoffrey Howe, and the events leading up to them; the impact of Michael Heseltine; the poll tax; and, not least, the character of Margaret Thatcher herself. To the last of these we now turn.

2

The Character of Mrs Thatcher

'The *Beast* stands for strong mutually antagonistic governments everywhere,' he said. 'Self-sufficiency at home, self-assertion abroad.'

Evelyn Waugh, *Scoop*

Mr Ridley has sought in his book not merely to exalt Margaret Thatcher's achievements, but to explain her downfall. He chooses to do so in terms of 'the enemies within' – the imagined treachery of some of her closest colleagues. But what his account in fact suggests is that one of the main causes of that downfall was an enemy even deeper within. That was the flaws within her own remarkable character.

Nigel Lawson, *Spectator*, 13 July 1991

Immediately after the 1987 election, Margaret Thatcher's power and reputation were at their height. For in politics, as in no other activity known to mankind except warfare, nothing succeeds like success. This is particularly true of Western democratic politics, where the very fact of re-election is taken to be an indication not only of success but of virtue also. It is most particularly true of Britain, whose Prime Minister is not bound by the different ropes – of law, of politics and of tenure – which tie down the First Ministers and Heads of State of France, West Germany and the United States. So it was that since the election there had been a tendency to bow down before Mrs Thatcher. This collective self-abasement extended from most of the Conservative Party, through David Owen and the *Independent* newspaper, to Bryan Gould, and on to Eric Hobsbawm and the *savants* of *Marxism Today*.

The worship of power

It was not that these people, and papers, wholly approved of what she was and what she had done (though some did). It was rather that they attributed extraordinary powers to her. She evidently contained the magic ingredient. Her combination of social authoritarianism and economic liberalism at home with national self-assertion abroad was supposed to make a unique appeal to what used to be called the working classes and now went by the name of 'the C2s' in the polling and market research trades.

Even the BBC, under the newly-installed Michael Checkland and John Birt, was not exempt from this massed fawning. The television news of 26 November 1987, on Mikhail Gorbachev's imminent stopover in Britain *en route* for the United States, was notably oleaginous. Mrs Thatcher was now, it appeared, the undisputed leader of the Western world. Moreover, Mr Gorbachev liked and trusted her. While not perhaps being prepared to go as far as he in trust and affection – for, we were to understand, she was not easily fooled – she was nevertheless prepared to 'do business' with him. Anyone would have thought that the intermediate-range missile agreement between the Russian and American Foreign Ministers was her own personal handiwork and that she had set up the forthcoming summit herself.

Despite Mr Birt's proclaimed new policy of analysing the news, explaining it and placing it in context, there was nothing about Mrs Thatcher's numerous past pronouncements on the evil nature of Soviet Communism, which had reached a peak of hysteria at the time of the shooting down of the South Korean aeroplane. Nor was there anything about her opposition to the agreement itself. There was no evidence that she had changed her mind. She would still have felt happier and more secure with cruise missiles at Greenham Common in Berkshire.

But, as Mrs Thatcher had now won three elections, people were somehow reluctant to regard her as the same as any other politician. There was supposed to be both a magic ingredient and a coherent body of doctrine called Thatcherism. In reality there was neither. She had won in 1979 entirely justly (insofar as justice has any part in these matters) because the Labour government had destroyed itself. She had won in 1983 because the Labour Party was a shambles and the Opposition was split between Labour and the Alliance. She had won in 1987 for the same reasons, even if Labour's campaigning had been more adroit on that occasion. Tactical voting had proved a chimera, with otherwise intelligent people insisting that they were going to vote for 'their' party (usually Labour rather than Liberal or Social Democrat), whatever the consequences might be. In all this adulation of Mrs Thatcher as a person, Thatcherism as a force, there was an unwholesome whiff of the worship of power for its own sake.

Mrs Thatcher is surprised

It was at once a strength and a deficiency in her that, at this stage, she was always being surprised. Every day was a new day, a fresh abuse becoming manifest, another scandal being revealed. The state of affairs which had been drawn to her attention or she had discovered for herself was, she would aver, nothing short of shocking, quite shocking. The Government really ought to do something about it. Indeed, the Government ought to have done something years ago. Valuable time had been lost; so a brisk start must be made now.

Not for her the modestly lowered eyelids of an A.J. Balfour, the sceptical resignation of a third Marquess of Salisbury, or the pessimistic yet oddly comforting scriptural reflection that we are all conceived in sin, and shapen in iniquity. 'Action this day!' she would demand, echoing Winston Churchill, to whom she had taken to referring with increasing familiarity as 'Winston', though they were never on close terms or, indeed, on any terms at all.

Normally vigorous Ministers became tired just by listening to her. She was as interventionist as Edward Heath; more so than

James Callaghan or Harold Wilson. Civil servants had traditionally inclined to the view that there was nothing much to be done about whatever-it-happened-to-be or that we had always done it this way, and doing it any other way would present insuperable difficulties or, at any rate, annoy lots of people. David Owen had often spoken of the dampening effect of this attitude as demonstrated to him as a Labour Minister. Mrs Thatcher's dismissal of it was one reason for his admiration of her. She was as busy as any Benthamite Utilitarian, as officious as any Fabian Socialist.

Admittedly some of her various initiatives trickled into the sands. For instance, she discovered that there was rubbish everywhere. But instead of placing the responsibility where it lay, with the Environment Department and the local authorities, she brought in Richard Branson, who created much publicity but did little to clear the rubbish. In fact Mr Branson subsequently denied that he had been assigned any specific task.

Then she discovered the 'inner cities' – a universal euphemism for decayed (or, more often, destroyed) nineteenth-century towns whose populations were disproportionately immigrant, especially black, in composition. The problem had been around for years, for even longer than the rubbish in the streets. The Conservative who first drew attention to it, well before Mrs Thatcher formed her 1979 administration, was Peter Walker. He should have been in charge of the whole programme and perhaps would have been, had she not imposed a doctrinal test and exiled him to Wales. The second Conservative to attend to the problem, at the 1981 Blackpool conference and on other occasions, was Michael Heseltine, but he removed himself from the Cabinet in 1986, to return only after Mrs Thatcher's departure.

Why had it taken her so long to find out about the cities? The explanation was perhaps that she travelled everywhere by car, avoiding trains, in fact hating them – always a bad sign in a person, along with a dislike of walking and of animals. If you travelled by car you tended to avoid city centres and, often, to bypass cities entirely. Mrs Thatcher did not travel by train during her election campaigns, but she was perforce transported into various towns, if only for enough time to have her picture taken.

What made the deepest impression on her was a scene less of dereliction than of enterprise. It was at Gateshead. It was what was described as 'the largest shopping and leisure complex in Europe' – rather like the biggest aspidistra in the world, of which Gracie Fields used to sing so affectingly. From that moment, there was no restraining Mrs Thatcher's enthusiasm. She brought the project up in an encounter with voters on television shortly before the 1987 election. Some of these citizens churlishly said they would prefer to have jobs, so providing them with money to spend in the shopping complex.

Her rewriting of history

It would be idle to deny, however, that Mrs Thatcher changed the present – even though the two changes for which she was most widely praised, the sale of council houses and the reform of the trade unions, were the work of political opponents who were in due course to leave her service, Michael Heseltine and Jim Prior respectively. But Mrs Thatcher also tried to change the past. We have already remarked her frequent invocation of 'Winston'. What, one wonders, would she have made of this exchange between Churchill and R.A. Butler during the former's post-war administration:

> *Churchill*: Walter [Monckton, Minister of Labour] and I settled the railway strike so you won't be troubled any more.
> *Butler*: On what terms have you settled it?
> *Churchill*: Theirs, old cock! We did not like to keep you up.[1]

If Mrs Thatcher had given in, she would not have admitted it. She was reminiscent of the advice commonly given to the faithless lover: deny, deny and keep on denying, whatever evidence may be produced to the contrary. Indeed, she possessed two methods of discourse, denial and assertion. It was difficult to

[1] R.A. Butler, *The Art of Memory* (1982), 137.

blame television interviewers for, on the whole, failing to respond adequately to her. Opponents across the floor in the House of Commons found it hard enough. Colleagues around the table in No. 10 found it even harder. It was a mistake to believe, as many did, that Mrs Thatcher's style of politics was founded on a fondness for facts and a distrust of vagueness and generalisation. On the contrary, it was a form of bullying.

But the voters loved it, for a time: just as they loved Ena Sharples of *Coronation Street* and Alf Garnett of *Till Death Us Do Part*. Anyway, they loved it when it was someone else who was at the receiving end, as it usually was: Neil Kinnock or Sir David Steel, David Dimbleby or Sir Robin Day (whom Mrs Thatcher once called 'Mr Day' throughout an entire interview). Despite the influence of Sir Gordon Reece over soft hairstyles and husky voices, Mrs Thatcher consistently broke the old rules of political television. When in difficulties, she talked faster and shouted louder.

This, curiously, worked to her advantage in television studios. So it did also, though less curiously, in the Chamber of the Commons, which was designed for this very kind of performance. But when the House came to be televised, Mrs Thatcher subtly changed her technique, becoming softer and quieter, except when her passions were aroused. It was a lapse in control by her which led to the resignation of Sir Geoffrey Howe.[2]

A consequence of her technique of assertion and repetition was the belief, common in the 1980s, that the present was quite different from the past. People thought that a fundamental change had occurred in the Conservative Party not merely after 1979 but when she became leader, in 1975. 'I have changed everything,' she said to her biographer, then her adviser, Patrick Cosgrave, in March 1976. He had asked her what difference her election as leader had made. This was on the evening of a defeat of the Wilson government on public expenditure brought about by a combination of Conservative Opposition and Labour Left. Mrs Thatcher thought Harold Wilson should have resigned. One

[2] See below, p. 146.

adviser – Dr Cosgrave does not say whether it was he – counselled caution: after all, she might find herself in the same position one day.[3] The sentence soon became part of the small change of political quotation, which was easily understandable. But it was also believed, taken at face value, which was not so understandable, unless we remember the power of simple assertion.

There were otherwise intelligent politicians and observers who believed that from the 1940s or the early 1950s (the date varied) until the advent of Mrs Thatcher we had lived through a period of political compromise or consensus which had been weak, wet, soggy or liberal (again, the adjective varied). And yet, if there was indeed a consensus during this remote, pre-Thatcher age, the Conservatives certainly chose colourful, even violent language in which to express its meaning. We have only to think of such performers as John Boyd-Carpenter, Charles Hill, Quintin Hogg, Iain Macleod and Peter Thorney-croft. 'Socialism' and 'the Socialists' were excoriated weekly, in and out of the House of Commons.

The truth is that there was no such consensus. The *Economist* cleverly invented 'Mr Butskell' to describe a composite of R.A. Butler as Chancellor of the Exchequer and Hugh Gaitskell as his shadow; the name stuck. But Macleod, with Enoch Powell, first proposed selectivity in the Welfare State. The parties were not at one. Conflict was real.

The influence of Sir Ronald

It was generally assumed that Mrs Thatcher possessed no sense of humour, though this was disputed by some of her admirers. Unfortunately they were, like the friends of Maurice Bowra, hard put to it to provide examples. Most of her public essays in this line were the work of her speechwriter, the affable playwright and man of the theatre Sir Ronald Millar. Sometimes they could be rather embarrassing:

[3] Patrick Cosgrave, *Margaret Thatcher* (1978), 196-7. However, in his *Thatcher: the First Term* (1985), 26, Dr Cosgrave gives the year as 1977, when James Callaghan was Prime Minister. The first version is probably the correct one.

Ladies and Gentlemen, I stand before you tonight in my green chiffon evening gown, my face softly made up, my fair hair gently waved ... The Iron Lady of the Western World? Me?[4]

It was Sir Ronald who suggested that she invoke the prayer of St Francis outside the front door of 10 Downing Street after winning the 1979 election:

Where there is discord, may we bring harmony. Where there is error, may we bring truth. Where there is doubt, may we bring faith. Where there is despair, may we bring hope.[5]

There was no limit to Sir Ronald's ingenuity in the service of his mistress. It was he who coined: 'You turn if you want; the lady's not for turning.' The preceding words were: 'To those waiting with bated breath for that favourite media catchphrase, the U-turn, I have only one thing to say.' The echo was of Christopher Fry's play *The Lady's Not For Burning*, first performed in 1948. It was doubtful whether many of those assembled at Brighton spotted the reference.[6] Sir Ronald puzzled Mrs Thatcher with one of his jokes. In October 1977 Peter Jay, James Callaghan's son-in-law, had recently been appointed Ambassador to Washington. He had made a speech comparing the Prime Minister, Mr (as he then was) Callaghan, to Moses, leading his people into the promised land. Moses, it may be remembered, had been given two tablets of stone. Sir Ronald's joke was: 'So my message to Moses is this: keep taking the tablets.' Mrs Thatcher could not understand it and thought 'keep taking the pill' would be funnier, even if it was on the *risqué* side. She was, however, prevailed upon to stick to the original version.[7]

---

[4] Speech at Finchley, 31 January 1976. The sobriquet 'Iron Lady' had been bestowed on Mrs Thatcher by the Soviet newspaper *Red Star*, 23 January 1976.

[5] Spoken on 4 May 1979; Nicholas Wapshott and George Brock, *Thatcher* (1983), 179.

[6] Speech to the Conservative Conference, 10 October 1980; Wapshott and Brock, op. cit. 161.

[7] Speech to the Conservative Conference, 14 October 1977; Wapshott and Brock, op. cit. 161.

Her other sayings

Though she was not a natural wit, Mrs Thatcher was the origin of numerous quotations, many more than had come from her predecessor, Edward Heath, even allowing for the disproportion in their periods of office as Prime Minister and leader of the party. Several of the best-known quotations are, however, difficult to track down precisely.

'Is he one of us?' was asked by Mrs Thatcher of colleagues about other colleagues and, less often, of colleagues about journalists. It was usually asked expecting the answer No. The criteria were political or economic rather than social. 'Wet' was used by her to rebuke colleagues who lacked her singleness of purpose or disagreed with her on economic or social policy. 'The Wets' was adopted as a description by the group themselves, of whom the principal members were Sir Ian Gilmour (dismissed 1981), Francis Pym (dismissed 1983) and Jim Prior (resigned 1984). Earlier, R.A. Butler had been described by political opponents as 'wet'. It was originally public school slang for boys who were considered to be ineffectual, wanting in resolution or foolishly sentimental, though it had enjoyed a circulation outside those schools or their products. 'There is no alternative' was attributed to Mrs Thatcher in relation to economic policy in 1979-81, which led to the nickname 'Tina' in Whitehall – though this never quite caught on and was not much heard after the early 1980s. Oddly enough, the same declamatory sentence was used by Labour Ministers, notably Harold Wilson and James Callaghan, in 1964-70 to justify various incomes policies. 'What is the alternative?' was also employed at this earlier period. The trade union leader Clive Jenkins said several times that the alternative was to refrain from having an incomes policy.

For someone who had been brought up as a Methodist (and married in Wesley's Chapel, City Road, EC1, before converting to Anglicanism), Mrs Thatcher was sparing in scriptural reference. But to one story she was attached. 'No one would have remembered the Good Samaritan,' she told Brian Walden, 'if

he'd only had good intentions. He had money as well.'[8] Mr
Walden was one of her favourite interviewers – perhaps her
favourite – as she was one of his favourite subjects, though
interviewing her on Nigel Lawson's resignation in October 1989
he was tougher than anyone else had been.[9] The story of the
Good Samaritan was invoked on numerous occasions both by
her and by Norman Tebbit, for whom it evidently held a similar
appeal. Neither made clear that the Samaritan not only paid
cash but also indicated his willingness to incur debt: 'And on the
morrow when he departed, he took out two pence, and gave them
to the host, and said unto him, take care of him; and whatsoever
thou spendest more, when I come again, I will repay thee.'[10]

It was Mr Walden who provided the occasion for her most
famous misquotation, 'Victorian values'. She never used the
words. Mr Walden did. He said that what she was expounding
sounded to him like Victorian values. She concurred, adding:
'They were the values when our country became great.'[11] Words
were put similarly into R.A. Butler's mouth when, at London
airport in December 1955, a Press Association reporter asked
him to assent to the proposition that Anthony Eden was 'the best
Prime Minister we have'. Butler duly agreed, and the words
were ever after attributed to him.[12] Similarly, James Callaghan
was saddled with 'Crisis? What Crisis?' This was a headline
summarising Mr Callaghan's remarks – again, at London
airport – on returning from the Guadaloupe Summit to snow
and strikes.[13] The exchange in question went: Journalist: 'What
… of the mounting chaos in the country at the moment?'
Callaghan: 'I don't think that other people in the world would
share the view that there is mounting chaos.' Butler and
Callaghan were damaged politically by their misquotations, but
Mrs Thatcher was undamaged by hers. Indeed, it is arguable
that she was in Mr Walden's debt, though the words gave rise to

[8] *Weekend World*, 6 January 1980.

[9] See David Cox (ed.), *The Walden Interviews* (1990), 30 ff.

[10] Luke 10:35.

[11] *Weekend World*, 16 January 1982. Mr Walden subsequently claimed paternity in the *Sunday Times*, 16 August 1987.

[12] See Anthony Howard, *RAB* (1987), 222.

[13] *Sun*, 11 January 1979.

various tedious and inaccurate attacks on the evils of nineteenth-century society by those who were politically ill-disposed towards her.

Broadly speaking, they were the same people who assaulted her for saying 'There is no such thing as society' to a magazine.[14] They represented her as lacking in 'compassion', as 'uncaring', as a believer in State-approved selfishness. Neither Mrs Thatcher nor her supporters responded combatively. They could have pointed to the misery which the theories of Rousseau, Hegel and Marx had brought about: but they refrained. Certainly Mrs Thatcher herself was averse to philosophical speculation, even though she often attended meetings of the Conservative Philosophy Group which were held at Jonathan Aitken's house in Lord North Street, Westminster, and where the ambitious Conservative politicians, journalists and dons present easily outnumbered the philosophers. 'Oh *really*, Enoch...' she would expostulate as Mr Powell was once again driving his train into the buffers.

Her private character

In private she was a considerate and conscientious person. There were abundant and well-attested stories of her kindness to colleagues and others who found themselves with health troubles or in matrimonial difficulties. Ministers commented not on a worldliness exactly but, rather, on a down-to-earth quality, a lack of censoriousness. 'Cecil, your first duty is to your wife,' she said to Mr Parkinson, which was sensible and well-intentioned, though as matters turned out he did not benefit. After national tragedies she wrote personal letters to the bereaved.[15] She liked and admired Eric Heffer, as he did her. When he died in 1991, she wrote to his widow Doris and, in July of that year, attended his memorial service at St Margaret's, Westminster.

A journalist was once interviewing her on an off-the-record basis. After half-an-hour or so he made as if to depart, saying

---

[14] *Woman's Own*, 31 October 1987.
[15] Hugo Young and Anne Sloman, *The Thatcher Phenomenon* (1986), 80.

that he had no doubt taken up enough of her valuable time. '*I'll* tell you when to go,' she said, and resumed her monologue.

But she was quite without side. She was famous for breaking off discussions to cook scrambled eggs or to make (usually instant) coffee. She once interrupted a meeting at No. 10 to go out to buy bacon for her husband Denis. When a civil servant told her that there were others who could save her trouble and do the job just as well, she replied that they would not know the kind of bacon her husband liked.[16] Peter Jenkins has written, however:

> Even more preposterous is the view that representing Finchley somehow made her into a suburban housewife. On marrying she moved into Flood Street, Chelsea, and from that day she was untouched by financial worry of any kind, spared from the economics of housekeeping, and materially for ever removed from the shopkeeping world in which she had grown up. Her little shopping expeditions, the apron at the sink, Denis's special breakfast bacon, were aspects of the politician's image.[17]

And yet, Mr Jenkins perhaps implies a greater degree of opulence than Mrs Thatcher in fact enjoyed during this period, even though financial worry may have been absent. There were no servants, though there may have been a cleaning lady. Certainly Mrs Thatcher did the cooking herself. She was a great believer in regular meals for the children, notably tea, with cakes baked by her. She would rebuke a neighbour, Joanna, Mrs Terence Kilmartin (the possessor of a warm heart but a hot temper), for occasionally smacking her own children, who were of roughly the same age as Mrs Thatcher's twins. Children, she said, should never be struck but, rather, told 'No' firmly and repeatedly. This was tiring, no doubt, more tiring than the odd cuff. But it was the proper way to go about things.

Her style of government

Her most famous remark of all predated her Premiership: 'As

[16] Young and Sloman, op. cit. 22.
[17] Peter Jenkins, *Mrs Thatcher's Revolution* (1987), 85-6.

Prime Minister, I couldn't waste time having any internal arguments.'[18] In 1979-83 she picked off dissentients one by one, or two by two. It is arguable that she did not have the Cabinet she really wanted until June 1987, and not wholly so even then. 'Mrs Thatcher's style of government' was a topic much discussed throughout the 1980s. The more general question of whether we were moving towards a more 'presidential' Prime Minister had been talked about, by politicians, journalists and academics – most of all, by academics – since Harold Macmillan's day. The first edition of John Mackintosh's *The British Cabinet* (1962) and R.H.S. Crossman's Introduction to the Fontana edition of Bagehot's *English Constitution* (1963) had played a notable part in the debate.

On the whole, the conclusion of the political classes was that we were indeed moving towards a more presidential system of government. Doubters included Ronald Butt in *The Power of Parliament* (1st edn 1967), Henry Fairlie in *The Life of Politics* (1968) and Ian Gilmour in *The Body Politic* (1969). The trouble was that, quite apart from the difficulty of arriving at agreement about the facts, the word 'presidential' was used in at least four senses. It was used to refer to the power of the Prime Minister over his (or, later, her) Cabinet; the allegedly absolute control exercised by the Government, doing the Prime Minister's bidding, over the House of Commons; the presidential nature of general elections, with a leader rather than a party against another leader; and the separation, deliberately created, between the leader and the party.

Harold Wilson had tried to draw a distinction between the Labour Party and the Labour Government. Mrs Thatcher attempted to distinguish between herself and a Conservative Cabinet.[19] Most Prime Ministers, such as Harold Wilson and James Callaghan, come to dislike their parties. Others, such as Winston Churchill, Harold Macmillan and Edward Heath, never liked them much in the first place. Mrs Thatcher never despised her followers, certainly not her followers in the country. They reciprocated with adoration, at any rate until the last phase.

[18] Interview with Kenneth Harris, *Observer*, 25 February 1979.
[19] See above, p. 31.

Her relationship with her followers in the House was more complicated. She was elected leader in 1975 partly because she was not Mr Heath: specifically, because she was prepared to listen and to be reasonably civil, as the grumpy organist had patently not been. Alas, these hopes, which had shone bright in 1975, and were still glowing four years later, were slowly to be extinguished.

Mrs Thatcher came to rival the late Stanley Holloway in the art of the monologue and was clearly unfamiliar with Dr Johnson's view that 'questioning is not the mode of conversation among gentlemen'.[20] What made matters worse was that she did not wait for the answers. Whether she listened or not, the spectacle of her bearing down on a hitherto jovial table of Conservatives in the dining-room, shepherded by her faithful Parliamentary Private Secretary of the moment, was enough to dull the heartiest appetite and to disturb the strongest digestion.

Ah, those Parliamentary Private Secretaries of hers, what a curious collection of characters they were! The first was Ian Gow, foully murdered by the IRA, though he had left his post as PPS seven years before his assassination. He was a clubman, a conversationalist, an authority on Aneurin Bevan. He was affable but at the same time slightly sinister, like his Eastbourne constituent Dr John Bodkin Adams. He was popular and gregarious but simultaneously somehow feared, as his mistress's eyes and ears. The universal view among MPs was that, after his departure in 1983 to become Minister for Housing and Construction, she failed to find any adequate successor.[21]

Gow was a solicitor who had been to Winchester. Though affluent enough by most people's standards, in the Conservative Party he was not considered a rich man.[22] Mrs Thatcher concluded that it was unfair to ask a backbencher who did not have substantial independent means to become her PPS. Certainly a person holding this unpaid position could expect to

---

[20] Boswell, *Life of Johnson*, March 1776.
[21] Ian Gow was appointed Minister of State at the Treasury in September 1985 but resigned later in the year in protest against the Anglo-Irish Agreement.
[22] He left £764,526: *Independent*, 20 October 1990.

work all day long and would have to rely on his parliamentary salary unless he had an additional source of income. But the MPs she did appoint lasted for an average of only something under two years. Surely, if Mrs Thatcher had offered a two-year stint, followed by a guaranteed promotion to the Government at, say, Minister of State level, she could have taken her pick?

In the event she appointed, after Gow, a succession of men who were variously described as 'political morons', 'Sloanes', 'hooray Henrys' and 'chinless wonders'. In short, they were thought to be out of touch with the modern Conservative Party. They were, in chronological order, Michael Alison (Eton and Wadham), Archie Hamilton (Eton), Mark Lennox-Boyd (Eton and Christ Church) and Peter Morrison (Eton and Keble).

There were some backbenchers, well-disposed towards her politically, who nevertheless considered Mrs Thatcher to be something of a snob on the quiet. She certainly had a sentimental affection for Belton, the grand house near Grantham, decorating No. 10 with prints of, and objects from, the estate.[23] The truth is that she had a generalised *tendresse* for tall, slim, good-looking men, whose looks partook of a certain women's magazine quality. Of her PPSs, only Mr Lennox-Boyd and, conceivably, Mr Alison fulfilled these specifications. She was fond of Humphrey Atkins, devilish handsome, with an eye for the girls. She wanted to make him Speaker, but the House was not having any of it and chose Bernard Weatherill instead. Perhaps the House was wrong and Mrs Thatcher right. But she did not erect any social barrier against her favourites, as the rise of Cecil Parkinson before 1983 demonstrated. Nor did she impose any doctrinal test on them, as the career of Sir Ian Gilmour showed until 1981, when he had really gone too far in public scepticism about her policies.

Her failure to prefer allies

Mr Parkinson was a doctrinal ally, none more staunch apart

---

[23] It was rumoured that one of Mrs Thatcher's grandmothers had been seduced by Harry Cust (d. 1917), journalist, MP, roué and heir to the third Earl Brownlow of Belton. See Angela Lambert, *Independent Weekend*, 20 July 1991.

from Nicholas Ridley. But his career after 1987, when he was restored to his place in political society as Secretary of State for Energy, exemplified her disposition to go off people. A lot of ink was spilt over her alleged tendency to pack her Cabinets with sycophants and cronies. What was striking, in fact, was how few of her personal and political supporters she appointed, at any rate to major offices. And those whom she did prefer were, at some stage or other, exiled to the plantations or even sent to the scaffold. Her weakness as a picker of men – on the whole, she did not pick women – was all of a piece with her failure to appoint, or anoint, a successor. The latter omission was but the particular illustration of the general case. Mr Parkinson she picked up, toyed with and discarded. Opinions differ as to whether John Moore was considered as a successor: the balance of Cabinet opinion is that, very briefly, he was.

Altogether, the notion of a slowly but ruthlessly constructed Thatcherite Cabinet was a myth. Sometimes opponents of the Prime Minister willingly implemented policies which had come to be associated with her. On other occasions she imposed an apparently impossible task on one of her colleagues. If he failed, he was punished. If he succeeded, he was inadequately rewarded and she claimed the credit. The Minister on whom the task had been imposed was sometimes disinclined to undertake it on political grounds. He had to go through with it all the same. Occasionally the Minister would approve of the object he had been set.

Thus Mr Moore wanted to reform the health service on free-market lines congenial to the Prime Minister. He failed, became ill, was dismissed and was replaced by Kenneth Clarke, who did not really want to change the service in this way. Instead he produced a botch, for which he was rewarded by being sent to the Department of Education weeks before Mrs Thatcher's own dismissal. There then was the case of Patrick Jenkin. He was the earlier version of Mr Moore, except that neither Mrs Thatcher nor anyone else ever considered him a possible leader of the party. The other difference was that he was not as enthusiastic about abolishing the GLC as Mr Moore was about reforming the health service. Lord (as he later became) Jenkin did not fail: he merely received a bad press, and was replaced by his junior Minister, Kenneth Baker.

It was the same story at Education, where Mr Baker replaced Mrs Thatcher's old mentor Sir Keith Joseph. Here again Mr Baker did (or appeared to do) his mistress's bidding without antagonising either his backbenchers or the public generally, though he did alienate the teachers. Chris Patten was another recipient of the great Can of State when he was sent to Environment to try to do something about the poll tax.[24]

Most conspicuously of all, the light of Mrs Thatcher's countenance failed to shine on Norman Tebbit. He had been appallingly injured in the Brighton bombing of 1984, and his wife had been paralysed. He had made an excellent recovery, though the strain of looking after her was great.[25] He was as sharp a debater and as effective an orator as he had been before the outrage. Indeed, he was even more impressive speaking to Conservative audiences, who reached out to him. There were some who claimed that his sense of humour was not what it had been. But if this was so – for there were others who could detect no change – who could blame him? In 1985 Mrs Thatcher made him chairman of the party, two years later he helped to win the election and immediately afterwards he retired from the Government, ministerial ambition at an end.

The usual explanation was that he departed because he fell out with Mrs Thatcher over the merits of two rival advertising agencies.[26] But even in the Conservative Party of the 1980s, obsessed as it was by advertising, it was unlikely that a Minister should fall because of a dispute between two sets of gentlemen with gold chains and blow waves. A more probable explanation was that he wished to spend more time with his injured wife. Nor should we forget that he had vigorously expressed his misgivings about Mrs Thatcher's support for the American bombing of Libya.

But the principal explanation was that Mrs Thatcher had gone off him at the time of the Westland affair. He had not

[24] See below, p. 70ff.
[25] See Norman Tebbit, *Upwardly Mobile* (1988), 225 ff.
[26] See below, p. 97.

plotted against her or formed an alliance with Michael Heseltine (even though they were later to work happily together in the Commons over such matters as the abolition of ILEA). His error had been to contemplate Mrs Thatcher's fall – to mention the unmentionable. As Mrs Thatcher had mentioned it herself, saying at one stage of the affair that she might not still be Prime Minister at the end of the day, her response to Mr Tebbit's similar thoughts may have been harsh or simply irrational. But there it was. To be fair to Mrs Thatcher, she may have had some right on her side. The chairman was the leader's creature and was expected to support him or her, as the case might be. That, after all, was what he was there for. As we have seen, the message was not lost on Mr Baker in the events of November 1990.[27]

John Biffen, again, was essentially a doctrinal ally. Like her, he was suspicious of Europe, believed in free enterprise and had early been influenced by Enoch Powell. But he hated her stridency. He was a sceptic, a philosophical Conservative with all the characteristics of the Cambridge historian of the 1950s which he was, carrying the marks of Kenneth Pickthorn and Herbert Butterfield (who, however, claimed to be an Asquithian Liberal). She could never have made a real ally of Mr Biffen, however hard both of them might have tried. And exactly the same might be said of Nigel Lawson and Sir Geoffrey Howe.

It can plausibly be argued that if she had appointed Nicholas Ridley instead of John Major as Chancellor in October 1989, she might have saved herself. This is certainly Mr Ridley's opinion.[28] She could have appointed him in July of that year instead of leaving Mr Lawson *en poste*. Such speculations are profitless.

It is equally without profit to speculate on what might have happened if she had found, in her words, 'another Willie' after Lord Whitelaw's retirement owing to ill-health from the Cabinet and the post of Deputy Prime Minister.[29] In Charles Powell's

[27] See above, p. 19.

[28] See Nicholas Ridley, *My Style of Government* (1991), 136 ff.

[29] Though he remained Deputy Leader of the Conservative Party until July 1991 and was not replaced.

view, it was Lord Whitelaw who erected the barrier against any further movement towards the ERM after the *ad hoc* Cabinet committee's holding operation in 1985.[30] When he departed, the movement started again. On the other hand, Lord Whitelaw did not favour Mrs Thatcher's continuation in office in 1990. And he certainly played his part in favouring the preferment of Ministers who were not to demonstrate unswerving loyalty to Mrs Thatcher at the crucial time.

In these promotions Mrs Thatcher tended to rely on the Whips. Tristan Garel-Jones saw to it that the Wets were not wholly unrepresented. Indeed, of those who had attended parties in the 1979-81 period whose theme was hostility to Mrs Thatcher's policies, Chris Patten and William Waldegrave were by 1990 in the Cabinet, John Patten was considered unlucky not to be in the Cabinet, while Mr Garel-Jones himself was a Minister of State at the Foreign Office, having been Deputy Chief Whip. It has been suggested that if he rather than Tim Renton had been Chief Whip in Autumn 1990, she would have survived as leader. On the one hand, he had worked on her behalf against Sir Anthony Meyer in 1989 and offered his services to her campaign team, such as it was, in the following year. But, on the other hand, he was her political opponent. Alistair McAlpine had earlier urged Mrs Thatcher, in her own best interests, to get rid of Mr Garel-Jones from the Whips Office.

Irrespective of whether Mr Garel-Jones as Chief Whip would or would not have saved Mrs Thatcher, her appointment of Mr Renton to the post was certainly odd. He was a sensitive, charming, scholarly Etonian, with an Oxford First in History. He was a friend and admirer of Sir Geoffrey Howe, but had earlier resigned as his Parliamentary Private Secretary in protest against a discriminatory levy on the banks' profits. Restored to the Government, his career as a Home and Foreign Office Minister, honourable and competent as it had been, hardly indicated that a glittering future awaited him as Chief Whip. In 1990 he behaved equally honourably, but he was not 'one of us'. Nor had he ever pretended to be.

---

[30] See Transcript, Nigel Lawson interview with Jonathan Dimbleby, *On the Record*, BBC1, 7 July 1991.

Her bombast and bluster

There was a good deal of bombast and bluster about Mrs Thatcher's style of government:

> A leader must lead, must lead firmly, have firm convictions, and see that those convictions are reflected in every piece of policy ... How can I change Margaret Thatcher? I am what I am ... I am not an 'I' person, I am not a 'I did this in my government', 'I did that'. I have never been an 'I' person so I talk about 'We' – the government. I cannot do things alone so it has to be 'we'. It is a Cabinet 'we' ... Yes, I do lead from the front. Yes, I do have fundamental convictions ... But we do have very lively discussions because that's the way I operate ... then we reach collective decisions. That's collective responsibility.[31]

In November 1989 she told Robin Oakley of *The Times* that she was 'happy to carry on', 'by popular acclaim'.[32] Altogether she appeared, as they say in Wales, to be going a bit funny. There were television pictures of her clearing up rubbish in St James's Park. There was something oddly disturbing about those disjointed, stabbing movements with a pointed stick, as if a freelance witch were doing unmentionable things with a hatpin. That the rubbish had been deliberately placed there for her to assault made the scene resemble the more strongly an illustration to one of the Grimms' fairy tales. Actions and movements are a surer guide to mental condition than those more conventionally accepted indicators, the eyes.

But Mrs Thatcher's eyes were by now disturbing as well. On television, in a disastrous European election broadcast, they had assumed a newly manic quality.[33] This, combined with teeth that looked as if they were about to gobble one up, was quite upsetting to sensitive spirits.

The tenth anniversary of her Premiership affected her oddly. She showed no sign of giving up: but she did not wish to be

---

[31] *Daily Express*, 28 October 1989; *The Times*, 24 November 1989; BBC, *Panorama*, 27 November 1989. Cit. Peter Hennessy, 'Central Administration' in Peter Catterall (ed.), *Contemporary Britain* (1990), 9 at 13.

[32] *The Times*, 24 November 1989.

[33] The broadcast was on 14 June 1989.

reminded, or for others to be reminded, that she had been Prime Minister for that length of time. She was no longer the regal figure she had been, despite the luxuriance of 'we's' in her various interviews. She had lost her complete self-confidence. The loss was compounded when she was challenged by the rogue baronet Sir Anthony Meyer. It was the attempt that was damaging. It was rather as if Princess Michael of Kent were calling on the Queen to abdicate in her favour. The princess would not get far – everyone knew that – but somehow the religious mystery that hedged the monarch had been taken away. And yet, the seeds of Mrs Thatcher's destruction had been sown 15 years earlier, when she was Shadow Minister of the Environment, and to the story of the poll tax we must now turn.

3

The Poll Tax

In the management of the revenue he disapproved the simple but oppressive mode of a capitation, and preferred with reason a proportion of taxes deducted on every branch from the clear profits of agriculture and commerce.

Edward Gibbon, on Amrou the Saracen,
The Decline and Fall of the Roman Empire

And it came to pass in those days, that there went out a decree from Caesar Augustus, that all the world should be taxed.

Luke 2:1

Twenty years ago there were numerous cries that would rouse a Conservative party conference: that we were an overcrowded island, that greater discipline (usually a euphemism for corporal, maybe even capital punishment) was required in home and school alike, that parents were responsible for their children's misdeeds, that the closed shop should be made illegal and that the rates should be abolished. Others were uneasy besides Conservatives from the constituencies on their annual outing to the seaside. There was Anthony Crosland, for instance, who as Secretary of State for the Environment told the local authorities in 1975 that the party was over. Crosland considered the rating system unsatisfactory but concluded typically – though in this case probably correctly – that there was nothing to be done.[1]

This was certainly the conclusion of the Layfield Committee

[1] Personal knowledge.

which reported in 1976.[2] Sir Frank Layfield had been confined to finance. Lord Redcliffe-Maude, whose committee had reported a decade earlier, had chosen to restrict himself to the function and organisation of local authorities, even though he could have included finance in his deliberations.[3] This had been the pattern of inquiries into local government: to separate function from finance. It was to be repeated in the 1980s over the poll tax. An excessively, even brutally, simple notion – that of a flat-rate impost on every adult over 18, subject to certain exceptions – was grafted on to a financial system which to describe as Byzantine would be to do an injustice to the straightforwardness and reputation for plain dealing of the imperial court at Constantinople.

The mischief lay in the Revenue (formerly the Rate) Support Grant. Roughly half of local authority income came or, under the reformed system, was to come from this central government source. A quarter came from the new uniform business rate and the other quarter from local residents. The grant was supposed to allow for the different levels of need in different areas and was calculated for each area using a complicated formula of 28 indices of need from poverty to bad housing, single parents to immigrants.

Wandsworth was only the ninth most deprived inner London borough according to the Government. It duly received the ninth highest grant a head of £1,332. But, because it spent less a head than other boroughs, its grant was highest as a proportion of its spending. Wandsworth's grant was 90 per cent of its expenditure, while Lambeth's was 78 per cent. Wandsworth's poll tax was £136, Lambeth's £590. After Norman Lamont's disbursement of £140 in his 1991 Budget, Wandsworth actually ended up owing its residents money – in fact it simply refused to collect any – whereas Lambeth's poll tax was reduced to £450.[4]

[2] Cmnd 6453 (1976).
[3] Cmnd 4040 (1969).
[4] Martin Linton in the *Guardian*, 21 March 1991.

A glint in Mrs Thatcher's eye

Such an outcome had not been expected or allowed for by
Edward Heath and Margaret Thatcher 17 years previously. For
it was then that the Conservatives promised to abolish the rates.
The reason was that they were thought to be unfair. A poor
widow living alone might find herself paying the full amount. In
an identical house next door, the same liability might be
distributed among a husband, a working wife and two grown-up
sons. More inequitable still, this industrious family might find
themselves inhabiting a council house and hence paying no
rates at all. Mr Heath, assisted by Peter Walker, had already
reformed the structure of local government. At any rate they had
changed it. Larger authorities had been created: Avon,
Humberside, Tameside, which happened to be in and around
Manchester. They had even abolished the county of Rutland.[5]

Mr Heath now found himself in opposition once again, but his
reforming zeal was unabated. His Shadow Environment
Minister was Mrs Thatcher. She had previously been famous, in
a small way of business, as Thatcher-the-Milk-Snatcher, the
Education Secretary. She now, in the period from the second
election of 1974, acquired a new renown as Thatcher-the-
Mortgage-Lowerer. She promised to lower (and to peg)
mortgages, and was treated with the elaborate scorn which
Anthony Crosland reserved for women who thought they were
clever. Her promise to abolish the rates aroused less scorn,
maybe because it had aroused less interest. The Conservative
Manifesto of October 1974 promised:

> Within the normal lifetime of a Parliament we shall abolish the
> domestic rating system and replace it by taxes more broadly
> based and related to people's ability to pay. Local authorities
> must continue to have some independent source of finance.

When this passage was quoted against him in later years, Mr
Heath was fond of italicising the six words 'related to people's
ability to pay'.[6] He was certainly entitled to do this: but the last

[5] See generally Peter G. Richards, *The Reformed Local Government System* (1973).
[6] See *The Times*, 17 July 1987.

sentence, which came after them, was less often quoted, by him or by anybody else. There was nothing discreditable about it. On the contrary: it implied that the Conservatives were contemplating a more general reform of local authority finances. This, indeed, was so. The abolishing of rates was only the second step. The first was the transfer to central government 'in the medium term' of the cost of teachers' salaries up to a specified number of teachers for each local education authority. Expenditure on the police and on the fire services would 'qualify for increased grants from the Exchequer'. The Conservative Government would see to it that this saving was 'passed on to the ratepayer' (which implied that the rates would not be abolished until a higher governmental contribution to local authority finance had been made).[7]

This was, by any standards, a more reasonable and reasonably expressed attitude than what appeared after the early 1980s. The promise or promises still avoided questions of function. There was to be no State education system or national police force. The British, anyway the English, continued to be alarmed by the story of the French politician who took out his watch and announced that he knew what, at this precise moment, every single child in France was studying. Likewise the radical Right and the libertarian Left combined to denounce a national police force, controlled – who could tell what might happen? – by an unscrupulous and ambitious Minister of Justice, as a development even more to be feared than the introduction of identity cards. There was, nevertheless, an inarticulate belief that local government had certain functions to perform, and that it should raise the money to perform those functions on its own.

In succeeding years even this belief, vague as it was, became submerged by the desire to *discipline* local government. This desire did not – or did not solely – come about through the urge to punish refractory Labour authorities such as those of Lambeth or Liverpool. Some of these councils undoubtedly needed to be disciplined; it is extraordinary that a Conservative government, led by Mrs Thatcher, allowed the Liverpool Council

[7] Conservative Manifesto, October 1974.

particularly to get away with as much inefficiency, vindictiveness and near-criminality as it did in the early 1980s.

At the 1979 election, however, the Conservatives were not greatly exercised by the reform of local government. The Manifesto stated that rates reform would have to await a decrease in general levels of taxation. It also contained one sentence giving the flavour of things to come: 'Other examples of waste abound, such as the plan to spend £50m to build another town hall in Southwark.'

The founding fathers

But interest was not completely dead. The first recorded mention of a poll tax, as far as can be established, was by Tom King, the newly appointed Minister for Local Government, in the House of Commons in November 1979.[8] He said that such a tax was being considered by the Government. In February 1981 a Conservative MP, Christopher Murphy, introduced a Bill to abolish the rates, and favoured a poll tax as the replacement.[9] In July 1981 it was reported that the poll tax idea had received 'enormous support' in the 'Tory grassroots' and had been 'promoted at Conservative conferences almost annually'.[10]

The post-1979 Environment Secretary was Michael Heseltine. We shall make a closer acquaintance with him in the next chapter. For the moment, it is enough to observe that in the Conservative performance of this period he filled much the same function as the Demon King. From time to time he would appear in a cloud of sparks, to be applauded by some and hissed by others. Mrs Thatcher was certainly among the hostile element in the audience, even though her disapproval might be suppressed. She neither liked nor trusted him. He, for his part, reciprocated, calling her 'the old cow' in private conversation.

---

[8] *The Times*, 22 November 1979.

[9] *The Times*, 3 February 1981. Mr Murphy's supporters included Richard Alexander, David Gilroy Bevan, Tim Brinton, John Carlisle, Den Dover, Robert Dunn, Ian Mills, Peter Griffiths, Warren Hawksley and James Pawsey, of whom the last-named was to give the Government considerable trouble over the poll tax in 1990-1.

[10] Muriel Bowen in the *Sunday Times*, 12 July 1981. Miss Bowen had been an active Conservative.

Though he had always taken some trouble to distance himself from the 'wet' element, there was no doubt about his position on the left of the party. Certainly there could be no doubt about it after his speech to the 1981 conference. Talking – or, rather, orating – on the problems of poverty, unemployment and deprivation in the inner cities, he inspired a generation almost as Iain Macleod had inspired an earlier one.

This was one side of Mr Heseltine, the 'caring' Mr Heseltine. But he had another side too, or several of them. One was as the hammer of 'spendthrift' – the favourite Conservative word – Labour authorities. To control their spending he invented rate-capping. At all events, he was the Minister who carried it out. He was said to suffer from dyslexia. In fact he had an aversion to ploughing through great piles of paper: a very different disability, if such it be. He much preferred to lie on a ministerial sofa in his shirtsleeves surrounded by his advisers, as if he were a puritan pasha. In this way he learnt quite a lot about local government finance. He certainly interfered in it repeatedly. Rate-capping prohibited councils from exceeding certain levels of charging. It was continued in substantially unmodified form as poll-capping by succeeding Secretaries of State for the Environment.

But Mr Heseltine was never taken in by the poll tax. That was one of his principal strengths in the leadership election of 1990. If he had been constrained to carry on at Environment, who can tell what his views might have been in 1985? But no: he was sent off to terrorise – and, in turn, to be terrorised by – the women of Greenham Common instead.

In December 1981 he published a Green Paper[11] saying that the rates should stay but that they could, conceivably, be supplemented by a poll tax. He said the aim was 'to produce proposals for a system which would remedy as fully as possible the shortcomings of the existing system of domestic rating and which would command the widest possible acceptance in the country as a whole'.[12] Mr Heseltine was never an enthusiast for the poll tax: but then, he did not care for the rates either. Hardly

[11] Cmnd 8449 (1981).
[12] *Daily Telegraph*, 17 December 1981.

anyone did. In the end Mr Heseltine settled on a policy of masterly inactivity. It was one of his wiser courses of action.

It was not true, though many have asserted that it was, that the 1983 Manifesto contained nothing about rates. The Conservatives claimed that they had checked the 'relentless' growth of local government spending. Manpower was now down to the level of 1974. The achievement of many Conservative authorities in saving ratepayers' money by putting services such as refuse collection out to tender had played a 'major part' in obtaining better value for money and in the level of rate increases. The Conservatives would encourage 'every possible saving' by this policy. There were, however, numerous 'grossly extravagant' Labour authorities whose 'exorbitant' rate demands had caused 'great distress' to both business and domestic ratepayers. They would legislate to curb 'excessive and irresponsible' rate increases by high-spending councils, and to provide a general scheme for limitation of rate increases for all local authorities to be used if necessary.

What this 'general scheme' was to be, the Manifesto perhaps wisely did not tell us. But this was the high tide of what was called 'Thatcherism'. The second term saw the movement at its zenith: the decline began after the collapse in the City of 1987. Mrs Thatcher's urge to do something about – to do something to – Labour councils, whether malign, as in Liverpool, or loony, as in Islington,[13] or a mixture of both, as in Lambeth, became a political force.

We name the guilty men

Her Environment Secretary was now Patrick Jenkin. Mr (later Lord) Jenkin was tall and dark, with the curly, high cheekboned look of the Highlander, though he had been educated at Clifton and Cambridge, and had practised briefly as a barrister before turning to industry and, later, politics. In 1964 Iain Macleod had

---

[13] In reality the Islington Council was remarkably sensible about most things, and was efficient in most of its undertakings, but had acquired a reputation for lunacy owing mainly to the supposedly high number of 'trendy lefties' who had taken up residence in the borough.

predicted great things for him. And he had risen quite high. Nevertheless, he was recognised, if at all, as the politician who had said during Mr Heath's power crisis that he cleaned his teeth in the dark. Though good-looking, which appealed to Mrs Thatcher, he was somehow limp, which did not. He was shortly to be roughly pushed aside by Kenneth Baker. He was certainly no match for Mrs Thatcher. He did what any sensible man would have done: he passed her demand for action on to a junior Minister.

This subordinate was William Waldegrave, a younger son of the present Earl. In his manner he combined diffidence with arrogance. He had been made a Fellow of All Souls and written a book on Conservative political theory. It is not unfair to say that he had been educated out of his wits. In his early time in Parliament, roughly 1979-81, he had been a member of a group whose leading members were Tristan Garel-Jones, John Patten, Chris Patten, Richard Needham and Robert Cranborne. They dined together, gave parties at their houses at which journalists from liberal newspapers were frequent guests, and were generally disobliging about Mrs Thatcher and, in particular, her economic policies. Mr Waldegrave was the first of this number to gain preferment, though others were to follow. Here he did what any sensible junior Minister would have done: he set up a committee.

Its members included: Professor (now Sir) Christopher Foster, then a Visiting Professor at the London School of Economics and formerly an adviser to Mrs Barbara Castle when she was at Transport; Dr Richard Jackman, also of the LSE; Lord Rothschild, formerly head of the Central Policy Review Staff and much else besides, who once said that 'what this country needs is a revolution';[14] Professor Tom Wilson of Glasgow, for many years an economic consultant to the Secretary of State for Scotland; Leonard (now Mr Justice) Hoffmann, QC; Dr Christine Whitehead; Daniel Hodson; and John Stancliffe. The committee's assistant was Oliver Letwin, later the Conservative candidate first for Hackney and then for Hampstead, and the

---

[14] Personal knowledge.

son of Professor William Letwin of the LSE and Shirley Robin Letwin, a publicist and philosopher of the libertarian Right.[15]

The committee rejected a local sales tax. Residents of a high-spending borough would simply go to its low-spending (and therefore low-taxing) neighbour for their purchases.[16] It is difficult to see why Mr Waldegrave's committee considered this a persuasive argument. For an adjustment mechanism would surely apply. The high-spending (and therefore high-taxing) borough would have to reduce its taxation, and accordingly its expenditure, in order to reattract custom. Likewise, a local income tax was rejected because it would not encourage 'accountability'. The assumption was made that only central government could collect taxes. But a locally set level of taxation would surely ensure local accountability as efficaciously as any device? Fatal word, accountability! Fetish-word of Tony Benn and his acolytes but a few years earlier, the cause of the mandatory reselection of Labour Members and the transform-ation of the party's electoral system: now to be the cause of misery as yet uncomprehended by the Conservatives!

Certainly the Adam Smith Institute did not foresee the future. One of its members, Douglas Mason, an economist at St Andrews University – which had produced many of Mrs Thatcher's aggressively radical young supporters – said that the wider the incidence of a tax, the more its scale was understood and the more widely its cost was spread throughout the population. It was for that reason that the institute regarded it as desirable that domestic rates should be replaced 'by a simple *per caput* tax or, as it is popularly known, a poll tax, covering everyone over the age of 18'.[17]

At about the same time another St Andrews alumnus, the Scottish politician Michael Forsyth, published a Conservative Political Centre pamphlet. The majority of voters, he wrote, were not householders. Rate rebates and the unified housing benefit scheme ensured that many millions contributed nothing to the running of the councils which they had elected. If ever

---

[15] See Paying for Local Government, 1986.
[16] *Sunday Times*, 1 April 1990.
[17] Adam Smith Institute, *Omega File* (1985), cit. ibid.

there was a 'recipe for political irresponsibility', the rating system was it. 'Clear accountability' was the outstanding virtue of a poll tax. Sharing the costs of a council's operations equally among those who benefited from them would make everyone equally liable for policies which they supported.

The amount payable would vary from council to council but 42.4 million adults would need to pay an average of £159 a year to replace the £6.5 billion raised by domestic rates.[18] The Adam Smith Institute estimated £180 a head.[19] Generally the proponents of the tax, including at a later stage the Government, predicted something in the low hundreds; while the opponents, including the professional and local authority organisations, predicted three or four times those amounts. For instance, the Chartered Institute of Public Finance and Accountancy (which probably had the best all-round record during this whole period) predicted a tax of £44 in Wandsworth, more than £450 in Westminster and almost £600 in Camden. Though it was wrong about Westminster – the Institute had clearly forgotten Lady Porter – it was right about the other two metropolitan boroughs.

The Scottish revaluation

The political impetus to change was provided by Scottish revaluation. Across Scotland in 1985, average rates bills had increased owing to a wholesale review of the value of business and domestic property. The worst affected were ratepayers in predominantly Conservative areas. In Barnton, one of Edinburgh's most prosperous suburbs, the rate bill for a large, four-bedroomed detached bungalow rose from £1,600 to £2,347. At Bearsden, a suburb of Glasgow, William Whitelaw was heckled.[20]

Now, it is not altogether easy to understand why revaluation should have brought about these sharp rises and the consequential outrage. For rates are calculated on poundage, as

---

[18] Michael Forsyth, *The Case for a Poll Tax* (CPC, 1985).
[19] Adam Smith Institute, op. cit.
[20] *Sunday Times*, 1 April 1990.

a proportion of rateable value. At a given level of expenditure, the proportion should fall. Evidently what the Scottish authorities did was to use the general confusion as a smoke-screen behind which to impose a substantial rise all round. But again, it is not easy to understand why this rapacity should not have been dealt with under Mr Heseltine's legislation or its Scottish counterpart or, if necessary, under new legislation.

Nevertheless, the candid chronicler will not – though he could – see Scottish revaluation as the pretext for the imposition of the poll tax by Mrs Thatcher. There was genuine alarm in the Conservative Party about the electoral consequences of the Scottish rises. They supplied, if you like, the trigger. So it was that in the spring of 1985 Mrs Thatcher convened several meetings at Chequers. The new tax was at this stage to be called 'the residents' charge' or 'the services charge': 'the community charge' came in later. In this chapter 'the poll tax' is used, not least because this is what people (including, in a moment of parliamentary inadvertence on 6 May 1987, Mrs Thatcher herself) called it throughout the story. The failure to make 'the community charge' part of the language demonstrated that government could do little to change popular usage – and also, perhaps, that the poll tax was generally disliked.

We name more guilty men

During these Chequers meetings Leon Brittan and the Home Office objected to the new tax, reportedly on democratic grounds.[21] Nigel Lawson and the Treasury objected because the rates were easy to understand and to collect. Mrs Thatcher was unmoved. Her eye fell on the Permanent Secretary at Environment, Terence Heiser. He was to set up a unit at his department to study the poll tax, working in tandem with Mr Waldegrave's group of *savants*, or as the rear of a pantomime horse.

This work found its way into a Cabinet committee whose

[21] Ian Aitken in the *Guardian*, 8 April 1985.

chairman was an increasingly bemused William Whitelaw. Mrs Thatcher charged the then head of the No. 10 Policy Unit, John Redwood, to keep a close watch on the progress of events, and in particular to be vigilant for any sign of backsliding brought about by the opposition of Mr Lawson, who was growing surlier by the month. To this end he recruited Mr Letwin, whom we have already met, and who was only recently down from Cambridge.

Mr Baker's scheme

In the earlier stages of this enterprise the Local Government Minister was Kenneth Baker. In autumn 1985 he supplanted the luckless Mr (soon to become Lord) Jenkin as Environment Secretary. Mr Baker had earlier been an acolyte of Edward Heath. Now, though he was a devotee neither of Mrs Thatcher nor of her doctrines, he had been careful not to place himself among the anti-party comrades who included such figures as Sir Ian Gilmour, Jim Prior and Francis Pym. Mr Baker was distrusted for his ambition, tolerated for his affability and admired for his political skills. Nevertheless he did not believe that politics was the whole of life. He had compiled several anthologies of English poetry and prose, which were made heavy work of by the brutalist critics of our progressive papers but were quite good of a kind. His hair appeared to have been painted with shellac, and he smiled a good deal. One of his colleagues said of him: 'I have seen the future, and it smirks.'

His one known weakness was for visual aids. He would display coloured lines and flashing lights before our wondering eyes with the dexterity of a conjurer at a children's party, and the dedication of a peddler of patent medicines in the last century. Having manipulated his visual aids, in January 1986 he produced his Green Paper *Paying for Local Government*[22] Introducing it to the Commons, he said that the 'central theme' was the 'need to bolster local democratic accountability'.[23] To this end, we needed a way of paying for local government which

22 Cmnd 1794 (1986).
23 90 H.C. Deb., c.797 ff, 28 January 1986.

narrowed the gaps that existed between those who used, voted for and paid for local government services.

Business and commercial ratepayers footed 60 per cent of the local tax bill but had no vote to influence local elections. For businesses, rates were uncontrollable overhead costs which could and did vary from year to year. They should not be a local tax. A uniform non-domestic rate poundage should be set centrally. All the yield of non-domestic rates would continue to support local government expenditure but it would be pooled and redistributed as an equal amount for every adult in all authorities.

Again, the then grants arrangements were 'unstable and complex'. They obscured the link between what people paid for local services and what they got for their money. He proposed, first, a needs grant, to compensate authorities for their different needs and, second, a standard grant, to reduce tax bills by a standard amount an adult. Both grants would be fixed in advance for the year in question; 'local authorities would then know where they stood'.

Every extra pound spent would be met in full by the local adult population (though Mr Baker in fact said 'local domestic ratepayers'). Every pound saved would benefit them in full. There would have to be assistance for those on low incomes. Each authority would set its own charge. There would be registers 'entirely separate' from electoral registers.

There would also have to be 'transitional and safety net arrangements'. In England and Wales (though not in Scotland), the community charge would start at a low level, with a corresponding cut in rates. The whole burden of any increased spending would fall on the community charge from the start, in order that a 'clear link' might exist between higher spending and a higher community charge. In subsequent years there would be further transfers from the rates to the community charge. In some areas the rates would disappear within three years, and in all areas within ten.

Such was Mr Baker's scheme. It was what was put before the country at the 1987 election. With one important exception – for the rates were abolished rather than phased out – it formed the basis of the Local Government Finance Act 1988. And it was (as the young women who are engaged to write reviews of novels in our great newspapers like to say) deeply flawed. The precise respects we shall examine shortly. At the moment, the response was gratifying, surprisingly so. The 1922 Committee welcomed Mr Baker's proposals.[24] Even the Labour Party was quiet, as it remained on this subject during the 1987 election. One exception was Jack Straw:

> There are some who think that the poll tax will go away if we pretend it is not there: that it will take two Parliaments to implement: that Kenneth Baker made the proposals in the expectation that they would be shelved. We should not be so complacent. This Government's record is of doing the immoral and the unthinkable, poll tax will become a reality in Scotland this side of the election;[25] we will have it in England and Wales too, unless we wake up the nation to its full, ugly implications, very soon.[26]

Mr Ridley takes charge

Whether Mr Baker thought the proposals would be shelved is disputable. What is certain is that he later maintained that what had been introduced was not his scheme.[27] Mr Baker's successor, Nicholas Ridley, had no doubts. Or, if he had, they concerned the delay of three to ten years – the so-called twin-tracking system – between the initial introduction of the poll tax and the final extirpation of the rates.

Mr Ridley seemed to have been intended by nature to be an evictor of widows and oppressor of orphans. He was as lean as an old racehorse, as lined as an Anatolian peasant. He was an English aristocrat. His sourness of disposition was confidently attributed to the evil of primogeniture. A younger son, he had eschewed the church, the army, the law and even public relations, and had made his way instead as an engineer, which was no doubt to his credit, but seemed to have done nothing to

[24] *The Times*, 29 January 1986.
[25] It was introduced on 1 April 1989.
[26] *Guardian*, 4 April 1986.
[27] Interview with Polly Toynbee, *Times Saturday Review*, 16 March 1991.

improve his temper. He smoked cigarettes with dedication, as if engaged in an athletic activity from which he hoped eventually to attain national recognition. He made no pretence of liking journalists, and was accordingly liked by some of them in return, because he clearly did not give a damn for anybody.

In October 1986 he told the Conservative Party conference at Bournemouth that they had a choice: either they went on legislating and legislating until they had a framework of law within which the abuses could be contained, or they could make local authorities 'fully accountable' to their electors and ensure that those who voted for 'local extravagance and depravity' paid for it.[28] This, it should be remembered, was the conference at which successive Ministers set out their stalls for the next year's election. Mr Ridley spoke mutedly but was heard enthusiastically. Others were not so approving. The municipal treasurers, chief executives and rating valuation officers all opposed the poll tax, as did also the Association of District Councils and the Inland Revenue Staff Federation.[29]

Mrs Thatcher had always made a show of refusing to submit to 'the interests' or even to consult them very much. This show was broadly justified, while the refusal was usually beneficial. Over the poll tax, certain groups – the Valuation and the Inland Revenue Officers particularly – would lose power and influence or even cease to exist altogether as a consequence of its introduction. And yet, there was something impressive about the weight of professional and also academic opinion which was against the tax.[30] Clearly not all the opponents of the tax were interested parties, Labour supporters or critics of Mrs Thatcher. But Mr Ridley said that Ministers were 'long past' the point where they were asking for suggestions of a different principle or nature. They had been doing that for 30 years 'to my personal knowledge. The system is rotten.'[31] So we arrived at the 1987 Manifesto:

[28] *The Times*, 9 October 1986.

[29] *Daily Telegraph*, 3 November 1986; *Guardian*, 5 November 1986; *Daily Telegraph*, 15 May 1985.

[30] See Tony Travers and John Gibson, *Tax Reform in Local Government: a Poll Tax* (Institute of Local Government Studies, Birmingham, 1985).

[31] *The Times*, 26 November 1986.

We will now tackle the roots of the problem. We will reform local
government finance to strengthen local democracy and accountability. Local electors must be able to decide the level of service
they want and how much they are prepared to pay for it. We will
legislate in the first session of the new Parliament to abolish the
unfair domestic rating system and replace rates with a fairer
community charge. This will be a fixed-rate charge for local
services paid by those over the age of 18, except the mentally ill
and elderly people living in homes and hospitals. The less well-off
and students will not have to pay the new charge – but everyone
will be aware of the costs as well as the benefits of the local
services. This should encourage people to take a greater interest
in the policies of their local council and getting value for money.
Business ratepayers will pay a unified business rate at a
standard rate pegged to inflation.

It could not be said that the Conservatives had omitted to give
due warning of their intentions. And yet, the commitment
played little or no part in the election campaign. In election
broadcasts it made a solitary, fleeting appearance in a
performance by Jack Cunningham, the Shadow Environment
Spokesman. There was also one omission from this section. It
concerned the timing of the introduction of the tax. This
reflected the division that existed in the Cabinet between the
Twin Trackers and the Big Bangers. Mr Baker and the majority
of the Cabinet belonged to the former group, Mr Ridley and Mrs
Thatcher to the latter. They wanted the poll tax to be introduced
at once or in a year rather than in a period of between three and
ten years. Others expressed doubts: the London Conservatives,
and John Biffen, who had been dismissed for cheek, and Sir
George Young, a lugubrious, bicycling baronet who had been
dismissed for wetness all round and was to prove one of the most
acute critics of the tax in the years ahead. Even Sir John
Hoskyns, formerly the head of the Prime Minister's policy unit
and now Director-General of the Institute of Directors, had his
reservations. In a letter to Mr Ridley, he wrote that 'further
study' of the 'entire system' of local government finance was
needed. He mentioned the removal of the cost of education from
local authorities, and possibly that of roads ('arguably a national
service') too. And he suggested that the provision of 'personal

social services' should be made by health rather than by local authorities.[32] The Gallup Poll showed a remarkable and, to the Government, worrying reversal of opinion since Mr Baker's Green Paper. The question was whether the poll tax was fairer than the rates:[33]

	February 1986	July 1987
Fairer	50	27
Not as fair	28	47
No difference	7	6
Don't know	16	19

Mrs Thatcher was unmoved. She proclaimed the poll tax as the 'flagship' of her third term at a meeting of the 1922 Committee, and placed Michael Howard as third in command, under her and Mr Ridley.

Mr Howard was Welsh, Jewish and a lawyer, accordingly triply qualified to undertake those difficult, dangerous, sometimes disagreeable tasks which a Prime Minister finds it necessary to call on a colleague to perform. Like that other Cambridge QC Leon Brittan, he was said to have 'a safe pair of hands' and to be 'really quite extraordinarily able'. A year and a half previously, Mr Brittan, as he then still was, had been dismissed from the field, a sacrifice to the anger, or maybe the prejudice, of the gentlemen in the pavilion. Mr Howard was to survive. He was undoubtedly industrious. Articles were written, speeches made: but somehow they did not convince very many people. Personally agreeable and politically intelligent though he was, Mr Howard gave the impression that he would take any brief if the fee was right, but that on this occasion the brief was a thin one.

Mr Ridley's views prevail

The Conservative conference of 1987 met in confident, even gloating mood, despite the warnings of Mr (as he then still was) Peregrine Worsthorne in the *Sunday Telegraph* to beware

[32] *Financial Times*, 7 July 1987.
[33] *Daily Telegraph*, 27 July 1987.

against 'bourgeois triumphalism'. And it persuaded the Government to change its policy on the poll tax. Or, rather, the conference gave the occasion for the Big Bangers, led by Mrs Thatcher and Mr Ridley, to defeat the more prudent Twin Trackers, whose policy had originated with Mr Baker. There had been nothing like it since the conference had forced the then chairman, Lord Woolton, to accede to a demand to build 300,000 houses a year. The instrument of change was Gerry Malone, who had recently lost his seat in Aberdeen South. The decision had already been taken to introduce the poll tax immediately in Scotland in 1989. In view of his own and others' experiences in that country, one might have expected Mr Malone to appreciate the merits of a more cautious approach. Not a bit of it:

> We've had the courage to take on the challenge. Let's do it properly. Let's do it as soon as we can.[34]

Mr Malone received a standing ovation, while Mrs Thatcher and Mr Ridley smiled on each other and on the eloquent young Scotsman.

Two days in mid-December were allotted to the second reading of the Local Government Finance Bill. Opening the debate, Mr Ridley said that, to help manage the change, the Government proposed transitional arrangements to phase in the community charge over four years. First, domestic rates would be abolished and the community charge introduced 'in one go' in 1990. Second, the new system would 'sweep away' the unfair system of resources equalisation whereby those in areas of high rateable value subsidised those in areas of low. The contribution to the safety-net – the four-year transitional period – would be limited to £75 an adult.[35]

The Conservatives won the vote by 341 to 269. A majority of 101 had fallen to 72. Those voting against included Edward Heath, Sir Ian Gilmour and Sir George Young; those abstaining included Michael Heseltine and Tim Raison. A table of Conservative MP voting against the Government in this and

---

[34] *The Times*, 7 October 1987.
[35] 124 H.C. Deb., c.1113 ff, 16 December 1987; see also c.1245 ff, 17 December 1987.

subsequent divisions on the poll tax is given at the end of this chapter. Over two years of parliamentary rows ensued which were debilitating to party morale.

The reasons for the failure

Let us at this stage, however, examine the reasons why the poll tax failed to work in the manner which had been so confidently predicted. The first reason lay in the replacement of the Rates Support Grant by the Revenue Support Grant. The new grant was allocated in two parts, though a single figure was paid to each authority. The first part of the grant equalised between authorities, taking account of their varying needs to spend. Needs assessments were determined by the Government after negotiations with the local authorities' associations. The grant that remained after the needs equalisation process was allocated among authorities on a *per capita* basis. Mr Ridley may have thought that the old system was 'unfair':[36] but the new system was grotesque in its inequity. Thus, owing to the redistribution of grants and non-domestic rates in 1988-9, the top five gainers (in pounds for every adult) were Epping Forest with £135, Elmbridge with £194, Chiltern with £196, Westminster with £200 and South Bucks with £203. The bottom five losers were Hackney with £238, Southwark with £253, Lewisham with £264, Tower Hamlets with £310 and Greenwich with £318.[37]

The second reason lay in what was known as 'gearing'. All marginal spending fell on the poll tax. If an authority decided to put up spending by £1, the full £1 fell on the tax. As the poll tax made up roughly 25 per cent of an authority's income, an increase of spending of 1 per cent (for example, from £100 million to £101 million) led to a poll tax increase of 4 per cent (from £25 million to £26 million).[38]

The third reason lay in the 'safety net' or, as they were sometimes called (for they were calculated on an area basis) the

[36] See above, p. 67.

[37] Department of the Environment, unpublished figures, Quot. Tony Travers, 'Community Charge and other Financial Changes', in John Stewart and Gerry Stoker (eds), *The Future of Local Government* (1989), 9 at 17. I am indebted to this article.

[38] Ibid. 22.

'safety nets'. During the four-year period of introduction, authorities gaining from the redistribution of the central grant[39] were required to contribute to a pool of money from which losing authorities would draw. Some authorities would accordingly levy a higher poll tax than they would otherwise have done, and other authorities a lower tax.[40] The difference between the domestic rate for every adult in 1990 and the poll tax in 1991 would be met with a grant of 100 per cent in 1991; of 75 per cent in 1992; of 50 per cent in 1993; of 25 per cent in 1994; and of nothing afterwards.

First of all, the grant was redistributed from the poorer to the richer authorities. Then, for four years, the richer authorities were to give to the poorer. Sir Rhodes Boyson, who had started off as an enthusiastic supporter of the poll tax, was saying by 1989: 'The community charge as it now stands is a Labour Party benevolent fund.'[41] This was not just Sir Rhodes in his customarily exuberant spirits: he was expressing a truth about the Conservative Party. It was now in a state of thorough alarm. This had come about gradually. The trouble was not that any notion of 'accountability' had long since been jettisoned, owing to the redistribution of the grants, to the safety nets and to poll-capping, successor of rate-capping. It was not even that the tax was inequitable, though in April 1988 Michael Mates took 37 Conservatives with him into the lobby, supporting his amendment that poll tax should be related to income, and there were 11 abstentions. The occasion was also notable for having brought about one of Mrs Thatcher's infrequent visits to the tearoom, which were made only in times of the gravest emergency.

The real trouble was that, for most voters, the tax was much *higher*, often by a factor of three or four, than the Government had predicted. Members such as Emma Nicholson thought about its effect on women in Tavistock; Members such as John Lee thought about its effect on his seat in Pendle, Lancashire, as did numerous other MPs, and not only those from the North.

[39] See above, p. 68.
[40] Ibid.
[41] *Observer*, 16 July 1989.

Mr Patten gives money away

Chris Patten succeeded the unlamented Mr Ridley, turned to his new Minister for Local Government, David Hunt, and said: 'It's not going to work, is it?'[42] Mr Patten's advancement could be regarded as a sign of Mrs Thatcher's desperation. Though he had written speeches for her in his time, he had also helped Sir Ian Gilmour with his productions. In 1979-81 he had been one of the principal doubters, but had been helped on his way through, it was thought, the influence of his friend and admirer, the Whip Tristan Garel-Jones, to whom demonic or anyway magical powers were commonly attributed by the Conservative Right. He was shortish, squarish, often with a hangdog expression. He cultivated liberal journalists but possessed a capacity to attract affection, even love. His assistant, Mr Hunt, was a solicitor, affable, reasonable. He was from Merseyside but did not make a fuss about it. They were an impressive pair, especially in the House, when they would each make excellent speeches without notes.

Mr Patten's principle was: 'Give him the money, Barney.' At the conference in Blackpool Mr Hunt announced the abolition of the safety net after one year. Thereafter the gainers would receive their gains in full, but the Treasury would find the £685 million it would cost to protect the losing authorities over the next three years. There would also be a new system of transitional relief, running for three years, to help people who would otherwise have faced the largest increases in the change to the poll tax. This would cost £300 million and a further £300 over the succeeding three years. The total cost of the relief was £1.3 billion.[43]

In February 1990 it was reported that the Conservative shires were planning to overspend. In Mr Baker's Mole Valley, the council was due to fix a charge of £292 a year, 30 per cent more than the Government's prediction.[44] Mr Patten offered an extra £21 million all round together with a free computer scheme.

[42] Private information.
[43] *The Times*, 12 October 1989.
[44] *Sunday Telegraph*, 11 February 1990.

He claimed that the shire counties were driving up their poll tax bills in order to replenish the funds used to fight local elections. Figures from the indispensable Chartered Institute of Public Finance and Accountancy showed that Labour authorities had overspent government estimates by 35 per cent, Conservative by 31.[45] The chairman of the Police Federation attacked the poll tax as a 'pernicious act of betrayal' because policemen would have to pay; in Glasgow, indeed, payment was already being extracted from their earnings at source.[46]

Wandsworth set a poll tax of £148, which was £23 below the Government's estimate; whereas Haringey set one of £573, which was 11p below. In March the Gallup Poll showed Labour as 19 points in the lead. The lead was increased to 23 points. Labour won the Mid-Staffs by-election, and Marcus Fox, a vice-chairman of the 1922 Committee, said that MPs were 'punch drunk' as they saw the figures being produced by different authorities and added: 'We should have known this would happen. Let us sort it out.'[47]

Saturday 31 March 1991 saw the most serious rioting in Central London of this century. Steve Nally of the Anti-Poll Tax Federation claimed credit but the police blamed the extreme Left and Neil Kinnock attacked 'toytown revolutionaries'. Three weeks earlier, 3,000-5,000 demonstrators, or some of them, had fought the police outside Hackney Town Hall. Demonstrations disrupted a meeting of Haringey Council before an alliance of Left-wing Labour councillors and Conservatives defeated a proposal to levy the charge of £573. During the evening, a stone smashed a council chamber window, two protesters leapt 15 feet into the chamber from the gallery, and demonstrators fought with police and spat at councillors. The start of the meeting was delayed for 95 minutes as 50 protesters 'chanted incessantly', showered the chamber with torn-up agendas and 'yelled obscenities' before police carried them away.[48] In Nottingham, demonstrators dressed as Robin Hood and his Merry Men, and

45 *The Times*, 16 February 1990; ibid. 10 March 1990.
46 *Daily Telegraph*, 3 March 1990.
47 *The Times*, 2 March 1990.
48 *Daily Telegraph*, 6 March 1990.

armed with imitation custard pies, broke up a meeting to set the poll tax. Several councillors, including a woman Conservative, were hit in the face by pies and many of those present (including the Sheriff in his ceremonial robes) ducked as the missiles were thrown. The 20 protesters in Lincoln green (including a man attired as Maid Marian) forced their way into the chamber, drowned the debate and threw papers in the air.[49]

More seriously for the Government, 18 Conservative councillors in West Oxfordshire resigned at having to set a tax at £159 above the government estimate, while 200 demonstrated outside the Shire Hall, Taunton, in protest at a recommended poll tax of £350, £100 higher than the estimate. Most seriously of all, there was rioting in Tunbridge Wells. The world was being turned upside down. On 1 April 1990 the poll tax replaced domestic rates in England and Wales. It had replaced them in Scotland a year previously. On 19 July Mr Patten announced an additional subsidy of £3.3 billion to hold down poll tax levels, and was applauded in the Conservative newspapers for an act of prudent statesmanship.

In November 1990 Mr Heseltine promised a review of the poll tax in the election for the party leadership, while Mr Major and Mr Hurd followed him. Indeed, in the opinion of Mr Major's campaign manager, Norman Lamont, his following Mr Heseltine in this matter was crucial to his victory.[50] In one decade, the 1980s, local government finance came to dominate the Conservative Party and the future of its leader as they had once been dominated by the Corn Laws, Irish home rule and tariff reform. It was odd; it was extraordinary. But the dark night of the poll tax was not over yet.

[49] Ibid.
[50] Private information.

Poll Tax Rebels 1987-90
Conservatives Voting Against

Member	Second Reading	Mates Amendment	Third Reading	Financial Provisions
R. Adley		x	x	
R. Allason				x
J. Aitken			x	
A. Beaumont-Dark	x	x	x	
W. Benyon	x	x	x	x
J. Biffen		x	x	
Sir N. Bonsor				x
Sir R. Boyson				x
I. Bruce				x
A. Buchanan-Smith		x		
Sir A. Buck		x		
P. Cormack	x	x	x	
J. Critchley	x	x		
T. Dicks				x
H. Dykes		x		x
C. Gill				x
Sir I. Gilmour	x	x	x	x
Sir P. Goodhart	x	x	x	x
J. Gorst		x		x
H. Greenway				x
K. Hampson		x		
K. Hargreaves	x	x	x	x
A. Haselhurst		x		
Sir B. Hayhoe	x	x	x	x
E. Heath	x	x		
M. Heseltine		x		

Member	Second Reading	Mates Amendment	Third Reading	Financial Provisions
R. Howell				x
R. Hicks		x		x
M. Irvine	x	x	x	
Sir G. Johnson-Smith		x		
D. Knox	x	x	x	x
J. Lee				x
J. Lester	x	x		x
M. Mates		x		x
R. Maxwell-Hyslop				x
Sir A. Meyer	x	x	x	
Sir C. Morrison	x	x	x	x
J. Pawsey				x
Mrs E. Peacock		x		
Sir T. Raison		x		
T. Rathbone		x	x	x
G. Riddick		x		
R. Shepherd			x	x
Sir D. Smith				x
R. Squire	x	x	x	x
A. Steen				x
Sir P. Tapsell		x		
P. Temple-Morris	x	x		x
C. Townsend		x		
B. Wells		x		x
J. Wiggin				x
T. Yeo		x		
Sir G. Young	x	x	x	x

Sources: H.C. Deb., 17 December 1987, 18 April 1988, 25 April 1988 and 18 January 1990.

4

The Impact of Mr Heseltine

Most men sink into insignificance when they quit office. Very insignificant men acquire weight when they obtain it.

Winston Churchill, letter to
David Lloyd George, 9 November 1921

When I told him that he would never get to the top unless he made friends, he said: 'Nonsense. Look at Ted and Margaret. They didn't have any friends, and they got to the top.'

Julian Critchley, *Heseltine: the Unauthorised Biography*

In 1954-5 the three successive Presidents of the Oxford Union were Michael Heseltine; Jeremy Isaacs, who was later to found Channel 4 and to be director of the Royal Opera House, Covent Garden; and Anthony Howard, who was later to be editor of the *New Statesman* and the *Listener*, deputy editor of the *Observer* and a notable biographer. They all got Seconds: Mr Howard in Law, Mr Isaacs in Classical Greats and Mr Heseltine in Politics, Philosophy and Economics. Mr Howard mused afterwards on the unfairness of life or, at any rate, of the examinations system. He himself, he said, was quite clever and had worked fairly hard. Mr Isaacs was quite clever too, had worked very hard and was, moreover, enthralled by his subject. Whereas Mr Heseltine was not very clever and had worked hardly at all. And yet they had all ended up with the same class of degree. There was no justice in the world.[1]

[1] Personal knowledge.

The dyslexia factor

There are some academically snobbish people who say, only half-jokingly, that it is possible to obtain a degree in PPE simply by reading the newspapers. This is not true. The course requires in those who take it a certain aptitude in conceptual thought. This Mr Heseltine has never made any pretence of possessing. Indeed, it is claimed that additionally he suffers from a mild form of dyslexia. As he has confessed:

> Although I have a certain fluency and familiarity with the spoken word, I find it less easy to absorb from or communicate through the written. In commerce that matters very little; in opposition politics some would say it is almost an advantage; but in government it is a massive burden.[2]

His unauthorised biographer Julian Critchley explained that his dyslexia was diagnosed at second hand by Mr Critchley's father, the neurologist Dr Macdonald Critchley, to whom he had sent his son Rupert. 'The condition,' Mr Critchley writes, 'has not been so severe as to prevent Heseltine from writing at all, only to discourage him from doing so.'[3] The condition did not prevent him from writing a resignation statement of 2,500 words in an afternoon, immediately after his resignation from the Cabinet over the Westland affair.[4] That anyone – whether Mr Heseltine or somebody else – could have composed this number of words in the time available to him remains one of the minor mysteries of the crisis.

Nor did his condition prevent him from writing the book referred to above; not to mention numerous articles in the four years following his departure from Mrs Margaret Thatcher's Cabinet. The letter to the electors of Henley which was the proximate cause of his challenge to her in 1990 – which made it impossible for him to turn back – had started life as an article for the *Sunday Times*. At least two other Welsh politicians,

---

[2] Michael Heseltine, *Where There's a Will* (1987, paper edn 1990), 3.
[3] Julian Critchley, *Heseltine: the Unauthorised Biography* (1987, paper edn 1988), 42.
[4] Ibid. 158.

David Lloyd George and Aneurin Bevan, have had a preference for receiving information through the spoken rather than the written word, though this did not prevent Bevan from writing *In Place of Fear*[5] or Lloyd George from compiling his outstanding war memoirs, largely on his own.[6]

A Swansea boy

It often surprises people when they learn that Mr Heseltine is Welsh. He does not have a Welsh name. He does not look Welsh. He does not, perhaps, look English either. There is something of the pine-forest about him. Certainly he sounds Welsh, but only to those with an acute sense of accent. Strictly, it is not an accent at all, but a timbre to the voice. He says from time to time that he comes from 'the South Wales commercial classes'. It is arguable that South Wales has never possessed any commercial classes – and that it might have been better for the region if it had. His father was a manager for the Steel Company of Wales, and liked to be known as Colonel Rupert Heseltine on account of the rank he held in the Territorial Army. His maternal grandfather had been a coal merchant.

He was brought up in Swansea, which was not a typical Welsh or even South Welsh town, but somewhere with a mysterious quality of its own. It was a frontier town or, rather, a town of several frontiers: between South Wales and West Wales, the English language and the Welsh, irreligion and Nonconformity, Wales and the rest of the world (for it was a leading seaport). It possessed a raffish, cosmopolitan quality. The evacuees who descended on its West Glamorgan and Carmarthenshire hinterland during the war appeared at least as strange as the youthful inhabitants of Acton and Greenwich who had travelled further for the same purpose. Swansea Bay was claimed by patriotic locals to rival the Bay of Naples; while the Swansea-to-Mumbles railway line was the first to be constructed in Great Britain. The town has lost some of its special quality with the decline of the coal, tinplate and metallurgical

---

[5] 1952, new edn 1976.
[6] 6 vols , 1933-6.

industries; what changed it most of all was Hitler's Luftwaffe. It has never recovered from those nights of destruction. But something of its pre-war quality can still be discerned. It was here that Mr Heseltine spent his early years.

But then he was sent away to school, to a preparatory school and afterwards to Shrewsbury. Wales has never been a great patron of the public schools. Doctors tended to send their sons to such establishments as Epsom and Bromsgrove. Mr Heseltine did not fit this pattern, and neither did Sir Geoffrey Howe (Aberavon and Winchester). At school Heseltine was contemptuous of authority.[7] Shrewsbury's principal effect on his life was that it enabled him to enter Pembroke College, Oxford, where Critchley and Ivor Richard were contemporaries, and which Denzil Davies was later to attend.[8]

He was famous at Oxford because he was a President of the Union of striking appearance. 'He looks like a Midwich Cuckoo,' a woman later remarked on seeing a group photograph of the Union committee with Mr Heseltine, in white tie and tails, in the middle of the front row. He was even more famous for introducing various celebrities of the early 1950s (notably Sir Bernard and Lady Docker) to the Union Society, for extracting money from them, for converting the cellars of the premises into a night club of a decorous kind and – through these and other stratagems – for turning round the debating society's finances. He had already acquired something of a reputation as an entrepreneur.

The foundations of a fortune

On leaving Oxford he tried to put off his period of national service for as long as possible, and accordingly embarked on a course in accountancy.[9] Alas, he found difficulty with his examinations. In later life he would make jokes about his

[7] Critchley, op. cit. 2.

[8] He had earlier applied to and been turned down by Bristol and Reading: Susan Crosland, 'Michael Heseltine' in *Looking Out, Looking In* (1987), 26.

[9] Ibid. 24. Many Oxford and most Cambridge colleges during this period insisted on their undergraduates' doing their national service before going up to the university. Pembroke College, Oxford, was exceptional.

failures. At the Mid-Staffordshire by-election of 1990, for instance, he commended the Conservative candidate to a village meeting on the ground that he had passed his accountancy examinations, whereas Mr Heseltine had failed his.[10] It cannot, however, have been so amusing at the time, particularly since it meant that the call-up could be postponed no longer.

Mr Heseltine joined the Welsh Guards, a curious regiment which has specialised in accommodating such characters as A.J. Ayer and Kenneth Rose, whose lack of any connection with Wales was fortified by their unsuitability for the military life. The regiment's history was certainly less distinguished than those of the two South Wales infantry regiments, the South Wales Borderers and The Welch, later to be amalgamated in the Royal Regiment of Wales. But this could hardly be helped, as the Welsh Guards had been established only in 1915, at a time of military enthusiasm in Wales.[11]

Mr Heseltine's military career did not last long. He became prospective Conservative candidate for the safe Labour seat of Gower in the forthcoming election, which turned out to be in 1959. In accordance with the rules then in force, he was automatically discharged. By 1962 the rules, or conventions, had become better-known. Over 600 national servicemen requested nomination papers as candidates at two impending by-elections. The practice of granting discharges in these circumstances was suspended, and a select committee of the House of Commons appointed to examine the problem. On this committee's recommendation, a special advisory committee, appointed by the Home Secretary, was set up to scrutinise the bona fides of hopeful candidates seeking their discharge from the services. Only one such candidate was recommended for release. Having been discharged, he announced that he had, after all, decided not to stand. The advisory committee still exists somewhere in Whitehall or Queen Anne's Gate, even though the reason for its creation – peacetime conscription – has ceased to apply.[12]

---

[10] Personal knowledge.
[11] See Kenneth O. Morgan, *Rebirth of a Nation: Wales 1880-1980* (1981), 160-1.
[12] S.A. de Smith, *Constitutional and Administrative Law* (5th edn 1985), 220.

It was Mr Heseltine's first footnote in constitutional history. Afterwards he would wear his dark red-and-blue Brigade tie almost as often as Harold Macmillan used to wear his. It was in frequent evidence when he was Secretary for Defence. Mr Critchley once asked a Grenadier general whether he objected to Mr Heseltine's wearing this tie. 'Not in the least,' he had replied, 'but I wish the chap wouldn't always tie it in a Windsor knot.'[13]

His first business was property development, on a not very large scale. Among his ventures was the conversion of a house in West London into lodgings, chiefly for foreign students. He supervised the hostel himself. He was once at a party when a young woman of socialist inclinations accused him of exploiting others. He said that he worked very hard and had, in fact, been up at six that morning. What, she asked, was he doing at that hour? He replied: 'I was mixing the butter with the marge.'[14]

He took up publishing as well, with an Oxford friend, Clive Labovitch. Handbooks and directories of various kinds offset losses from *Topic*, a pioneering attempt at a news magazine on *Time-Newsweek* lines which anticipated, and was in some respects the superior of, the magazine founded by Sir James Goldsmith two decades later. *Town* magazine, previously *Man About Town* and *About Town*, was an even more superior production, whereby an obscure magazine concerned with gents' outfitting had been converted into perhaps the best – certainly the most original – of the magazines of the 1960s which were to be epitomised by *Queen*. Financial trouble ensued because these publications were unprofitable and because there was a slump in the property market. It did not prevent him from marrying in 1962 Anne Williams, the daughter of a London solicitor of Welsh origins.

> I remember a moment in my business life when every Friday the company finance director used to bring in the list of outstanding creditors. There were three columns headed: solicitors' letters, writs received and writs whose time limits for reply were about to expire. The bills in the last column we paid.[15]

[13] Critchley, op. cit. 96.
[14] Private information.
[15] Heseltine, *Where There's a Will*, 35.

This quotation does perhaps less than justice to Mr Heseltine's conscience over the repayment of debt. He was proud of having paid off all his creditors. By the time he became MP for Tavistock (succeeding the equally elegant but politically different Sir Henry Studholme), Haymarket Press, the foundation of his fortune, was returned to profit, and he was on the way to becoming a rich man.[16] He thought, rightly, that he was fortunate to enter Parliament when his party was in opposition rather than in government. It gave him a greater opportunity to become noticed. He also believed that the length of time he spent in opposition, four years, was about right. Where he considered himself most fortunate was in catching the eye of Peter Walker, then opposition spokesman on transport.

A junior Minister

Mr Walker had been compelled to strive even harder than Mr Heseltine for his financial success, which he had found in the City, notably in insurance, rather than in property or publishing. But, though Mr Walker had been an early opponent of our entry into the Common Market (before 1964, indeed, entering into a correspondence with Lord Beaverbrook on the matter[17]), he was the same kind of Conservative as Mr Heseltine. They believed in social responsibility allied to personal reward. In Edward Heath's government he was rewarded with a parliamentary secretaryship at Transport. This lasted less than six months.

'Pussy.' That's what they called us. We were the scum of the earth – tolerated by the civil servants ... In private office I had the nicest but totally inexperienced kids straight out of university. If they went along to some senior civil servant and said, 'My boss has asked if you will do this,' they were told where to go. I blew my top. 'You're not going to use me to train your officials. I'm going to have more experienced civil servants to help me do my job. This is my private office.'[18]

[16] See Dominic Prince, 'A Very Private Fortune', *Independent on Sunday*, 12 May 1991.

[17] Personal knowledge.

[18] Crosland, art. cit. 29.

In October 1970 he was moved sideways to become
Parliamentary Under-Secretary at the Department of the
Environment. It was as Minister for Aerospace at Trade and
Industry that he became notorious. He was accused of lying to a
Commons select committee, though there seemed no point in
doing so. He had to come to the House to explain that he had not
intended to mislead the committee. It was at around this period
that Mr Heseltine began to acquire his nicknames: 'Tarzan',
though, as Mr Critchley points out, he had always been notably
unathletic; 'Goldilocks', which is, or was, self-explanatory as far
as the hair was concerned, though no three bears were in
evidence; and 'Brilliantine', though this could with greater
accuracy have been used of Kenneth Baker or Cecil Parkinson,
Mr Heseltine being recognisable by the tossed mane rather than
by the plastered-down thatch. The equally inappropriate
'Michael Philistine' came later.

The episode of the mace

It was in his second period of opposition, 1974-9, that he found
true fame. The cause was the episode of the swinging mace. The
occasion was the debate on the second reading of the bill to
nationalise the aircraft and shipbuilding industries. The Labour
government had just won a crucial division by one vote. Minutes
earlier, the Conservative opposition had believed that they had
won or, at least, that the vote had been tied. The whisper went
round the Conservative benches like a spark through a fuse:
Michael Cocks, the then government Whip, had persuaded one
of his charges to break a 'pair'. This is an agreement between
two opposing Members that neither will vote on a certain
evening or in a specific division. At times of acute political
ill-feeling pairing arrangements have sometimes been suspended. This had not happened in 1976, though the government's
majority varied between one and three, depending on how many
Irishmen chose to turn up.

That there was nothing in the Conservative belief made no
odds. 'Cheat,' they yelled. Some Labour MPs retaliated by
singing 'The Red Flag', the first time this melancholy ditty (as

Bernard Shaw remarked, like the funeral march of a fried eel) had been heard in the Chamber since 1945. It was at this point that Mr Heseltine, who, having wound up the debate, was opposite the dispatch box, seized the mace and advanced on the government front bench. Whether he meant to present it ironically to Michael Foot, who had wound up the debate against him, or to James Callaghan, who was beside Mr Foot, is still disputed, some believing that he intended to do them a mischief. Mr Heseltine supports the more pacific version, and points out that he apologised to the House next day.[19]

The elders of the party in Parliament were furious, William Whitelaw notably so. But Mr Heseltine became something of a hero to the party outside, even though in 1975 he had supported first Mr Heath and then Mr Whitelaw. Mrs Thatcher punished him by moving him from his beloved Industry to shadowing Environment. This change did little to impede his other road to fame, which was to be via the party conference.

Fame at the conference

The Conservative Party had possessed other post-war platform orators. Lord Hailsham had rung his bell in the 1950s. Iain Macleod had done his annual turn in the next decade. Honourable mention should perhaps be made also of Ted Leather, who was Canadian, and Peter Thorneycroft, whose brand of Belgravia Cockney recalled a more spacious age. But a whole decade, 1975-85, belonged to Mr Heseltine. He would begin by replying to the debate, complimenting the speakers, and then say something about his area of responsibility, successively the Environment and Defence. Then, before 1979, he would attack the Labour government and, afterwards, the Labour Party. The assembled Conservatives cheered and cheered. The standing ovation, often a forced affair with other speakers, was never less than wholehearted.

His colleagues hated it and often hated him. He was going through a routine which they found disagreeable – which they

[19] Ibid. 30.

performed only under compulsion – with every appearance of enjoyment and, what was worse, with every sign of success. The story became current that the party managers so arranged matters that Mr Heseltine was cut off in full flood by *Playschool*, which always interrupted the morning's television coverage of the conferences. Mr Heseltine's reputation, with the Conservative loyalists and the Labour Party alike, was made as an opponent of socialism. There was accordingly a disposition to place him in the middle or on the right of his party.

Even after his Blackpool speech of 1981, which was notable for his denial of Mrs Thatcher's major premise – that people were responsible for their own lives – there was learned argument about where he really stood in the Conservative Party. For not only did he attack Labour every autumn by the seaside with a vigour which had not been witnessed since the death of Macleod. As Secretary of State for the Environment he was the hammer of the Left. Or he liked to appear as such. It is arguable that, if he had been more effective before 1983, the poll tax would not have acquired the place in Mrs Thatcher's affections which it did.

Then there was his period at Defence. There is no doubt that he behaved unconstitutionally – it may be illegally – before the 1983 election. He took over in January 1983, and had talks with the director of MI5, Sir John Jones. These involved the drawing up of an MI5 briefing paper on the Campaign for Nuclear Disarmament. There were proposals that leading members of CND should be reported on and have their telephones tapped. MI5 was also persuaded into agreeing to supply 'open' material from published sources on CND activists to one of Mr Heseltine's civil servants. This official was instructed to set up a pre-election anti-CND propaganda section, DS 19. The material, which was assembled by the MI5 officer Cathy Massiter, was passed on to the civil servant responsible for the propaganda group by Sir (as he later became) Peter Blaker, one of Mr Heseltine's junior Ministers.[20]

[20] David Leigh, *Observer*, 17 May 1987. This story was derived from the script of a programme in the *Secret Society* television series by Duncan Campbell. The BBC programme was withdrawn and not shown until 1991, on Channel 4. Cathy Massiter, however, made her allegations in another programme, on Granada television. Ms Massiter, unlike Clive Ponting, went unprosecuted under the Official Secrets Acts.

After the Westland affair

Though enlightened and progressive opinion did not hold Mr Heseltine in high esteem, neither did the Prime Minister. She did not like or trust him. Nevertheless his walk out of the Cabinet over the Westland affair caused general surprise. It is unnecessary to go over the story again here. It has already been well-told.[21] He resigned over Europe and over the way in which Mrs Thatcher was running the Cabinet. What was surprising was the speed with which he made his peace. Within weeks he was saying publicly that one of the most extraordinary resignations since 1945 should now be forgotten.

His principal ally on the back benches, Michael Mates, adopted a similar approach. Mr Heseltine's other ally was Dr Keith Hampson. He was a doctor not of medicine but of philosophy; his subject was history. He was a clever and affable man, better-liked than Colonel Mates but still not regarded as quite 16 annas to the rupee.[22]

Later, in 1990, Mr Heseltine's campaign team was to be joined by Neil Macfarlane and Sir Peter Tapsell. Mr Macfarlane had been Minister for Sport, was a golfing partner of Denis Thatcher, played cricket, watched rugby football and possessed an air of rotarian good fellowship. Sir Peter was one of the cleverest men in the House and had made himself a millionaire through his connection with the stockbrokers James Capel. He was an economic expansionist and an opponent of monetarism who had consistently been denied office. He was not a bitter but he was certainly a disappointed man, with good reason. He possessed weight but did not command any following. For the next four years and more, however, Mr Heseltine's principal supporters were limited to two, Colonel Mates and Dr Hampson – the colonel and the doctor – with backing in the public prints from his friend of long standing, Julian Critchley. He possessed, Mr Critchley told us regularly, that streak of vulgarity without which it was impossible to succeed in modern, certainly in

---

[21] See Critchley, op. cit. 129 ff; Peter Jenkins, *Mrs Thatcher's Revolution* (1987), 185 ff; Magnus Linklater and David Leigh, *Not With Honour* (1986).

[22] For descriptions of Colonel Mates and Dr Hampson, see below, p. 189.

Conservative, politics.

Mr Heseltine's first movements were pacific. The Westland affair was still rumbling on when he called for peace all round, and for bygones to be treated as bygones. His most aggressive action was to stage yet another angry walkout, this time from the studio of *Channel 4 News*. He had just learnt that the programme was to include a filmed interview with Clive Ponting, whose acquittal on charges under the Official Secrets Acts in 1985 had caused embarrassment to Mr Heseltine and to the government as a whole. It was reliably reported that the presenter, Peter Sissons, 'looked stunned', as Mr Heseltine 'pulled a small microphone from his tie, slammed it down and walked away'.[23]

In February 1986 he abstained in a division about selling off bits of British Leyland to the Americans. There were 'jeers and counter-jeers' when he addressed the Young Conservatives at Blackpool. He said that he would like to give a 'new impetus' to industrial policy. He did not believe that the machinery of government was adequate to 'cope with the effort Britain must make to build and restore our industrial base'.[24] In March he told *Weekend World* that for too long, and for historical reasons, the Treasury had dominated the country's industrial policies.

Later in the month he put forward his programme, or a good part of it. First, single-purpose development corporations, similar to those for new towns, should be established to take charge of the revival of deprived areas. Second, local government Ministers should be appointed to be responsible across government departments for the interests of such cities as Birmingham, Newcastle, Liverpool and Manchester. And, third, there should be 'new measures' to encourage business back into the inner cities, such as a special initial subsidy for the first year of the life of these businesses, or an exemption from rates for the first two years.[25]

People believed that it had taken a riot to make the politicians 'stop, listen and perhaps begin to understand'. People were, he

[23] Julia Langdon in the *Daily Mirror*, 17 January 1986.
[24] *Daily Telegraph*, 10 February 1986.
[25] *Sunday Times*, 23 March 1986.

added somewhat obscurely, 'wrong', but this is what they did believe.[26] He told a Merseyside conference on urban regeneration at Knowsley that a 'national urban agency' should be set up to promote up to 100 trusts which would sponsor 'joint private sector and local authority redevelopment'.[27] There had been nothing like it since the policy-making heyday of the old Liberal Party in the period before David Steel and David Owen. Mr Heseltine had a policy for all occasions. He was evidently enjoying himself.

> I can say what I like. I have been in chains. I have been imprisoned for years ... I will do what I can to get the Tory Party re-elected.[28]

He said at Liverpool that

> What jobs are offered, I intend to take. I've always taken the jobs I've been offered. People like to succeed. I've never been an exception to that rule. I share that ambition with every member of the Cabinet. In my experience there are few shrinking violets around when the call comes, however loud the protestations.[29]

He drew large crowds in the Derbyshire West and Knowsley North by-elections.[30] He called for the phasing out of mortgage tax relief, for 'closer co-operation' between government and industry, and for a 'new industrial strategy'.[31] He incorporated these and other ideas in a substantial book, *Where There's a Will*, which was published in March 1987 and briefly topped the best-seller lists. It is almost unheard-of for works of political analysis by practising politicians – or, indeed, by anyone else – to top these lists, or even to appear in them at all. Perhaps the purchasers thought they were getting Mr Heseltine's memoirs. If so, they were disappointed. But the success of the book provided some guide to the fame of the

[26] *Guardian*, 27 March 1986.
[27] *The Times*, 25 April 1986.
[28] Press Association, 4 March 1986.
[29] *Daily Telegraph*, 24 April 1986.
[30] Press Association, 30 April 1986; *The Times*, 31 October 1986.
[31] *Sunday Telegraph*, 26 October 1986; Press Association, 11 February 1987.

author. Other politicians who have resigned from Cabinets have continued to make speeches, as Mr Heseltine did; few (the sole exception since 1945 is perhaps Aneurin Bevan) have continued to be recognised by the public as Mr Heseltine was. Not only did they recognise him: they quite liked what they saw. Of supporters of all political parties canvassed by the MORI organisation in March 1987, 24 per cent preferred Mr Heseltine as Mrs Thatcher's successor, 15 per cent Norman Tebbit and 12 per cent Sir Geoffrey Howe. Of Conservative supporters, 28 per cent preferred Mr Tebbit, 21 per cent Mr Heseltine and 14 per cent Sir Geoffrey.

A brief spell of favour

Though Mrs Thatcher disliked and distrusted Mr Heseltine as strongly as ever, the party managers decided that they could not afford to allow such a populist talent to remain buried. They determined to make use of it in the forthcoming election. Mr Heseltine, for his part, welcomed his return, if not to respectability – for he had never been wholly respectable, even at the high tide of Thatcherism – then at least to political acceptability. It was, however, cautiously reported that he would not 'play a role in any kind of inner team'. Nor would he be 'part of any central focus'. But he would be 'doing a little more than might have been expected'. This was, it appeared, 'a sign that his steadfast refusal to rock the boat any further since his departure from the Cabinet has been noted and welcomed'. His personal relations with the chairman, Mr Tebbit, 'have always been reasonable' (which was true enough). The party had also tried to 'smooth out the difficulties between Mrs Thatcher and Mr Heseltine at the time of the Westland affair' (endeavours that had not been successful).[32]

He visited 99 constituencies but his path did not cross Mrs Thatcher's.[33] Otherwise he was in fine abusive form. He described Labour's policies as 'wall-to-wall whitewash' and its

[32] *The Times*, 20 April 1987.
[33] Ibid. 22 May 1987.

campaign 'a three-week journey from red rose to red flag'.[34] But there was no place for Mr Heseltine in Mrs Thatcher's new Cabinet. Of the departments which he might have occupied, Defence went to George Younger, the Environment to Nicholas Ridley, and (the department he really coveted) Trade and Industry to Lord Young. Lord Young's representative in the House of Commons, with membership of the Cabinet thrown in, was Kenneth Clarke, who became Chancellor of the Duchy of Lancaster and Minister for Trade and Industry. Mr Clarke had joined the Cabinet, again as Lord Young's Commons representative, in 1985, when he had been Paymaster-General and Minister for Employment.

Mr Heseltine would not have relished representing Lord Young in the Commons or anywhere else. But could he not have been fitted in somewhere? There is no evidence that he expected a recall but, if he had been offered a post, and accepted it, political history would have been different. Certainly not only the tone but also the content of his speeches changed after the election. He talked more about Europe, fatal topic of Mrs Thatcher's last term, responsible for the successive political deaths of Mr Heseltine, Mr Lawson, Mr Ridley, Sir Geoffrey Howe and, finally, Mrs Thatcher herself. In autumn 1987 he called for co-operation with France on nuclear weapons and for full British membership of the European Monetary System.[35]

He delivered the Macmillan Lecture at the party conference – he now made an annual major speech on the fringe of the conference rather than from the platform – and defended the Macmillan years, saying that he had 'laid the foundations for housing ownership opportunities'. It was, however, characteristic of Harold Macmillan and the Conservative Party of his time that they 'did not see the success of the free market of itself as sufficient'.[36] This was what became known in the 1980s as a 'coded message'. Thus in the first half of the decade any reference to Disraeli was taken to be a flag of defiance towards Mrs Thatcher. So too was any mention of his phrase 'one nation'

---

[34] *Daily Express*, 20 May 1987; *Sunday Times*, 31 May 1987.
[35] *The Times*, 25 September 1987.
[36] Ibid. 7 October 1987.

– even though the One Nation Group of the 1950s, as one of its original members, Enoch Powell, has pointed out, was dedicated among other objectives to greater selectivity in the social services.[37]

But Mr Heseltine had another, sterner side, more consonant with Mrs Thatcher's views. This was most in evidence in matters of foreign policy and defence. One commentator wrote: 'He is clever enough to be even-handed in some areas.'[38] Mr Heseltine thought of everything in political terms. Nevertheless, it is doubtful whether he was, in this period, consciously trying to play the patriotic card. Indeed, had he been a more calculating politician, he would have responded more sweetly – as, after all, Mrs Thatcher herself did – to the popularity of Mr Gorbachev in the beauty contest of national leaders. As it was, hardly a week went by when Mr Heseltine did not try to make our flesh creep with tales of the Russian menace and warnings about the perils of lowering our defences.

And he was hot for security too. So, occasionally, was Neil Kinnock – when he thought he could use an alleged lapse as a stick with which to beat the government. We have already seen something of Mr Heseltine's discreditable role in relation to CND before the 1983 election.[39] Mr Kinnock, in the House, attacked the government's dilatoriness in failing to suppress the *New Statesman*, which was carrying an article by Duncan Campbell on the *Secret Society* affair.

> *Kinnock*: Why did the Government delay until yesterday seeking to take action against Mr Campbell? Why did they fail to secure the prevention of the publication in a magazine?
>
> *Heseltine*: Does my Right Honourable Friend [Mrs Thatcher] recognise that we are concerned, not with the competence of the Government, but with the irresponsibility of an organ of left-wing opinion? Does she further recognise that this is one more example of the failure of the Left to distinguish between the privilege of

[37] Enoch Powell, in a discussion on Iain Macleod, BBC Radio Scotland, 20 March 1991.
[38] *Daily Express*, 19 April 1988.
[39] See above, p. 84.

freedom of speech and a licence to peddle the nation's security?[40]

An alliance with Mr Tebbit

Then there was his alliance with Mr Tebbit, which was at its most vigorous over the abolition of the Inner London Education Authority. He urged Kenneth Baker, the then Education Secretary, to abolish it immediately. He warned that allowing the ILEA to 'wither on the vine' could store up potential electoral damage. And he called on Mr Baker to overcome his 'characteristic tolerance' by taking even greater powers over school closures, so that local education authorities could not defer them in the face of parents' threats to opt out.[41] He later continued with Mr Tebbit to warn the House of Lords not to reject the speedy abolition of the ILEA.[42]

Mr Tebbit had quarrelled with both Mrs Thatcher and Lord Young during the election campaign, or they had quarrelled with him – at any rate, there was a *froideur* between him and the Prime Minister. After the election he had left the Cabinet, to devote more time to his wife, who was confined to a wheelchair after being badly injured in the Brighton bombing of 1984. There were some who expected great things of the Heseltine-Tebbit alliance: that they would unite to embarrass the Government, or perhaps carve up the future leadership of the party between them. Mr Critchley had long maintained that the contest would be between Mr Heseltine and Mr Tebbit. With them in alliance, who could tell what might happen? In the end, very little did. They went their separate ways.

Though Mr Heseltine became more critical after 1987, he never tried seriously to embarrass the Government. Of the poll tax, he said in the debate on the Queen's Speech:

> I recognise that I am unashamedly a prisoner of my past. Twice I have advised Conservative Cabinets and Shadow Cabinets against this form of local authority finance, and twice, at least,

[40] 108 H.C. Deb., c.1021, 22 January 1987.
[41] 123 H.C. Deb., cc. 819-24, 1 December 1987.
[42] *Daily Express*, 9 May 1988.

they have accepted my advice. I must say that I have not yet seen any reason to change my mind.[43]

Over the poll tax his way was more-in-sorrow-than-in-anger rather than I-told-you-so. In the end (he told an interviewer) he was a Conservative. He did not believe that the poll tax justified a vote against the Government in a general election. He wanted the Conservatives to win, and would do nothing to prejudice that position.[44] Though attempts were made by 10 Downing Street to link him with Colonel Mates's poll tax amendment, his quarrels with Mr Ridley were more about, in his view, undesirable developments in the Green Belt and elsewhere than about local authority finance.[45] Mr Ridley replied in an Open Letter that it was he, Michael Heseltine, who had done more than anyone to relax planning controls when he had been at Environment.[46]

This was all innocent political fun. So was his campaign against Rowntrees' being taken over by Nestlé's or Suchard, his proposal to link benefits with work or training, and his idea that houses should be built on army land.[47] Even his call for credit controls, heretical though it might have been, could be regarded as playful:

Nigel [Lawson] would be better advised to attack the heart of the problem as opposed to risk spoiling what has been a very successful Chancellorship by long-term high rates of interest which, while choking off the consumer boom, do a lot of harm to the industrial base.[48]

The question of Europe

Europe was a different matter. Not only did he believe in it, and write a good book about it.[49] He had resigned from the Cabinet because of it. It was now a cluster-bomb with a multiple-firing

---

[43] 118 H.C. Deb., c. 281, 29 June 1987.
[44] Interview with Anthony Bevins, *Independent*, 10 October 1989.
[45] *Guardian*, 12 April 1988.
[46] Ibid.
[47] *The Times*, 3 May 1988; *Sunday Times*, 12 June 1988; *Daily Mail*, 14 June 1988.
[48] *Guardian*, 27 August 1988.
[49] *The Challenge of Europe* (1989).

device. Every so often a part of it exploded. The Government (he told an interviewer) had taken Britain into Europe further and more irrevocably than any previous administration. The Macmillan government applied to join. The Heath government signed the Treaty as it was: but at that stage the member-States retained the veto which had been injected by General de Gaulle into the original treaty. It was Mrs Thatcher who signed the Single European Act, which was 'the biggest transfer of sovereignty undertaken in any period of our history'. From that moment, we were committed to a process which required majority voting and to which we were subject. The conclusions from that were 'of profound consequence'.[50]

They were indeed. No one could deny that. The trouble was that Mr Heseltine seemed disinclined to draw them or, at any rate, to act upon them.

> I have made it clear [he said] that I will not challenge Mrs Thatcher. That remains my position.[51]

He continued to do well in the polls. In October 1988 MORI had recorded the following preferences among all voters: Mr Heseltine 22 per cent, Mr Tebbit 15 and Sir Geoffrey 14. Among Conservative voters the figures were: Mr Tebbit 26 per cent, Mr Heseltine 20 and Sir Geoffrey 17. In December 1989 the Gallup Poll found that as leader he would do more than anyone else to attract the wavering vote back to the Conservatives.[52] He told the television programme *Agenda*:

> I think ambition is a very laudable human quality and if, in the service of the party, I had a chance to play the ultimate role, it would be a huge honour.[53]

Throughout autumn 1989 there was increasing pressure on Mr Heseltine to stand against Mrs Thatcher, as the rules allowed. It was believed that Colonel Mates had 110 pledges of

---

[50] Bevins, art. cit.
[51] *The Times*, 24 November 1989.
[52] *Sunday Telegraph*, 10 December 1989.
[53] *The Times*, 20 November 1989.

support, though the precise figure varied in accordance with one's informant. Mr Heseltine hesitated, withdrew and left the fight to Sir Anthony Meyer.[54] It was never contemplated that Mr Heseltine would win. It was said, rather, that he would be a superior breed of stalking horse.

This was, however, a misuse of the phrase. There was no intention to put up another candidate if (as happened in the following year) Mrs Thatcher failed to win outright in the first ballot. Everyone assumed she would win outright, against Mr Heseltine or anyone else. Mr Heseltine's function, it was hoped, would be to act as a focus of discontent, to amplify the voices saying to Mrs Thatcher: So far, and no further. He would then be in a position to reap his reward in one, two, three years.

Mr Heseltine refused to see the future in quite this way. He did not want to use up any credit at this stage. The one flaw in his front of sincerity was that, to make his chances of succeeding Mrs Thatcher realistic, the Conservatives had first to lose the election. Or so it was believed in 1989. And yet, here he was, saying in speech after speech that he had no intention of challenging Mrs Thatcher and was working for a Conservative success in the election.

He was certainly one of the most assiduous speakers in by-elections. He went to the Vale of Glamorgan. He went to Mid-Staffordshire, where he managed to make a speech which was both rousing and amusing but omitted to mention Mrs Thatcher once by name.[55] When taxed with this neglect on the *Question Time* television programme on 10 May 1990, he replied breezily that it was a 'rubbish point'. This programme was notable because one of the panellists, the Shadow Minister of Transport, John Prescott, succeeded in provoking Mr Heseltine into making his firmest declaration so far that he would not challenge Mrs Thatcher.

On 30 October 1990 Mr Heseltine came to lunch at the *Observer*. Two days previously the leaders of the European Community had voted 11-1 (Mrs Thatcher dissenting) to agree to 1 January 1994 as the date for the start of the next stage to

[54] See below, p. 176.
[55] Personal knowledge.

economic and monetary union. Mrs Thatcher had made disobliging noises. Mr Heseltine had an issue. He was asked at the lunch: Would he now stand? He was firm that he would not. He had, he said, spent four hard years building up a position unique in modern British political history. He did not propose to throw it away at this stage.

5

The Perils of Abroad

That takes off a little of my esteem for this thing of yours – that it
goes on abroad. Hang 'abroad'! Stay at home and do things here –
do subjects we can measure.

Henry James, *The Lesson of the Master*

Miss Prism: Cecily, you will read your Political Economy in my
absence. The chapter on the Fall of the Rupee you may omit. It is
somewhat too sensational.

Oscar Wilde, *The Importance of Being Earnest*

Immediately after the 1987 election, the most popular man in
the Conservative Party was Nigel Lawson. He had delivered a
victory, not perhaps against the odds, but certainly after a series
of trials and alarms. In 1985 the Conservatives had lost the
Brecon by-election to a Liberal candidate (then still part of the
Alliance) after complaints about the inadequacy of public
services, particularly in matters of transport and health, and
expressions of dislike for 'that bloody woman', the Prime
Minister. In January 1986 she had, in her own opinion, at any
rate, come close to being supplanted over the Westland affair,
though by whom she and others found it difficult to say.

The 1987 election

Nor had the election itself been an affair of sweetness and light.
The Labour Party's election broadcasts, showing, among other
affecting scenes, Neil Kinnock and his wife Glenys walking

hand-in-hand along a beach, had been admired and envied on account of their polish and 'professionalism'. Few commentators noticed that nearly 30 years previously Labour's broadcasts, in which Tony (then Anthony Wedgwood) Benn had played a principal part, had been praised for precisely the same reason. And yet in that 1959 election the Conservatives under Harold Macmillan had obtained a majority of 101 over the other parties.

Not many observers expected the party under Margaret Thatcher to win a majority of 124 – only 41 fewer than it had won in 1983. Certainly Mr Kinnock did not expect it. On election night, briefly buoyed up by some misleading intelligence from the BBC, he had believed he would win. Hugh Gaitskell had possessed the same conviction at Leeds Town Hall in 1959, even though it had been brought about in different circumstances and for different reasons. Mrs Thatcher did not expect to win by this margin either. At one period in the campaign she thought she might lose, and exchanged harsh words with the party chairman, Norman Tebbit, on that account.

The dispute, resembling as it did one between the Blues and the Greens in Imperial Constantinople, concerned the merits of two advertising agencies: the one, Saatchi and Saatchi, which formally held the Conservative Party account and enjoyed the support of Mr Tebbit, and the other, Bogle Bartle Hegarty, whose principal admirers were Lord Young and Tim Bell, a somewhat louche character with a blow-wave whose place in Mrs Thatcher's affections was attributed to his ability to make her laugh and to his ingenuity in thinking up slogans and wheezes of a populist character. Mrs Thatcher's daughter Carol (who deserves as much credit as her father Denis for preserving her independence and dignity in often trying circumstances) advised her to 'get your act together, Mum'. Lord Young and Sir Timothy, as he later became, triumphed over Mr Tebbit in the great advertising agency dispute, though the former's victory was short-lived, as these things go. Whether this controversy made much difference to the result is doubtful. Anyway, it was all right on the night.

The character of Mr Lawson

Mrs Thatcher had made Mr Lawson Chancellor in 1983, after the election, together with Leon Brittan as Home Secretary. Both appointments were courageous, even rash. Both politicians were Jewish. Mr Lawson at 51 was comparatively young; Sir Leon at 43 was very young.[1] Neither was popular in the party. In 1986 Sir Leon was made a blood-sacrifice on the altar in Committee Room 14 specially reserved for these occasions by the Conservative backbenchers. In subsequent years he was to create trouble in Europe for Mrs Thatcher. Both were clever, and both were supercilious, or appeared to be so: but Mr Lawson was always a tougher, more robust political character.

At the same time he was a sensitive spirit. Though he did not take offence himself, and was not averse to giving offence to others, his interests were intellectual and artistic. As is not unusual with people who possess such interests, he had an extensive collection of *Wisdens*. He did not drink much (chiefly whisky or white wine) but he ate a good deal. When he was editor of the *Spectator*, his then foreign and arts editor, Malcolm Rutherford[2] was asked to call on him quite early one morning to discuss some matter or other. Mr Rutherford was astonished to find Mr Lawson breakfasting to the background of a sideboard bearing dishes of bacon, eggs, sausages, perhaps even kedgeree also. He said afterwards that he had no idea that such extravagant habits of life were maintained any longer. Mr Lawson's son used to enjoy holidaying with his father in France partly because he was expected to eat so much.[3]

Perhaps his chief characteristic was that he was a gambler. In the mid-1960s he once asked his political columnist on the paper whether he did the football pools. The columnist said he did not, though his father did: it gave him, a retired schoolmaster, something to think about, an additional interest. Mr Lawson

---

[1] Mr Brittan was knighted in 1989 on becoming a Vice-President of the European Commission.

[2] Later political editor of the *Financial Times*.

[3] Nigel Lawson was editor of the *Spectator* 1966-70; Dominic Lawson was editor 1989-.

said that he did the pools too, every week. His colleague objected that the odds against winning were very high. The editor replied that the sums that could be won were very high too. In the early 1970s he inherited 'a fair amount of money' from his aunt. When he had possessed a small amount of money, he had invested it himself. But when he had his aunt's money – supplemented by some from his then wife, the former Vanessa Salmon[4] – he thought:

> This is a serious business now; life's too short to spend the necessary time analysing company accounts and all that; I can pay a professional to do that ... I made a big mistake. He pretty well lost it all. He had also geared up my borrowing: in order to repay it I had to sell my house in Hyde Park Gate.[5]

Subsequently at social gatherings Mrs Lawson would point to her husband and say: 'There is the man who lost all my money.' This was perhaps unfair, in that the money had been lost through being put in the hands of someone else entirely.

Shortly afterwards they went their separate ways, she with Sir Alfred Ayer, he with Mrs Thérèse Medawar, a researcher in the House of Commons library. Mrs Medawar gave birth to a boy. A few years later Mr Lawson moved into her small house in Wandsworth. In 1980 they married. Their second child, a girl, was born a year later.[6] Cecil Parkinson had a child by his mistress, refused to leave his wife for her and was excluded from the government for four years on that account. Mr Lawson left his wife, had a child by his mistress, married her, had another child and remained a Minister without his private life's being questioned in any way.

A pioneer of monetarism

Mr Lawson was an influential Minister before becoming Chancellor. As Secretary of State for Energy from 1981 to 1983

---

[4] Vanessa Salmon, 1936-85. m. 1st, Nigel Lawson, 1955 (m.diss. 1980), one s., three d.; 2nd, 1983, Sir Alfred Ayer (d. 1989).
[5] Susan Crosland, 'Nigel Lawson' in *Looking Out, Looking In* (1987), 49 at 53.
[6] Ibid. 54.

he was widely credited with building up the coal stocks which helped to defeat Arthur Scargill's miners' strike.[7] As Financial Secretary to the Treasury from 1979 to 1981 he was regarded as a stern paladin of monetarism and the author of the medium-term financial strategy followed by Sir Geoffrey Howe as Chancellor. Monetarism was the belief – derived from the Chicago economist Milton Friedman and ultimately from Stanley Jevons's quantity theory of money – that control of the money supply, however defined, was both a necessary and a sufficient condition for controlling inflation, and that Keynesian demand management was irrelevant and even damaging.[8] The medium-term financial strategy was that monetary and Public Sector Borrowing Requirement targets would not just be specified for the year to come but instead be tightened over a sequence of years.[9] The Public Sector Borrowing Requirement was what the government had to borrow to make up for any discrepancies between its income and its expenditure.

In the 1970s monetarism was, in one form or another, embraced by figures as diverse as Sam Brittan, who was a liberal; Peter Jay, who claimed to be both a socialist and a believer in the free market; Denis Healey, who was Chancellor of the Exchequer; and James Callaghan, who was Prime Minister. Indeed, there are those who believe that the high tide of the doctrine, as far as its governmental application was concerned (what economists and economic commentators call 'policy'), occurred in 1978-81, when, for part of the time, a Labour government was in power.[10] Nevertheless, despite its ecumenical nature as a doctrine, monetarism was the distinguishing sign – even one of the conditions – of membership of those Conservatives who gathered round Sir Keith Joseph and the Centre for Policy Studies and who supplied Mrs

---

[7] It is necessary to emphasise Mr Scargill's personal responsibility for this disastrous episode in the history of the British working class. The miners who were doubtful about the wisdom of the action, not to mention its constitutionality, came not only from areas of traditional moderation such as Nottinghamshire but also from areas of traditional militancy such as South Wales.

[8] See generally William Keegan, *Mr Lawson's Gamble* (1989); Alan Walters, *Sterling in Danger* (1990); Tim Congdon, *Monetarism Lost* (CPS, 1989).

[9] Congdon, op. cit. 13.

[10] See Congdon, op. cit. Ch. 2.

Thatcher with most of her higher-grade political ammunition.

A belief in monetarism usually accompanied an even stronger belief in the merits of floating exchange rates. Britain had floated the pound under Anthony Barber (the forgotten Chancellor) and Edward Heath in 1972. It marked the collapse of the post-war international economic settlement inaugurated at Bretton Woods in 1944. Flotation was also followed by a period of unprecedently high inflation. Again, it had been urged by figures as varied as Mr Brittan and Enoch Powell as 'the price of economic freedom'.[11] Some leading members of the Labour Party, scarred as they had been by the sterling crises of 1931, 1947 and 1966, took a similarly favourable view of floating rates; though Lord Lever, who had a more extensive experience of practical finance than any of them, considered flotation to be an engine of instability.

By the beginning of the 1980s, accordingly, monetarism and floating rates were in theory politically neutral, jointly and severally. Men of the Right and of the Left could favour either or both of them promiscuously, without causing adverse comment as to their doctrinal soundness. True, a belief in both tended to indicate a member of what came to be called the Radical Right: but there was no logical or necessary connection. As the decade progressed, however, a belief in monetarism and floating rates came to be seen as a necessary condition of soundness as a Conservative and of loyalty to Mrs Thatcher. Yet both causes sank: floating rates in 1990, when we joined the exchange rate mechanism of the European Monetary System, and monetarism at an earlier period in the decade whose precise time is a matter of dispute. Mr Lawson played a substantial part in these defeats of the Prime Minister.

It was not that he had any doctrinal objection to monetarism, floating rates or both. He was not so much a pragmatist as an enthusiast. His enthusiasms would last for a year or so, sometimes longer. William Keegan has suggested that, in his conduct of economic policy, he tended to look for a discipline – for a hook on which to impale himself.[12] When he was Financial

[11] See Samuel Brittan, *The Price of Economic Freedom* (1970).
[12] Keegan, op. cit. *passim*.

Secretary, it was monetarism which fulfilled this function.

With him it had not always been so. In the mid-1960s he was a Keynesian, an expansionist, a sceptic about the evils of inflation and an urger of devaluation upon the Wilson government. His most consistently held beliefs were negative, though none the worse for that. He was against equality and against incomes policies. He used to believe that there was a correlation between unemployment and electoral success. In 1966 he wrote a leading article for the *Spectator* on the Wednesday upon the assumption that Harold Wilson would win a massive majority in the election on the Thursday, as turned out to be the case. He was, he said, sure of the result because of the rate of unemployment. Immediately afterwards he was criticised by the simpler members of his party for 'disloyalty' in anticipating a huge Labour victory but he bore this attack with his customary fortitude and equanimity, which became in his critics' eyes a form of scorn, as indeed it was.

The character of Sir Alan Walters

Sir (as he was finally to become) Alan Walters was a different kind of man. It is one of the errors of life, perpetuated by marriage bureaux, to suppose that similar people with like interests will get on well with each other; just as it is to suppose that dissimilar people with incongruous interests will get on badly. Mr Lawson came from a prosperous Hampstead household, his father was a tea-broker, he had enjoyed a privileged education and he had met with little but success in life – apart from his rejection by the civil service after Oxford, his failure to win Eton and Slough in 1970 and his dismissal as editor of the *Spectator* at the same time, though it must be said that even the best editors are liable to be sacked by capricious, malign or merely stupid proprietors. Sir Alan had had an altogether harder life. He had been brought up in Leicester, where his father was a bus-driver. He had failed the eleven-plus examination but had managed to attend Alderman Newton's School in the city, *alma mater* of C.P. Snow and J.H. Plumb. Like them, he had gone on to University College, Leicester, but had taken his first economics degree as an external student of London University. Physically he was the opposite of Mr Lawson: above medium height, fair, lined, spare, even stark, with staring eyes which did not, however, convey any impression of instability, though they contained a hint of fanaticism. He was addicted to jogging.

When he arrived for his first stint as economic adviser to Mrs Thatcher, British industry was already being laid satisfactorily to waste under the medium-term financial strategy. It was monetarism's finest hour. Perhaps it was altogether too glorious. 'In retrospect,' Sir Alan wrote in 1990, 'the squeeze was overdone.'[13] Mr Congdon agreed with him. Though the shock might have been inevitable and could be interpreted 'largely as a corrective to years of industrial over-manning' rather than as the by-product of a 'transient phase in macroeconomic policy', nevertheless 'in certain respects monetary policy clearly contributed to the harshness of the slump'.[14]

A few definitions

Here we must pause for some definitions. The narrow monetary base was the commercial banks' deposits with the Bank of England. The wide monetary base further included cash – notes and coins – in commercial banks ('till money'), together with cash circulating with the public. The narrow and the wide monetary bases comprised the measure known as sterling M0. Sterling M1 was M0 together with bank deposits ('sight deposits') which could be withdrawn on demand. Sterling M2 was a measure which fell out of fashion and happily need not detain us. Sterling M3 was M1 together with 'time' deposits, whose interest rates were geared to the length of time for which they were deposited. And sterling M4 was M3 together with deposits with building societies.[15] Most monetarists favoured M3 as the correct measure of the money supply, though Mr Congdon later came round to believing that M4 was the better

[13] Walters, op. cit. 91.
[14] Congdon, op. cit. 18.
[15] Keegan, op. cit. 236.

indicator.

In the early 1980s, M3 was growing above its target. An increase in interest rates was recognised as an antidote to excessive monetary expansion. The government accordingly raised interest rates to unprecedented levels. High interest rates were undoubtedly the cause of the appreciation in the exchange rate. Sterling's rise against the deutschmark[16] began shortly after the increase in Minimum Lending Rate to 17 per cent: 'the chain of connection is too logical and obvious to deny'.[17] Minimum Lending Rate or MLR was the same as the old Bank Rate, the rate at which the Bank of England lent funds to the banking system as lender of last resort. Though MLR was abolished in 1981, the Bank continued to have dealing rates at which it performed the same function. After abolition, bank base rates became the criterion for the level of interest rates.

During the 1980s, however, monetarism in its fullest rigour fell out of favour. Mr Congdon dates its decline to the 1982 Budget, when Mr Lawson was not even Chancellor.[18] Mr Keegan chooses Mr Lawson's Mansion House speech in October 1985, when 'he coolly announced that, in making policy decisions, he was simply going to suspend the M3 target for the rest of the financial year'.[19] Mr Lawson said that the government could maintain, and was maintaining, progress towards its inflation objective while M3 was growing at a rate well above the top set in the year's Budget Statement. To try to bring it back within the range, 'which, with the benefit of hindsight, was clearly set too low', would 'imply a tightening of policy which the evidence of other indicators of financial conditions tells us is not warranted'.[20] But Sir Alan Walters selects a slightly later date:

> If ever one is to put a date on the 'end of monetarism', then I think the middle of 1986 has a good claim. Of course it may be argued that this was nothing more than the usual pre-election expansion to give the voters an aura of prosperity in which, it is hoped, they

[16] Hereinafter referred to as 'the mark'.
[17] Congdon, op. cit. 18.
[18] Ibid. 19.
[19] Keegan, op. cit. 176.
[20] Speech at the Mansion House, 8 October 1985, quot. ibid.

will re-elect the incumbents. But it was more than that. The boost persisted for three years, long after the election.[21]

At first Mr Lawson was lucky. Public spending was held under such tight control and tax revenues were buoyed up so strongly by a general economic boom that the PSBR continued to decline and was eventually transferred into a budget surplus.[22] He also had the benefits of North Sea Oil and the receipts of the government's privatisation policy. This was a means of mutual enrichment – Conservative government and private capitalist benefiting alike – comparable to the dissolution of the monasteries under Henry VIII, the sale of monopolies under Elizabeth I or the appointment of commissioners under Sir Robert Walpole. As a piece of plunder it had numerous historical precedents. It had come about largely by accident but was a huge success. It was popularly thought that Harold Macmillan, by now Earl of Stockton, had compared it to 'selling the family silver'.

What Macmillan said about the silver

In fact this was not what Macmillan said but, rather: 'First of all the Georgian silver goes.' The words were spoken at a dinner of the Tory Reform Group at the Carlton Club on 8 November 1985. He said that the sale of assets was common with individuals or States when they encountered financial difficulties. After mentioning the Georgian silver, he continued: 'And then all that nice furniture that used to be in the saloon. Then the Canalettos go.' Profitable parts of the railways and the steel industry had been sold, along with the telephone system: 'They were like the two Rembrandts still left.'[23] The speech aroused much comment, and some amusement, both among opponents of Mrs Thatcher's government and among its supporters. The latter claimed that the components of the analogy – Georgian silver, furniture in the saloon, Canalettos and Rembrandts –

[21] Walters, op. cit. 103.
[22] Congdon, op. cit. 22-3.
[23] *The Times*, 9 November 1985.

illustrated how out-of-touch the almost parodically Whiggish Macmillan (or Stockton) was with the age of popular capitalism. He felt impelled to explain himself further in the House of Lords:

> When I ventured the other day to criticise the system I was, I am afraid, misunderstood. As a Conservative, I am naturally in favour of returning into private ownership and private management all those means of production and distribution which are now controlled by state capitalism. I am sure they will be more efficient. What I ventured to question was the using of these huge sums as if they were income.[24]

The distinction between capital and income – and how a failure to observe it led to bankruptcy, exile or worse – was a feature of his speeches in the Lords from his ennoblement to his death.

No such simple principle of accountancy was available for Mr Lawson to break in his managing of the exchange rate and the domestic rate of interest. Indeed, the wisest persons proffered the most conflicting advice. Mrs Thatcher was in favour of floating rates provided they led to a strong pound.

> I like a strong pound [she was to say when matters had become much worse]. Most Chancellors and most Prime Ministers *like* a strong pound.[25]

At the same time, she wanted a low domestic rate of interest. In Mr Lawson's opinion, she was obsessed by the rate of interest.[26] It was one of the factors in their falling out. She was passionate because she was concerned about mortgage rates rather than about British industry or small businesses. Simultaneously she believed – as she was, somewhat unhelpfully, to say to the House of Commons shortly before Mr Lawson's 1988 Budget – that 'you cannot buck the market'. This was also Sir Alan Walters's view. With him it at least had the

[24] 468 H.L. Deb., cc.390-1, 14 November 1985.

[25] Interview with Brian Walden, 29 October 1989, in David Cox (ed.), *The Walden Interviews* (1990), 30 at 51.

[26] Personal information.

merit of consistency. By 1985 he had returned to the United States, though he still made his opinions known to Mrs Thatcher. Mr Lawson's views were more complicated. He was at that point in favour both of official intervention in foreign exchange markets and of interest rate policy. But he had his doubts about fiscal policy, as did Mrs Thatcher and Sir Alan too.

Mr Lawson decides to join the ERM

In 1985 he decided that he wanted Britain to join the exchange rate mechanism of the EMS. The EMS had been founded in 1978 by Giscard d'Estaing of France and Helmut Schmidt of Germany. Neither was Mrs Thatcher's favourite continental character. Who was? Perhaps François Mitterrand of France, though he was not to arrive on the scene till later. When Giscard and Mr Schmidt founded the system (which came into operation in March 1979), James Callaghan was Prime Minister. Barbara Castle, then a newly-elected Member of the European Parliament, took up an entire train journey from Blackpool to Euston explaining its iniquities to her husband, the late Lord Castle, to Sir Robin Day and to the present writer. She was none too sure of Lord Callaghan's steadiness on parade when it came to the ERM.

She called it the EMS, as almost everyone else did, up to and including our entry in October 1990. Britain was a member of the EMS, but the other 11 countries were members of the ERM, whereas Britain was not. The ERM was an arrangement between governments to limit fluctuations in their exchange rates against the currencies of other members of the European Community. Governments were constrained to intervene in the markets to hold to agreed fluctuation limits: plus or minus 2.25 per cent for the more prosperous members, 6 per cent for Italy and Spain. They had to hold interest rates at levels which made this possible. Realignments had to be agreed by all member-countries. National currencies continued to exist. It was always open to a government to leave the ERM, as France had left its predecessor, the so-called 'snake'.[27]

Entry by Britain had been considered and rejected in 1981-2.
Mr Lawson reopened the question because of the sterling crisis
of January 1985.[28] Unfortunately 'floating' could still lead to
sterling crises. Neither Sir Alan Walters nor Mrs Thatcher
approved of joining the ERM in 1985 or, indeed, in any
circumstances. Sir Alan believed that Mr Lawson may have
been influenced by his experience of fixing the Hong Kong dollar
in October 1983 – a course which Sir Alan, as an enthusiast for
stability in certain circumstances, approved.

> In retrospect [Sir Alan wrote], the widely reported intransigence
> of the Prime Minister to entering the ERM was a godsend. If we
> had entered, then raising interest rates to new highs in late 1985
> and throughout 1986 would have jeopardised, even ruined, the
> Conservative Party's prospects in the election of 1987.[29]

Mr Lawson goes abroad

Prohibited by the Prime Minister from entering the ERM, Mr
Lawson nevertheless determined to exercise influence abroad.
Previously, he had never cared much for Abroad. A civilised
man, he had enjoyed visits to France.[30] But Abroad in the
ministerial sense – now getting into aeroplanes, now getting out
of them – had never greatly appealed to him. Long flights
affected one's pattern of sleep, short flights one's digestive
system: what was the point of it all, except to be photographed
and to impress one's more gullible followers as an international
statesman? Certainly Prime Ministers, from Harold Macmillan
to Margaret Thatcher, had been quick to seize this last benefit.
Mr Lawson neither was nor wished to become Prime Minister.
Still, he now began to enjoy foreign trips. Why was it, Mrs
Thatcher complained in 1986, that 'something always goes
wrong when Nigel goes abroad'?[31]

[27] See Sarah Hogg, *Independent*, 28 January 1989.
[28] Keegan, op. cit. 156.
[29] Walters, op. cit. 101.
[30] See above, p. 98.
[31] Keegan, op. cit. 188.

The late 1980s were distinguished by the number and frequency of economic summits, at which Mr Lawson liked to cut a dash. The first in time, and the second most famous, took place at the Plaza Hotel, New York, in September 1985. According to the Bank of England's version, the five leading industrial nations agreed that

> exchange rates should better reflect fundamental economic conditions and that a further orderly appreciation of the main non-dollar currencies against the dollar was desirable. They stood ready to co-operate more closely to this end, and each government itemised its own policy intentions. In its explicit admission of the problem, and in the specific commitments to action, the Plaza statement impressed the markets. The dollar turned down, and the impact was then reinforced by a powerful burst of co-ordinated exchange market intervention in which, importantly, the United States was seen to be participating.[32]

Sir Alan Walters was less impressed. The fall in the dollar began in February 1985, some seven months before the start of the implementation of the Plaza Agreement.[33] 'This in no way inhibited the participants from admiring their own perspicacity.'[34] To be fair to them, the Treasury Committee acknowledged this fall, dating it from March.[35]

The most famous meeting of this period produced the Louvre Accord of February 1987. The problem now was that the dollar was too low rather than too high. By the end of 1986, there were fears of an undervalued dollar. The accord aimed at supporting it at the position which it then occupied, on the assumption that the prevailing rates were exactly right. The agreement failed. The dollar continued to depreciate. The financial markets were not impressed. It was apparent that the difference between the US and her partners remained unresolved.[36]

Meanwhile Mr Lawson had taken a step of his own in the

---

[32] Treasury and Civil Service Committee, International Monetary Co-ordination, H.C. 304 of 1988-9 (1989), 133 (Memorandum by the Bank of England).

[33] Walters, op. cit. 57.

[34] Ibid.

[35] H.C. 304 of 1988-9, xix, para. 19.

[36] H.C. 384 of 1988-9, xx; see also Walters, op. cit. 58.

direction of financial internationalisation. In 1986 he decided that sterling should shadow the mark. Maybe he was influenced once again by his experiences with the Hong Kong dollar in 1983, which was tied to the US dollar. Or perhaps he hoped to demonstrate to Mrs Thatcher that she need not fear for sterling's stability within the ERM.[37] At any rate, in the last years of Mr Lawson's Chancellorship, the shadowing of the mark was depicted by Mrs Thatcher's supporters as the cause both of the post-1987 inflation and of the *froideur* which developed between her and the Chancellor.

One version is that senior officials at the Treasury were surprised by Mr Lawson's announcement at the IMF in 1987 that exchange rates were the main guide to interest rate policy. The decision to shadow the mark had not been considered in detail by officials. It was the consequence of a number of discussions between Mr Lawson and the Permanent Secretary, Sir Terence Burns.[38]

Mr Lawson's version is different. It is that Mrs Thatcher was fully apprised of the decision to shadow the mark. Whether or not she approved of it – and it would have been surprising if she had, completely – she certainly knew about it.[39] His explanation of the hostility that developed between them after 1987 is that she was angry, at least piqued, at his being regarded as the principal architect of the victory in the election. The credit, she thought, properly belonged to her. Mr Lawson makes the comparison with Lord Hailsham's treatment by Harold Macmillan after the Conservative win in 1959. Not only was Mr Lawson being hailed as a saviour: he was even being talked about as a successor. Mr Lawson makes another comparison, this time with Norman Tebbit. He too was seen as a successor (though before the election rather than afterwards). He too was cut down, like one of Elizabeth's courtiers.

And did the decision to shadow the mark cause the inflation? Lord Bauer considers it unproven. But it is generally agreed that the failure of the Louvre Accord partly caused the stock

[37] Keegan, op. cit. 193.

[38] Walters, op. cit. 137, citing with approval Keegan, op. cit.

[39] See below, p. 123.

market crash of October 1987.[40] And the response of the authorities to the crash, certainly the British authorities, helped bring about the inflation of the succeeding years which ended the political careers of both Mrs Thatcher and her Chancellor. As an official of the Bank of England told the Treasury Committee on 22 June 1988:

> This last year has been such a tumultuous and difficult one, because it was punctuated by the stock market crash of 19 October which changed everyone's perceptions. I think we all loosened monetary policy, consciously, after 19 October, because of fears of the damage that could be done if policy was too tight at a time when financial institutions were under extreme strain. That was one of the reasons why, over the last three months of last year, United Kingdom base rates came down in three separate half-point moves. I think the experts and the forecasters got it wrong ... [41]

Mr Lawson's credit boom

There was also a credit boom, which was led by lending to finance the purchase of houses. As the price of houses is regulated by the availability of finance rather than by the cost to the borrower of that finance, the result was inflation in house-prices, which led a broader inflation. Mortgage credit from the banks alone – and it was the banks, rather than the building societies, which were rushing to lend – quintupled from £2,043m in 1984 to £10,041m in 1987. The total of advances for house purchases (banks, building societies and other sources) increased from £17,072m in 1984 to £29,763m in 1987.[42]

Mrs Thatcher regarded the increase in house prices as virtuous, as the outward and visible sign of the correctness of her policies. The beneficiaries, or apparent beneficiaries, agreed with her – for a time. There was a period when no dinner-party in North London would be considered over until the guests had exchanged boasts about the increase in the value of their houses in the past month. Several years were to elapse before the boasts

[40] H.C. 384 of 1988-9, xx.
[41] Ibid. Q.111, evidence of A. Loehnis.
[42] Congdon, op. cit. 28.

turned sour.

In his interview with Brian Walden, Mr Lawson had little doubt about what had happened:

> *Walden*: But you boosted demand?
>
> *Lawson*: No I didn't. I didn't boost demand at all. So far from boosting demand by pouring money into the economy, the budget surplus increased. We had the biggest budget surplus we've ever had.
>
> *Walden*: But the money got there somehow, Nigel, didn't it?
>
> *Lawson*: Yes, yes, it did ... As a result of financial freedom, and as a result of the great upsurge of confidence there was in the country, we got people borrowing on an enormous and unprecedented scale. Just think of two figures alongside each other. The tax cuts in the 1988 Budget – which I think are highly desirable and will have continuing beneficial effects – they amounted to four billion. The increase in personal borrowing amounted to forty billion. It was this huge upsurge of borrowing, far greater than anything I expected.[43]

Sir Geoffrey Howe had begun the process of deregularisation by abolishing exchange controls when he was Chancellor in 1979. France and Italy did not abolish theirs till much later, a delay of which Mrs Thatcher was to make something when she was opposing Britain's entry into the ERM. In 1983 he became Foreign Secretary in succession to Francis Pym.

Mr (now Lord) Pym had been compared by Bernard Ingham to Mrs Mopp in the wartime show ITMA. The catchphrase was: 'It's being so cheerful as keeps me going.' Sir Bernard had got the catchphrase right but the character wrong. Mrs Mopp's line was: 'Can I do you now, Sir?' a question which perhaps would have been apt for other members of the administration. Sir Bernard meant Mona Lott, an error for which he subsequently and untypically apologised.[44] As Foreign Secretary during the Falklands War, having succeeded Lord Carrington, he had demonstrated an unwholesome tenderness for the Secretary-General of the United Nations and the Peruvian peace terms. His most grievous error, however, had been to state on television

[43] 5 November 1989, in Cox, op. cit. 53 at 71-2.

[44] See Robert Harris, *Good and Faithful Servant* (1990), 91. Mr Harris misquotes Mrs Mopp's catchphrase as: 'Shall I ...'.

during the 1983 election that he did not look forward to a landslide majority. Very large majorities, he said, presented problems of their own. To Mrs Thatcher this showed faintheartedness, even outright defeatism. Clearly the man had to go. 'Francis,' she said to him on Friday 10 June 1983, 'I want a new Foreign Secretary.'[45]

The character of Sir Geoffrey Howe

Sir Geoffrey Howe was, with Michael Heseltine and Tristan Garel-Jones, one of those Welshmen who had been sent away to school, in his case Winchester. His father was a well-known solicitor in Port Talbot, a coastal steel town some miles east of Swansea. His formidable but engaging wife Elspeth – who never cared for Mrs Thatcher, any more than Mrs Thatcher cared for her – was supposed once to have said: 'When I married Geoffrey, he was a fiery Welshman.' Whether Lady Howe ever said this or not (and no very convincing authority exists one way or the other), it is doubtful whether Sir Geoffrey ever possessed the attribute in question. In the early years of his post-war army service, before going up to Trinity Hall, Cambridge, he was compelled to enter a boxing competition, and was awarded the prize for being the best loser. The impression he conveyed was of unforced affability.   Nor was this impression misleading. His political career contained only one thoroughly disgraceful episode: his prohibition (urged on by Mrs Thatcher) of trade union membership at GCHQ, Cheltenham, over whose legal basis he initially misled the House of Commons.[46] Generally he was regarded as a thoroughly nice man. He was also, unlike Mr Lawson, naturally industrious. While Mr Lawson looked on the world as a philosopher or mathematician, seeking the flash of an inspired generalisation, Sir Geoffrey plodded through life as a painstaking lawyer.

[45] Francis Pym, *The Politics of Consent* (1984), ix.
[46] The matter is too complicated to go into fully here, but essentially Sir Geoffrey claimed, as Foreign Secretary, to be exercising powers which he did not possess either statutorily or under the royal prerogative. See also J.A.G. Griffith, *The Politics of the Judiciary* (4th edn 1991), 30, 125, 155, 278, 315-16; K.D. Ewing and C.A. Gearty, *Freedom Under Thatcher* (1990), 130ff.

He had done the State some service in his time. As Solicitor-General in Edward Heath's administration, he had seen through Parliament not only the government's trade union legislation but also the European Communities Act 1972, which is still law. The statute[47] recognised the concept of 'directly applicable' Community rules. For even at this stage of the Community's development, both the Council of Ministers and the Commission were empowered to make regulations having direct effect in member-States and creating individual rights and duties enforceable in national courts.[48] He was a European enthusiast, as Mrs Thatcher was not. She must have known this when she made him Foreign Secretary.

She also knew that he irritated her. He had done so since entering Edward Heath's Cabinet in 1972 as Minister for Trade and Consumer Affairs, when she was Education Secretary. 'Most of her senior Ministers she treated reasonably if patronisingly,' according to Jim Prior, 'although her treatment of Geoffrey Howe was sometimes really awful.'[49] She clearly enjoyed using him as a punchbag. Sir Geoffrey did not retaliate. Punchbags merely sway slightly. Even in private, he retained a modicum of civility. Unlike, say, Michael Heseltine and John Biffen in their ministerial days, he did not refer to her in conversation as 'the old bag' or 'the old cow'. He was always the gentleman – or the best loser in the boxing competition.

The character of Sir Charles Powell

By contrast, she got on well with Charles Powell. He spoke rapidly and made her laugh, whereas Sir Geoffrey did neither. Mrs Thatcher valued the ability to amuse her. Those in positions of power frequently value it, provided it is not taken too far. Sir Charles (as he was to become) was a civil servant and knew the limits. He was also young. When he first came to Mrs Thatcher's attention, as special counsellor for the Rhodesia negotiations, he

[47] S. 2(1).

[48] See *R. v. Secretary of State for Transport, ex parte Factortame Ltd* [1990] 2 A.C. 85 and Lords Judgments, 11 November 1990; *Independent*, 26 July 1991. See also Geoffrey Howe, 'Sovereignty and Interdependence', 66 *International Affairs* (1990), 675.

[49] Jim Prior, *A Balance of Power* (1986), 135.

was 38. Though he was not exactly good-looking in the women's magazine style favoured by the Prime Minister, he was tall, strong and reliable, with a firm handshake and abundant curly hair. He had a lively wife, Carla, who was Italian and had several friends among influential journalists. The Powells were a couple, even though Charles worked very long hours after moving to No. 10 in 1984 as Private Secretary to the Prime Minister. They moved in the *beau monde*. People talked, American fashion, of 'the Charles Powells'. No one ever said 'the Bernard Inghams'.

Sir Charles was also sceptical about Europe. He had gained a First in History at Oxford and professed an exaggerated regard for the virtues of the nation-State. Moreover, he did not wholly like or trust the Community officials from what he had seen of them, as First Secretary in Bonn and, later, as Counsellor to the UK Permanent Representative to the European Communities. Sir Geoffrey was thought in No. 10 to have 'gone native' in the Foreign Office, whereas Sir Charles was considered in the Foreign Office to have betrayed his vocation in No. 10.

The Single European Act

In the early part of the decade Mrs Thatcher put up a rousing annual performance in which she banged the table and demanded 'our money' from assorted alarmed representatives of the Community and apprehensive heads of government. These exhibitions of tantrums met with some initial success. The view of the Foreign Office was that, so long as they kept her happy, no great harm was done, and some good might even emerge. The culmination of this earlier period was the Single European Act 1986 which Sir Geoffrey introduced into the House of Commons. In 1991 Mrs Thatcher was to say that she had not properly understood it at the time; rather as she declared in the same year that entering the ERM under her Premiership had been 'a mistake'. Yet the provisions of the Act were modest.

By 1 January 1993 capital and labour were to be free to move across Community borders without restriction (though Greece, Portugal and Spain were given periods of grace before they had to remove restrictions on outward capital movements). This was a restatement of one of the terms of the Treaty of Rome 1957. Procurement by public authorities in each Community country was to be opened up to competition by firms in all Community countries. Technical standards for a particular product or trade were to be recognised by all other Community countries, while minimum standards were to be agreed on and given statutory force. This implied an end to the non-tariff barriers erected by several Community countries on imports from other such countries. It required a Community agreement on the restrictions, if any, to place on imports from outside the Community. There was to be some progress towards harmonisation, though not full equalisation, of rates of indirect tax on goods, such as VAT and excise duties, to that point where scrutiny of flows of goods across internal boundaries would all but cease.[50]

This Act caused no great fuss at the time. The European Communities Act 1972 had aroused more controversy – with, it must be said, greater cause. The Conservative Manifesto of 1987 was unaggressive about Europe, asserting that 'this government has taken Britain from the sidelines into the mainstream of Europe', applauding 'the opening of the market in financial and other services' and promising only to safeguard 'our essential national interests'. And then something happened. David Howell, the chairman of the Commons Foreign Affairs Committee and a former Minister, considers that it was not so much Mrs Thatcher that changed as the European Commission: that the Community was no longer the club which we had originally joined. Sir Geoffrey Howe believes that in 1988 Mrs Thatcher came to see Europe as a new, populist cause which would revive her and her party's fortunes.

We should also remember Mrs Thatcher's instinct to oppose. If you agreed with her in conversation, she would immediately alter her original position to cause a disagreement, about which a brisk argument could then ensue. She was not of a philosophical turn of mind, yet this habit of hers was oddly

[50] See Peter Sinclair, 'Britain's Foreign Trade, Payments and Exchange Rates' in Peter Catterall (ed.), *Contemporary Britain* (1990), 229 at 237.

reminiscent of R.H.S. Crossman. Labour came round to being the party of good Europeans. This was a change that was brought about partly by political expediency, partly by Neil Kinnock's travels abroad and partly by his son's embarking on Modern Languages at Cambridge.

The Delors Plan and the Bruges Speech

Mr Kinnock and Labour were also well-disposed towards the new President of the Commission, Jacques Delors. They were even better disposed towards his Plan or, at any rate, towards that part of it which involved a scheme, or social charter, governing workers' rights. The plan was, like all proper plans, composed of stages. Here there were three. The first stage called for 'increasing co-ordination' of monetary policies and the inclusion of the remaining Community currencies (Britain, Portugal and Greece) within the ERM. The second stage, in addition to the social charter, called for a European system of central banks which would begin to take decisions on monetary policy 'independent of political control'. While the third stage called for 'irrevocably locked' exchange rates and for the pound and other national currencies to be replaced by a single European currency.

Now, Mr Delors was a socialist, an intellectual, a Frenchman, a man. It was difficult to think of a collection of attributes less calculated to appeal to Mrs Thatcher. In September 1988 he received the kind of reception at the Trades Union Congress formerly reserved for dissident Spanish miners in the days of General Franco. The enemy was plain in view. The Prime Minister made a speech to the European College at Bruges. The occasion had been long arranged. Indeed, Mrs Thatcher had looked forward to it as a slightly tiresome engagement. Afterwards neither she nor Sir Charles – who wrote most of the speech – could understand what all the fuss was about. To this extent, the Bruges speech was not a reply to or an attack on Mr Delors. It stood on its own.

Mrs Thatcher said that 'willing and active cooperation' between 'independent sovereign states' was 'the best way to build a successful European Community'. Suppressing nation-hood and concentrating power at the 'centre of a European conglomerate' would be 'highly damaging'. Europe would be stronger 'precisely because' it had 'France as France, Spain as Spain, Britain as Britain, each with its own customs, traditions and identity'. The 'key issue' was not whether there should be a European Central Bank. The 'immediate and practical requirements' were to implement the commitment to free capital movement; abolish exchange controls, as Britain had in 1979; establish a genuinely free market in financial services; and make greater use of the ecu.[51]

Alas! Britain's proposal for the ecu as a kind of second-degree, optional currency did not gain favour. In these circumstances, all the liberal changes which Mrs Thatcher claimed to support implied a common currency. On the whole, she genuinely favoured these changes. She had, it is true, some difficulty with borders and their policing. Free trade did not entail the free entry into Britain of pornographers, drug dealers or mad dogs. Mrs Thatcher was much concerned with laxity at the ports. Nevertheless, she was in theory as much a free trader as Richard Cobden. It was a pity she did not wholeheartedly embrace the gold standard, for which, indeed, there is much to be said.

The European elections

The speech so moved Patrick Robertson, an Oxford undergra-duate of 20, that he relinquished his studies (to which, as he confessed, he was not specially suited) and founded the Bruges Group. It was composed largely of Conservative MPs, together with Peter Shore. Its spokesman was William Cash, the Member for Stafford, a solicitor, who was honest but tedious. The Bruges speech had, in fact, anticipated both the detailed proposals for monetary union and the social charter, which were published in spring 1989. Edward Heath appeared on television and made a speech in Brussels attacking Mrs Thatcher for

[51] *The Times*, 21 September 1988 and text, CPC, October 1988. See generally Stephen George, 'Britain and the European Community' in Catterall, op. cit. 63.

insularity and for misleading the people. Nevertheless, the Conservatives went into the European elections on 15 June 1989 under the slogan that a failure to vote would result in 'a diet of Brussels'. It is doubtful whether most people had much idea of what this meant. Certainly the results were chastening for the party:[52]

Party	Seats (UK) 1989 (1985)	Votes % (GB) 1989 (1985)	Votes % (GB) 1987 general election
Conservative	32 (45)	34.7 (40.8)	43.3
Labour	45 (32)	40.1 (36.5)	31.5
Liberal/SDP	–(–)	6.7 (19.5)	23.1
Green	–(–)	14.9 (0.6)	0.3
Other	4 (4)	3.6 (2.7)	1.8

The Madrid summit

Conservative MPs began to think that they might lose the next election and that, if they did, Mrs Thatcher would be largely responsible. Mr Lawson and Sir Geoffrey decided to present a united front to her before the Madrid European Summit. If she would not accept their terms, they would resign. It was the first occasion on which they had done anything of this kind. They were not close. Sir Geoffrey did not consider Mr Lawson to be a dedicated European, despite his recent enthusiasm for the ERM. This was the core of their demands. She must lay down the conditions for membership and not content herself with 'when the time is right'.

In the event she specified four conditions. She said that they were laid down in the first stage of the Delors Report: completion of the internal market, abolition of exchange controls, implementation of a free market in financial services and strengthening of competition policy. 'In these circumstances, and provided inflation is brought down significantly as we intend, the conditions would clearly exist for sterling to join the ERM.'[53] She added that the Delors Report 'spelled out' the 'fundamental nature' of European monetary union and the

[52] David Butler, 'Elections in Britain' in Catterall, op. cit. 46 at 47.
[53] *The Times*, 27 June 1989.

'transfer of sovereignty' which it would involve. These proposals, 'as they are now in the report' would not 'command the support of the British Parliament'.[54]

As things turned out, Mrs Thatcher once again found herself in a minority of one – no doubt to her gratification – because President Mitterrand, whom she was coming to regard as an increasingly sinister figure, had insisted on all three stages of the report's being taken as one. But she had surprised most people by accepting the first stage and Britain's entry into the ERM. She had even surprised herself. She had been forced into it. Someone would now have to pay.

Mrs Thatcher punishes Sir Geoffrey

Sir Charles Powell's view is that at Madrid Mrs Thatcher 'called their (that is, Sir Geoffrey's and Mr Lawson's) bluff'. This is a curious assessment. She approved neither of our entry into the ERM nor of the first Delors stage, as her several speeches from November 1990 onwards were to demonstrate. Mr Lawson and Sir Geoffrey had forced her into accepting both – or appearing to do so. Mr Lawson as Chancellor was in too strong a position to be disciplined. Sir Geoffrey had to pay instead.

In his place she appointed John Major, who had been in the Cabinet as Chief Secretary to the Treasury since 1987. She could have appointed Douglas Hurd, who was languishing at the Home Office but had regarded his life as one lengthy preparation for the Foreign Secretaryship. It appeared that he was condemned to be refused the job he really wanted. This, indeed, was one of his failings in Mrs Thatcher's eyes: he was too keen, too professional and – above all – too sympathetic to Europe. Mr Major did not, or appeared not to, possess any of these failings. Sir Geoffrey was shocked. Only a few weeks previously he had entertained week-end guests (including Lord Young, still then a Cabinet colleague) at his official country residence, Chevening in Kent.

Chevening is a large red brick house of the early eighteenth

---

[54] Ibid. See also 155 H.C. Deb., cc. 1109 ff, 29 June 1989 for Mrs Thatcher's Statement to the House.

century near Sevenoaks, carefully restored. It used to be the seat of the Stanhope family, who included Philip, Lord Chesterfield, author of *Letters to my Son*. The seventh Earl Stanhope died in 1967, having left the estate to the nation under terms set out in the Chevening Estate Act 1959. It was controlled by a trust whose chairman was the Lord Privy Seal and whose members included the Director of the Victoria and Albert Museum and persons appointed by the Prime Minister and the Environment Secretary. The Prime Minister had the responsibility of nominating the person to occupy the house. He or she could be the Prime Minister; any Cabinet Minister; the Queen Mother (as widow of George VI) or a lineal descendant of George VI; or the spouse, widow or widower of such a descendant. Chevening had not, however, proved strikingly popular either with members of the Royal Family or with Ministers of the Crown. Since 1973 Lords Barber, Hailsham, Carrington and Pym had each stayed for only a year or so; Prince Charles had stayed for six, from 1974 to 1980. In 1989 Sir Geoffrey and Lady Howe were the oldest inhabitants. Sir Geoffrey showed his guests the portraits of assorted Pitts, Stanhopes and Chesterfields as if they were of ancestral Howes of Port Talbot. He and his wife were distressed at having to leave, though he was later to claim that 'country houses had nothing whatever to do' with his negotiations with Mrs Thatcher.

She offered him the Leadership of the House and he asked to be Deputy Prime Minister as well. Lord St John of Fawsley says from time to time that this post is 'unknown to the constitution'. On this occasion Bernard Ingham echoed him in more forthright language, so annoying further those who already considered that Sir Geoffrey had been shabbily treated. The truth is that the post comes and goes, according to political convenience: it has been held, for instance, by C.R. Attlee, R.A. Butler and William Whitelaw.

Even so, Sir Geoffrey would have been better advised to accept the Home Office, which Mrs Thatcher threw in as a late alternative offer. It would certainly have been better for her if he had. For what turned out to be fatal to the Prime Minister was not so much that Sir Geoffrey was resentful as that he was, on account of his post, provided with ample time and opportunity to interest himself in matters European. This he proceeded to do, at fringe meetings and on special occasions.[55] When he made his first appearance before the House of Commons as its leader, a roar of approval went up from the Conservative benches. It was the clearest sign yet that she was in serious trouble with her backbenchers.

Mr Lawson punishes Mrs Thatcher

Meanwhile Sir Alan had recrossed the Atlantic for another spell of advising. In his absence, he had continued to make his views known to Mrs Thatcher by letter and by other means. Mr Lawson had tried to persuade her not to bring him back, but to no avail. Sir Alan, though of an ascetic disposition, had taken to touring the directors' dining (in practice, lunching) rooms of the City of London where, over avocado mousse and beef Wellington, he would cast doubt on the Chancellor's policies. An article expanding on his views was shortly to appear in a learned journal and was already circulating in Whitehall. Nevertheless, Mr Lawson would have been satisfied if Sir Alan had been eased out by the end of the year.[56] There seems little doubt that he made his views known to her.

Mr Lawson resigned. To claim that his resignation was due to a misunderstanding is idle. This is what some (though not including Mr Lawson) have claimed. Sir Alan apart, there was a clear difference of policy between the Prime Minister and the Chancellor. The Chancellor believed that the exchange rate should be 'an essential element of financial discipline, with the rider, incidentally, that exchange rate stability is itself an economic benefit'.[57] Indeed, a close reading of his resignation speech made clear that the exchange rate was to be not merely

[55] See e.g. Speeches to Bow Group, Conservative Party Conference, 11 October 1989; Anglo-Spanish Conference, Bath, 28 October 1989; Bow Group, Conservative Party Conference, 11 October 1990; and message to East Surrey Conservative Association, 30 December 1989.

[56] Interview with Brian Walden, 5 November 1989, in Cox, op. cit. 54-5.

[57] Resignation speech, 159 H.C. Deb., c.208, 31 October 1989.

an essential element but the governor of economic policy. Mrs Thatcher, on the other hand, believed that it was wrong to put exchange rate stability before monetary indicators.[58]

In the ensuing reshuffle Mrs Thatcher placed Mr Major at the Treasury, Mr Hurd at the Foreign Office and, to most people's surprise, David Waddington at the Home Office. From her point of view, Mr Major and Mr Hurd were to turn out to be an even more awkward combination than Mr Lawson and Sir Geoffrey. She had won a false triumph at Bruges and been humbled in Madrid. But the real perils of abroad were yet to be faced at Rome and in Paris.

---

[58] Interview with Simon Jenkins, *The Times*, 29 June 1991. In this interview Mrs Thatcher admits that she knew about Mr Lawson's shadowing of the mark. She says that to allow it was her 'great mistake'.

6

The Last Phase

Must I at length the Sword of Justice draw?
Oh curst Effects of necessary Law!
How ill my Fear they by my Mercy scan,
Beware the Fury of a Patient Man.

John Dryden, *Absalom and Achitophel*

It is not a principle of the Conservative Party to stab its leaders in the back, but I must confess that it often appears to be a practice.

A.J. Balfour, after the Carlton Club meeting, 1922

At the beginning of 1990 Mrs Thatcher resembled a woman whose husband wanted to go to Germany for their holidays. He had wanted to go there for years, for the last five in fact. She preferred Cornwall, with occasional forays into Switzerland, which, however, she did not much like. She would go when the time was right, but the time was not yet. Six months before, admittedly, that time had been brought closer by the threat of resignation of Nigel Lawson and Sir Geoffrey Howe. As Mr Lawson was to put it later on:

Geoffrey Howe felt that his position was becoming impossible in his negotiations that he was conducting with these counterparts in Europe and that British foreign policy was being screwed up by her handling of the European issue. And he felt that his position was becoming impossible and he could no longer carry on if there was no progress at Madrid. He could no longer carry on as Foreign Secretary. That was his decision. And out of solidarity with him I made it clear that, if he felt that he had to go, then I would go too because otherwise she might have thought: 'Oh well then, I can put Nigel into the Foreign Office and then Geoffrey Howe's resignation doesn't really make any difference.'[1]

As things turned out, Mrs Thatcher degraded Sir Geoffrey as a punishment; replaced him with the wholly unsuitable John Major; lost Mr Lawson; replaced him again with Mr Major, who was in danger of becoming the utility half-back of the government team; and appointed Douglas Hurd as Foreign Secretary in his place. This was a job that Mr Hurd had always wanted, which was one reason why Mrs Thatcher had refrained from giving it to him six months previously and on even earlier occasions when a change might have been possible.[2]

The character of Mr Hurd

He was the grandson of a Conservative MP and the son of another, who had been a farmer and agricultural correspondent of *The Times*. In the election later that year Mr Hurd was to bring about much innocent amusement through his endeavours to appear lowlier than thou. He resembled a bishop of orthodox views, forcefully expressed, or a public school headmaster who was both scholarly and stern. In the nineteenth century he would have combined both callings. He had written several good political thrillers and perhaps the best book about the Heath government, *An End to Promises*.

After leaving the diplomatic service he had been political secretary to Mr Heath in both government and opposition. Like Kenneth Baker, he was a reconstructed Heathman. But, again like Mr Baker, he had never become assimilated into the new regime. To an even greater extent, he was not one of us. Nor did he try to be. From time to time he would deliver speeches in which such unfashionable words as 'society' and 'community', 'duty' and 'obligation' made fugitive appearances. At Eton he had been known as 'Hitler Hurd' on account of his disciplinary

[1] Transcript, *On the Record*, BBC1, 7 July 1991.
[2] Mrs Thatcher was not alone in refusing to make ambitious and well-qualified people Foreign Secretary. Harold Wilson in 1964-70 and 1974-6 and James Callaghan in 1976-9 both neglected to give the post to Denis Healey.

proclivities. He was tall and spare, and tended to wear grey suits emphasising the premature whiteness of his hair which, though abundant, was cut with severity. He always wore a white handkerchief in his breast pocket. In private he had a loud, barking voice which, in public, conveyed reassurance to his auditors. In Mrs Thatcher's last phase Hurd shares rose steadily on the political exchange.

The position of Mr Major

No one thought seriously of Mr Major in this connection. He was currently considered to be Mrs Thatcher's man, and accordingly ineligible to contest the leadership with her. Among the political classes the consensus was that she would retire some time after the election, though estimates varied as to how long this would turn out to be. At one extreme, Kenneth Clarke thought she would try to go on for ever, at any rate as Prime Minister, and would have to be carried out of Downing Street kicking and screaming. Mr Clarke, as we have seen, turned out to be correct, though not entirely in the way he had imagined.[3] If she lost the election, the leadership would be contested – in 1992, 1993 or even later – by John Major, representing the Right, Chris Patten, representing the Left, and Michael Heseltine, representing the Spirit of Adventure. In 1993, however, Mr Hurd would be 63, to Mr Major's 50 and Mr Patten's 49.

It would clearly benefit him to have a contest before then. In the first four months of 1990, when the Conservatives lost the Mid-Staffs by-election to labour and interest rates under Mr Major had been higher than under Mr Lawson, it was considered likely – certainly it was considered desirable – that a challenge to Mrs Thatcher should be made in the autumn. The people who thought this were ordinary Conservative MPs who were in fear of losing their seats. They were worried not only by interest rates but, to an even greater extent, by the poll tax, which was due to come into operation in April 1990, and by what came to be known euphemistically as 'the Prime Minister's style'.

[3] See above, Ch. 1.

The Prime Minister's style

This phrase did not refer to Mrs Thatcher's habits of intervening in departmental matters, of asking Ministers awkward questions and of setting up *ad hoc* committees in place of the more regular Cabinet committees (which, paradoxically, had themselves been seen by a earlier generation as one of the principal causes of the decline of Cabinet government).[4] It was not that MPs thought that Mrs Thatcher was unduly bossy in her dealings with Ministers. Indeed, some of them considered that she was not bossy enough, as she had demonstrated by allowing the Westland affair to drag on for weeks. It was rather that her mental stability was giving increasing cause for concern. It was written of Bishop Butler, the moral philosopher of the early eighteenth century:

> The late Dr Butler['s] ... custom was, when at Bristol, to walk for hours in his garden, in the darkest night which the time of the year could afford, and I had frequently the honour to attend him. After walking some time he would stop suddenly and ask the question: 'What security is there against the insanity of individuals? The physicians know of none; and as to divines, we have no data either from Scripture or from reason to go upon relative to this affair.'[5]

Though Mrs Thatcher had softened her approach after the televising of the House had started in autumn 1989, nevertheless there were some alarming outbursts. Neil Kinnock often found himself at the receiving end. There was an illustration during Prime Minister's Questions in February 1990. Mrs Thatcher said she thought Mr Kinnock possibly took his instructions from the African National Congress. There was, quite properly, uproar. Mrs Thatcher then tried a second answer: she said that she did not take her instructions from the ANC. There was more uproar. The Speaker asked her to try again. She began: 'The ANC believes in comprehensive economic sanctions ...' The uproar continued. She replied: 'I said I would

---

[4] See John P. Mackintosh, *The British Cabinet* (1962), *passim*.
[5] Quot. Austin Duncan-Jones, *Butler's Moral Philosophy* (1952), 21-2.

start my reply again having withdrawn my previous words.'[6] She had, of course, done nothing of the kind. In October 1990, a month before her fall, the Speaker rebuked her for calling Mr Kinnock a 'crypto-Communist'.[7]

Newspapers such as the *Daily Mail*, the *Daily Express* and the *Sun* – and even, occasionally, the BBC – tended to depict outbursts of this nature as 'battling Maggie', as they termed her, in action. Indeed, there was in Mrs Thatcher's very stridency and unamenability to reason something which appealed to the brute instincts of working-class men, especially in South-East England, those famous C2s again. And not only working-class men either. Immediately after her fall a remarkable television programme was shown in which women writers of humane education and enlightened views – they included Beatrix Campbell, Germaine Greer, Isabel Hilton, Melanie Phillips and Marina Warner – praised Mrs Thatcher for exactly this quality of unreason.

Nevertheless, her supporters in Parliament were worried. The introduction of the poll tax saw inflation rise from over 7 to 9 per cent, and the worst scenes of middle-class disorder since the agitation for the repeal of the Corn Laws. Various schemes for jettisoning Mrs Thatcher were discussed by Ministers in this period. In March and April 1990 Labour's lead in the opinion polls was 23 per cent. Something had to be done. The most popular course was that it should be done to Mrs Thatcher. Unhappily, the obvious person to do it – and to profit from the deed – was Michael Heseltine. This was not at all to the taste of Ministers who had been canvassing the merits of Mr Hurd and, at a pinch, Sir Geoffrey.

If they were agreed with Mrs Thatcher about one matter, it was that they did not want Mr Heseltine to lead their party, still less to become Prime Minister and to be in a position to boss them about. He had not borne the heat and burden of the day as they had for the past four years. Instead he had toured the country, an even more popular figure with the party faithful than Jeffrey Archer. Alas, any scheme for disposing of Mrs

---

[6] 167 H.C. Deb., c. 137, 13 February 1990.
[7] 177 H.C. Deb., c. 1375, 18 October 1990.

Thatcher was bound to involve the intervention of Mr Heseltine at some stage. There were, admittedly, some Ministers who did not view a Heseltine Premiership as the end of the world: David Hunt, David Mellor, Norman Lamont. But they were comparatively junior.

Mr Heseltine appears to resolve matters

Then, in May 1990, Mr Heseltine resolved matters, or appeared to do so. Thursday 10 May 1990 was a notable day. Even Mrs Thatcher was polite about him at Questions. She might have been a tetchy schoolmistress paying reluctant tribute to a previously delinquent member of her class who had at last decided to make a contribution; while suspecting that he still had a couple of mice concealed in his desk ready for release at some date of his own choosing. Later that day, on *Question Time*, the message was that the boy had no mice in the desk. They were being kept safe at home, to be released at some time after the next election.

Mr Heseltine now said – what he had not been entirely clear about before – that he would not challenge Mrs Thatcher this side of the election. He went further, and predicted that any foolish fellow who was so misguided as to try it would come a cropper. He also gave his opinion that party elections were not a good idea anyway, being bad for morale and causing trouble and disturbance all round. Mr Heseltine now accepted not only Mrs Thatcher but also, in principle, her poll tax, rather in the spirit of the lady who informed Thomas Carlyle that she accepted the universe.

Throughout the summer, from May to September, the Labour lead in the opinion polls shrank steadily from 15 per cent to 11. The local elections of May 1990 also demonstrated that things might have been a great deal worse for the Government. In this respect they were the mirror-image of the European elections of the previous year. The results were as follows:[8]

---

[8] David Butler, 'Elections in Britain' in Peter Catterall (ed.), *Contemporary Britain* (1991), 59 at 61.

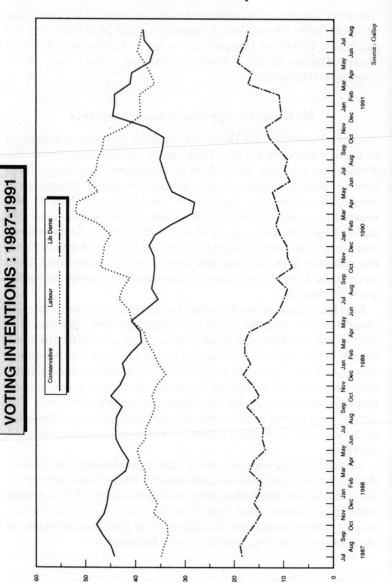

VOTING INTENTIONS : 1987-1991

Conservative
Labour
Lib Dems

Source : Gallup

	Con	Lab	SLD	SNP
London Boroughs	37.3	37.6	14.9	–
Change since 1986	+2.2	0.0	–7.7	–
Provincial England	27.3	51.9	14.7	–
Change since 1986	–3.6	+ 8.1	–8.6	–
Change since 1988	–7.5	+ 6.0	+0.6	–
Scottish Regions	20.0	44.6	8.4	22.2
Change since 1988	+2.7	–1.0	7.1	+3.6

Mr Baker's victory

Politicians read what they want to read – or what they want us to read – into the results of by-elections and local elections alike. Thus Sir Anthony Meyer said that the 1990 crop demonstrated that it was time for Mrs Thatcher to go. They did not demonstrate anything of the kind. The results were good for Labour but not outstandingly so. If the People's Party had taken over not only Bradford, as it did, but Wandsworth and Westminster as well, the pressure on Mrs Thatcher might have proved irresistible. As it was, Labour was the more badly bruised in London.

The 1990 local elections were primarily a victory for the Chairman of the Conservative Party, Kenneth Baker. He successfully presented the avoidance of a humiliating defeat as the winning of a famous victory. It was widely believed, not unreasonably, that he had saved Mrs Thatcher's bacon. The local elections were a victory also for the Keep Calm Party, whose leader had become Mr Major. The programme of this party was to retain Mrs Thatcher as Prime Minister but to take the country into the ERM in the autumn and generally to make friendlier noises in the presence of the Europeans. The aim was to contain Mrs Thatcher, chiefly through the agencies of Mr Major and Mr Hurd – and, incidentally, to win the approval of the editor of the *Daily Telegraph*, Max Hastings, and the new editor of *The Times*, Simon Jenkins.

This desire to impress enlightened opinion, an exercise in which our entry into the ERM played the principal part, was not one in which Mrs Thatcher had traditionally shared. Indeed, she rather despised enlightened opinion. That was one of her attractions, as much in the eyes of the neo-populists of the

Sunday Telegraph 'Comment' section – no longer, alas, the force it was – as of the *Sun* newspaper. Her view, which she took from Sir Gordon Reece, was that only the cheap papers were important politically, together with the *Jimmy Young Programme* and the women's magazines. Hence Mrs Thatcher's knighthoods for the editors of the *Sun*, the *Daily Mail*, the *Sunday Express* and the *Daily Express*, and peerages for the successive proprietors of the *Express* (the proprietor of the *Mail* having a perfectly good one of his own already).

The ERM exercise

The exercise to get us into the ERM, by contrast, made copious use of the City editors and economic columnists of the more expensive papers.[9] Sir Terence Burns and Sir Peter Middleton of the Treasury, who had once enjoyed favour as Mrs Thatcher's more official economic advisers, had both become converted to the cause. For once the Treasury, traditionally lukewarm in matters European, walked hand in hand with the more ardent Foreign Office. Indeed, it was Mr Hurd who was given the credit, or the blame, for converting Mr Major to the ERM. He performed his feat over a series of breakfasts at his London residence in Carlton House Gardens.[10]

Mr Ridley, for one, seemed to consider that this smacked of sharp practice.[11] But if blame was to be attributed, it was to be to Mr Hurd. Mr Major was 'popular in the party and his appointment was rightly welcomed'. He 'more or less continued his predecessor's economic policy and managed to persuade her to join the ERM'.[12] In fact, according to one observer less friendly to Mrs Thatcher, she became quite skittish about the prospect:

> Mrs Thatcher was tending to say when she bumped into officials in the summer, not 'Why are we going in?' but 'When are we going in?' And she got quite excited about the actual timing of the event.

[9] Transcript, 'A Very British Recession,' *Dispatches*, Channel 4, 13 March 1991.
[10] Philip Stephens, ibid. and *Financial Times*, 18 June 1990.
[11] Nicholas Ridley, *My Style of Government* (1991), 217.
[12] Ibid.

And I remember being told late in July by a senior official involved in it all, who certainly knew – I said, well, was it safe to go on holiday in August? And he said 'August, yes' implying that from September onwards it could be any time.[13]

Accordingly, here was Mr Major, having himself been converted by Mr Hurd (though the Foreign Secretary may have been pushing at an open door), himself converting Mrs Thatcher. It seems a little hard to treat Mr Hurd as if he were a sixteenth-century Jesuit – or a twentieth-century Scientologist – bringing innocent minds to the service of strange faiths. Mr Major must be assumed to have had a mind of his own. We know Mrs Thatcher had one. But 'Mrs Thatcher regarded John Major as a favourite son, almost a crown prince, so he was in a position to put arguments to her that she would not have taken from either Mr Lawson or Sir Geoffrey'.[14] Just so. Another way of putting it is to say that Mr Major deceived Mrs Thatcher – or that she deceived herself about Mr Major. Perhaps it was a bit of both. At any rate, as early as 1989 it was clear that Mr Major was not truly one of us, if he ever had been.

The fall of Mr Ridley

Mrs Thatcher might have stood up to Mr Major and Mr Hurd, Sir Terence and Sir Peter – not to mention Sir Geoffrey, whose function was now largely restricted to the delivery of lectures on Europe, which read surprisingly well. She might have stood up successfully to all these, and others, if she had enjoyed the continuing support of Nicholas Ridley in the Cabinet. But Mr Ridley gave an interview to Dominic Lawson, the young editor, in the *Spectator* of 13 July 1990, in which he said, in the course of other observations hostile to the European ideal: 'I'm not against giving up sovereignty in principle, but not to this lot. You might just as well give it to Adolf Hitler, frankly.' The cover of the magazine displayed a coloured cartoon by 'Garland' (Nicholas Garland) depicting a small Mr Ridley running away

---

[13] William Keegan, Transcript, *Dispatches*.
[14] Bruce Anderson, ibid.

from a big poster of Mr Kohl, having just daubed the German Chancellor's face to make him look like Hitler. Continental opinion was outraged, though more by Mr Garland's drawing than by Mr Ridley's words. The Germans, notoriously incapable of appreciating a joke unless about lavatories or gallows, were particularly incensed. They would have liked Mr Garland to be required to resign as well, but that was hardly practical politics. They had to be content with Mr Ridley's head instead.

He tried to endure for two days. On the Saturday (for the interview had first become available on the Thursday before) he talked twice on the telephone to Mrs Thatcher. He had been in Eastern Europe when the article first appeared. According to him, they agreed that they could have 'battled it out' but that this course would not be worth 'the indignity and the stress'.[15] He resigned, and was replaced by Peter Lilley, who was not to prove steady on parade.[16]

At the time the impression was not the same as Mr Ridley gave in his account. On the Thursday Mrs Thatcher had even tried to invent a new constitutional doctrine: that ministerial withdrawals – for Mr Ridley had withdrawn the offending observations – were not subsequently questioned. She was evidently confusing such retractions with personal statements made to the House: a very different matter. The evidence is that Mr Ridley wanted to stay, that Mrs Thatcher wanted him to stay, but that her hand was forced by her advisers at No. 10 and by representatives of the backbenchers. Sir Leon Brittan, we may remember, met his fate through the application of the same lynch law.

Mr Ridley claimed that his remarks about the Germans came at the end of his interview with Dominic Lawson.[17] This was not so: they occurred about two-thirds of the way through the tape-recording.[18] But this, a few Conservatives suggested at the time, did not dispose of the matter among gentlemen. For who, after all, fetched young Dominic from the station? Why, Judy

---

[15] Ridley, op. cit. 224.
[16] See above, p. 18.
[17] Ridley, op. cit. 224.
[18] Dominic Lawson, *Spectator*, 6 July 1991.

Ridley. And who – crucial question – cooked the lunch? Mrs Ridley again. In these circumstances (the argument ran) a decent chap, once he had discovered the indiscreet nature of his host's observations, would have telephoned him to inquire whether he had meant to say all he had said. In fact a complete transcript was sent to Mr Ridley's office, at their request, on the day the interview was published, though this could hardly have been of much help to Mr Ridley.[19]

It is the same with many rows in English life, in ordinary daily existence as much as in politics and the law. The game of Hunt-the-Issue is played enthusiastically. And the Issue glides from what was said, and whether it was true or false, to whether so-and-so was entitled to say it, and, if he was entitled, whether he was wise to say it, not to mention whether such-and-such was entitled or wise to pass it on. Truth and falsehood become subordinated to the *locus standi* of the speaker; while questions of manners are allowed to determine scales of value.

At all events, Mr Ridley's enforced departure left Mrs Thatcher without a single committed supporter inside the Cabinet, though the Downing Street press office emphasised that Mr Lilley's appointment left the 'political balance' of the Cabinet unchanged; Cecil Parkinson being by this time an apparently ineffective Minister of Transport who certainly enjoyed no longer the favour of his mistress. She had lost three Ministers, Michael Heseltine, Nigel Lawson and (in the sense that she had deliberately depoliticised him) Sir Geoffrey Howe over Europe. Now she had lost Nicholas Ridley over the same part of the world. The Curse of the Lawsons had struck again. Indeed, such was the jumpiness of Bernard Ingham at No. 10 that he seriously considered the possibility of a conspiracy between young Dominic and father Nigel.[20]

If Mrs Thatcher had not served Europe well – a matter about which there was dispute inside the Conservative Party – there was no doubt that, however one looked at it, Europe had not served Mrs Thatcher. Other parts of the globe, however, appeared more promising from her point of view. In 1989, at the

---

[19] Ibid.
[20] Private information.

party conference, she had claimed much of the credit for the revolution in Eastern Europe. Czech dissidents briefly occupied the place of honour traditionally allotted to Spanish miners at Labour conferences. But somehow it was not wholly convincing.

No comfort from Kuwait

Saddam Hussein's invasion of Kuwait on 2 August 1990 appeared more profitable. The particular British contribution to the ensuing developments was hard to disentangle. It was clear that Anglo-American consultation began at the very start of the crisis, when Mrs Thatcher was in the United States to deliver a lecture at the Aspen Institute of Colorado, and that co-operation continued to be close.[21] For their handling of the Kuwait crisis, it would be wrong to take anything away from Mrs Thatcher and the Cabinet. Nevertheless, the Iraqi invasion possessed a domestic political dimension which her supporters were not slow to appreciate.

To begin with, an effort was made in Conservative newspapers, notably the *Sunday Telegraph*, the *Daily Mail* and the *Daily Express*, to depict Mrs Thatcher as a world leader who, owing to her fortuitous presence in the United States, had marvellously fortified President Bush's resolve to resist aggression. Even if this stirring version of events was not accepted, as some did not accept it, nevertheless the government benefited, on the basis that it was well-known that, in time of international trouble, public opinion moved towards the government of the day – the more so if that government happened to be Conservative. In fact the opinion polls recorded no such movement. They recorded average Labour leads of 12 points in August, 11 in September, 13 in October and 11 in November, before the fall of Mrs Thatcher.

Not only was it believed that the government would benefit. It was also thought that the invasion of Kuwait had provided the Prime Minister with a new security of tenure. The doubts about her position which had been revived with the resignation of Mr

[21] Peter Catterall, 'Introduction: the Year in Perspective' in Catterall (ed.), *Contemporary Britain* (1991), 1 at 9.

Ridley were now stilled. True, there was a fine old British tradition of getting rid of Prime Ministers in wartime, H.H. Asquith in 1916, Neville Chamberlain in 1940. But they had been jettisoned because they were Men of Peace, unable or unwilling to stiffen the nation's sinews. No such charge could ever be made against Mrs Thatcher. She appeared to agree with the scriptures that the Lord was a Man of War.[22] She could plausibly be depicted as the woman for the moment.

And yet, oddly enough, this was not a factor which weighed with politicians in Mrs Thatcher's last phase. If fighting had broken out, as it had not – one of her last acts in government was to be to increase British troop strengths in the Gulf – her position might have been different. As it was, the Gulf crisis did nothing to secure her position, any more than it assisted the government in the opinion polls. The politicians' eyes were still fixed on Brussels and Bonn. On 7 September 1990 Mr Major, the Chancellor of the Exchequer, told the BBC *Today* programme:

> This weekend we're certainly not going to join the mechanism, no. I think there's no doubt in anyone's mind that we have crossed the Rubicon – that we have decided to join the exchange rate Mechanism. We set out the circumstances in which we would do so some time ago and as soon as those are met we will join.

At last, entry in the ERM

In fact Mrs Thatcher had never posited the equality of British and European inflation rates as a condition of our entry into the ERM.[23] What she said to the House of Commons after the Madrid summit was: 'I reaffirmed our intention to join. We must first get our inflation down …'[24] Three days previously she had said in Spain: 'Provided inflation is brought down significantly as we intend, the conditions would clearly exist for sterling to join the ERM'.[25] Even so, the government's self-imposed condition, looser than the popular version of it though it may

[22] Exodus 15:3.
[23] See e.g. Transcript, *Dispatches*, 13 March 1991.
[24] 155 H.C. Deb., cc. 1109 ff, 29 June 1989.
[25] *The Times*, 27 June 1989.

have been, was hardly being satisfied: *au contraire*, as the late George Brown would have said. The figures for 1990 were then as follows:[26]

	per cent
January	7.7
February	7.7
March	7.5
April	8.1
May	9.4
June	9.7
July	9.8
August	9.8
September	10.6

Accordingly there was more than a touch of sleight-of-hand in Mr Major's announcement at an IMF meeting on 26 September that, in timing ERM entry, 'prospective' inflation was more important than 'current' inflation. The truth was that Mr Major and Mr Hurd had talked themselves into joining the ERM. They had created a want which only entry could satisfy. On 10 September sterling fell heavily on fears of delay in entering the ERM. On 19 September Karl Otto Pohl, the President of the Bundesbank, was quoted as saying: 'Without naming names, can a country with an inflation rate three times that of Germany peg its currency to the mark?' Though there were claims that he had been misreported, sterling fell, as it did two days later with fears of further delay.

Economic commentators noted that 'these things are always done on a Friday'. They agreed with the politicians that the most likely date was 28 September. This would have the advantage of partly spoiling the Labour Party conference which was to start on 1 October. Older Conservatives still had bitter memories of how Harold Wilson used to ruin *their* conferences in the 1960s by announcing government 'initiatives' of one kind or another in the week of the gathering. Nor would such timing be spoiling for its own sake. It would make a political point too. It would deprive John Smith of his trousers. For Mr Smith had for some

---

[26] The figures are for the month in which the announcement was made and refer to the preceding month.

time urged entry into the ERM upon the government, partly because he knew that it was a cause of embarrassment inside the Cabinet.

But Mrs Thatcher had by now been converted, much as an infidel might have embraced Christianity under a threat of painful death. Unlike such forced converts, Mrs Thatcher had been able to extract a price. This was a cut of one point in the rate of interest to 14 per cent. It was to be a present to the Conservative Party Conference, which was to begin on 9 October at Bournemouth. Friday 5 October would accordingly be a convenient date on which to announce our entry. It would be both an aperitif to the Conservative gathering and a chloroform pad on Labour's remarkably successful week in Blackpool. In the course of this Peter Mandelson had caused the ranks of boiler-suited harridans to disappear and to be replaced by a set of nicely-spoken Labour ladies, identically dressed likewise, with large bows affixed to the front of their blouses or dresses, as the case might be.

On Wednesday 3 October Mr Major went from 11 Downing Street to see Mrs Thatcher at No. 10. He was accompanied by his senior officials, Sir Peter Middleton, Head of the Treasury, and Sir Terence Burns, Chief Economic Adviser. She said something like: 'I've been waiting, I've been waiting.' They said something like: 'Right. We think we do it, and we should do it this week.'[27] On 5 October Mrs Thatcher said:

> You will, of course, have heard the announcement that the interest rates are to be reduced by one percentage point on Monday, and that we have applied this weekend to join the exchange rate mechanism. The fact that our policies are working, and are seen to be working, have made both these decisions possible.

This was rich, not to say fruity. Indeed, it did not convince even the Conservative conference, which turned out to be a low-key, even dispirited affair, on account partly of the murder in July of Ian Gow by the IRA in his nearby constituency of

---

[27] William Keegan, Transcript, *Dispatches*.

Eastbourne. The party managers fixed the by-election for 18 October, clearly hoping that the cause would benefit from the conference. We had applied for ERM membership at a core rate of DM2.95. This was considered too high by economists.

No excitement in Bournemouth

The representatives who assembled at Bournemouth on the Monday evening held no discernible opinion on the subject. The international monetary system was a remote concern. And yet, if the occasion had a theme at all, it was Europe. The villain of the week was Jacques Delors. The Conservative conference traditionally has a villain to make the representatives' flesh creep. They keep their spirits up by booing or hissing him (for there has never been a her). They can, however, accommodate only one villain at a time.

Mr Delors was the latest in a distinguished line that included Aneurin Bevan, Tony Benn, Bernie Grant, Ken Livingstone and Arthur Scargill. Mr Delors was also described by Mr Hurd on *Newsnight* as a Cartesian. He was trying to be nice. What he meant, he explained, was that Mr Delors was one of your hard, logical Frenchmen who believed in centralisation, whereas he was more of a muddler through. Indeed, if the week produced a disruptive influence, it was Mr Hurd rather than Sir Geoffrey Howe, who was now restricted to fringe meetings as if he were a disgraced member of the old Politburo. Not only did the Foreign Secretary try to show some understanding of the hated Mr Delors. He also said, in his conference speech, that we must not be sulky about Europe. But Mrs Thatcher had never been anything else. In fact sulkiness was the mildest of the emotions she had displayed.

The other notable feature of the conference was Mr Major's speech, which was a triumph, certainly compared to his effort of the year before, when he was Foreign Secretary. He spoke movingly of equality of opportunity. Mrs Thatcher looked on with evident approval. He was spoken of – and written about in the newspapers – as the next leader of the party. He would become so, it was generally assumed, after Mrs Thatcher had voluntarily surrendered the leadership, almost certainly at some time after the general election. Statements made something over a month later that Mr Major had 'come from nowhere' were wide of the mark.

On 18 October the Conservatives lost the Eastbourne election to the Liberal Democrats, who won 49.8 per cent of the vote to the Conservatives' 40.9 and Labour's 19. This was a swing of 20 per cent from the Conservatives to the Liberal Democrats. Conservatives blamed the defeat on complacency, an unattractive candidate and the moral blackmail of the electors, who were informed that, if they did not vote for Gow's prospective successor, they would be giving aid and comfort to terrorism. The loss of Eastbourne, like the resignation of Mr Ridley, played a perhaps underestimated part in the sapping of Conservative morale. It demonstrated that the local election results (as interpreted, admittedly, by Kenneth Baker), the Gulf crisis, the diminution of Labour's poll lead from March's nightmarish 23 per cent, the entry into the ERM: all had no real effect. And the old third-party peril had returned. No matter that seats such as Eastbourne normally reverted to the Conservatives at the general election; no matter, either, that strong third parties could be perilous for Labour as well, as the elections of 1983 and 1987 had conclusively demonstrated; the Conservatives were still alarmed.

The Rome summit

Mrs Thatcher departed for the European summit at Rome leaving a distressed and divided party behind her. The meeting was held to prepare for an inter-governmental conference in December on economic and monetary union, a development to which Mrs Thatcher had offered vociferous opposition. There were two elements that were involved. The Italians were understandably irritated by adverse British criticism of their spell of European presidency, as embodied in Gianni de Michelis, who to English eyes recalled Hilaire Belloc's lines:

> The most degraded of them all
> Mediterranean we call.
> His hair is crisp, and even curls,
> And he is saucy with the girls.

Indeed, Mr Michelis deserves a place (chronologically, the first place) among the men who brought down Mrs Thatcher – Sir Geoffrey, Mr Heseltine and Mr Garel-Jones – three Welshmen and an Italian. The other element was that the majority of the Europeans wanted to cement a newly united Germany into Europe. Accordingly they did not wish to do anything to diminish Chancellor Kohl's enthusiasm for economic and monetary union.[28]

Mr Michelis pushed through a vote on a timetable for implementing stage two of the Delors Plan on monetary union. The vote had not been expected. In the weeks before the meeting both Jacques Delors and Helmut Kohl had said that they did not want to see Britain isolated. But once the Italians had called the vote, that was that, and Britain went down 11-1.[29]

François Mitterrand, whom to begin with Mrs Thatcher had found sympathetic, was not specially helpful either. At a pre-summit meeting on 27 October he and Mrs Thatcher had a row over farm subsidies. Moreover, in a letter to Mr Delors she accused the Commission of 'bouncing' member-States into providing economic aid to other regions of the world. The European leaders agreed on 1 January 1994 as the date for the start of the next stage of economic and monetary union. Some said that they were ready to introduce a single European currency before the end of the decade. Mrs Thatcher stated:

> It seems like cloud cuckoo land … If anyone is suggesting that I would go to Parliament and suggest the abolition of the pound sterling – no! … We have made it quite clear that we will not have a single currency imposed on us.

This, we may note, was the first of Mrs Thatcher's famous No's. It was uttered not to the House of Commons but as her first response to the summit. And it worried Sir Geoffrey Howe. True,

[28] Catterall, art. cit. 2.
[29] Stephen George, 'Britain and Europe' in Catterall (ed.), op. cit. 75 at 80.

he was no longer Foreign Secretary, but he often behaved as if he still was. He had a near-mystical regard not so much for Europe and its institutions as for something which he called The Policy. This was a kind of Platonic bundle of the attitudes to and even prejudices about the European Community embraced by successive Conservative administrations over the years. As a metaphysical construct it bore certain resemblances to the Party Programme of This Great Movement of Ours.

Custodian of The Policy

Sir Geoffrey regarded himself as chief custodian of The Policy. This was understandable enough. Had he not piloted the European Communities Act 1972 through the rocks of the House of Commons when he was Solicitor-General? This was the statute which had deprived Parliament of its sovereignty, though neither Sir Geoffrey nor Edward Heath was specially keen to emphasise this aspect of the matter at the time or, indeed, subsequently.[30] Mrs Thatcher was, in his view, ruining The Policy. She was certainly presenting it incorrectly. He thought that the change had occurred in her at some time in 1988, when she saw hostility to Europe as a good populist cause to pursue.

He objected also to her conduct of business, in particular to her bypassing of Cabinet committees in favour of unofficial groups of favourites or compliant persons. He believed, for example, that the poll tax would not have been introduced if it had been considered in detail by a Cabinet committee. But his main concern remained The Policy. He claimed to find the Leadership of the House an interesting post, though that was not always apparent to the casual observer. He claimed also that any disagreement he might have with Mrs Thatcher had nothing to do with great houses and who should occupy them. Likewise, he said that his disputes had nothing to do with his wife Elspeth and any antipathy existing between her and Mrs Thatcher.

[30] On the 1972 Act and sovereignty see *R*. v. *Secretary of State for Transport, ex parte Factortame Ltd*, above, p. 119.

Elspeth was certainly a formidable woman. She would have been called a feminist in the days before the word acquired its modern, more aggressive connotation. She came from that section of the female middle class – educated, politically progressive – which believed in good works. It also often believed in knowing best. This last belief might have commended her to Mrs Thatcher. But no. The two women circled each other like unfriendly cats who nevertheless had no wish to have a fight. Or, as Sir Geoffrey put it, they were polite but distant. He admired his wife for her independence, for her having made a career for herself. He had always found her a support and a comfort in his various trials. He thought it ridiculous for her to be compared to Lady Macbeth, as she sometimes was by hostile journalists.

Throughout the difficult months at the end of 1990 he became angry only once. That was about the profile of Lady Howe which appeared in the *Sunday Telegraph* of 25 November. When an acquaintance said 'I hope Elspeth wasn't hurt by it' he replied shortly: 'Of course she was.' He reverted to the subject in his speech accepting an award at the *Spectator* 'Parliamentarian of the Year' luncheon on 28 November. On Sunday 28 October, while Mrs Thatcher was still in Madrid, Sir Geoffrey appeared on Brian Walden's television programme. This was a long-standing engagement which had been confirmed at the party conference. Sir Geoffrey saw this as a welcome opportunity to restate The Policy. Mrs Thatcher may not have welcomed it as warmly as he: but neither she nor anyone else raised any objection; indeed, Sir Geoffrey became an expositor of government, anyway of Foreign Office, policy; and on the Sunday morning the faxes flew between London and Madrid. Sir Geoffrey talked of catching the European train. His political imagery at this period was much preoccupied with the railways (not, notoriously, among his mistress's enthusiasms). He also said:

I have attended a number of summit meetings with the Prime Minister at which in this preliminary stage we have found ourselves taking an apparently sharply differing view ... At the end of the day, by hard negotiation we achieved results which Parliament endorsed.

The Bruges Group were displeased. They were taken more seriously in the papers (and by the political correspondent of the *Spectator*) than their importance perhaps warranted. They now called for Sir Geoffrey's sacking or resignation and denounced him for 'irresponsible, unstatesmanlike and unconstitutional' talk of catching the European train. For the moment, Sir Geoffrey stayed put.

Mrs Thatcher's fatal outburst

On Tuesday 30 October Mrs Thatcher came down to the House to report on the weekend's stirring events in Rome. She looked well. She was wearing a bright blue outfit, a single string of pearls and, while she was reading her statement, spectacles. At first all went smoothly enough. Sir Geoffrey, who now regarded himself as a kind of supernumerary Foreign Secretary, was not wholly displeased with what he heard, sitting just below her on her right:

> On economic and monetary union, I stressed that we would be ready to move beyond the present position to the creation of a European monetary fund and a common Community currency which we have called a hard ecu. But we would not be prepared to agree to set a date for starting the next stage of economic and monetary union before there is any agreement on what that stage should comprise (*Hear, hear*). And I again emphasised that we would not be prepared to have a single currency imposed upon us, nor to surrender the use of the pound sterling as our currency.[31]

Mr Kinnock was combative but not specially so. In the course of his observations he mentioned Sir Leon Brittan and his divergence from the Prime Minister's views. This appeared to annoy her disproportionately:

Leon Brittan is a loyal member of the Commission. Yes, the

[31] 178 H.C. Deb., c.870, 30 October 1990. The Official Report does not, however, record the 'Hear, hears'.

Commission wants to increase its powers. Yes, it is a non-elected body and I do not want the Commission to increase its powers at the expense of the House, so of course we differ. The President of the Commission, Mr Delors, said at a press conference the other day that he wanted the European Parliament to be the democratic body of the Community. He wanted the Commission to be the Executive and he wanted the Council of Ministers to be the Senate. No. No. No.[32]

Clearly, The Policy was in ruins. Sir Geoffrey was particularly exercised by a story going around that Mrs Thatcher was contemplating a referendum on Europe. By eight o'clock on the Thursday morning it was clear to his PPS, David Harris – a cautious man, formerly political correspondent of the *Daily Telegraph* – that he intended to resign.

This, it should be remembered, was the period between the reassembly of Parliament and the Queen's Speech setting out the programme for the new session. For politicians it is something of a limboland, rather as the period between Christmas and the New Year is for other people. Thursday's Cabinet was chiefly concerned with new Bills which Sir Geoffrey would have to steer through the House. What he called 'those damned dogs' – canine rather than political – were causing trouble again. There was a dispute between Mrs Thatcher and Sir Geoffrey about compromising with the Lords, with the Prime Minister taking the Lower House's side. Several Bills had not been produced by the responsible departments. Mrs Thatcher was cross. So was Sir Geoffrey. She had undoubtedly been beastly to him over the years: but that was not the reason he resigned.

Sir Geoffrey resigns

Shortly after four on Thursday afternoon he telephoned No. 10, spoke to Andrew Turnbull, the Principal Private Secretary to the Prime Minister, and arranged an appointment at six. He also spoke to Douglas Hurd and to Tim Renton and told them what he intended to do. The Prime Minister did not know quite

[32] Ibid. c.873. The Official Report misprints 'We' for 'He'.

what to make of his decision. But she could see that his mind was made up and did not try to dissuade him. Sir Geoffrey was much concerned about getting his point of view across on the evening's television programmes and afterwards declared that he was well-pleased with the professionalism of those concerned. He wrote to her that he was

> deeply anxious that the mood you have struck – most notably in Rome last weekend and in the House of Commons this Thursday – will make it more difficult for Britain to hold and retain a position of influence.

Mrs Thatcher replied:

> Your letter refers to differences between us on Europe. I do not believe these are nearly as great as you suggest. We are at one in wishing to preserve the sovereignty of Parliament.

This was not so. They were not 'at one'. Sir Geoffrey's complicated view of the juridical nature of sovereignty was very different from Mrs Thatcher's simple view.[33] Nevertheless his resignation was unexpected. He had put up with so much in the past. Certainly Peter Morrison was surprised, a condition in which he was regularly to find himself in the weeks ahead:

> I happened to be away that particular day. I'd gone on to my home in Scotland and I was, as it so happens, having a bath at about 7.15 that evening, listening to *The Archers* and there was a newsflash saying that Sir Geoffrey had resigned. And I must tell you that nobody was more surprised than me that was so. And the reason why I say that is that the night before in no sense had I possibly anticipated, nor I think had the Prime Minister anticipated that would be the case.[34]

Chris Patten was similarly surprised, saying that Sir Geoffrey 'was almost a permanent part of the British Constitution'. It was 'as though we'd suddenly heard that Christmas was being

---

[33] See Geoffrey Howe, 'Sovereignty and Interdependence: Britain's Place in the World', 66 *International Affairs* (1990), 675, an edited version of the 1990 London School of Economics Alumni Lecture, given at the LSE on 8 June 1990.

[34] Transcript, *The Thatcher Factor Special*, Channel 4, Brook Productions 1990, 103.

cancelled'.[35] Mrs Thatcher, in her fifth reshuffle of the year, replaced Sir Geoffrey with John MacGregor as Leader of the House, and Mr MacGregor with Kenneth Clarke as Education Secretary.

Mr Heseltine writes a letter

Michael Heseltine was surprised as well. On 30 October, at lunch at the *Observer* – Mrs Thatcher's outburst at the Commons was to follow within hours – he had told the assembled journalists that he did not intend to make any move until after the election. On the same day he had written a prominently displayed article in the *Daily Mail* urging the cause of Europe on the government. He was now about to write another article, along similar lines, for the *Sunday Times*. What Mr Heseltine lacked in grace he made up for in industry. He also communicated with Sir Geoffrey, complimenting him on his action and wishing him well. He had been through it himself, he said: he knew what it felt like. The two had never been close – had never liked each other much – but in the succeeding weeks there were stories, by no means discouraged by No. 10, of a Swansea-Aberavon axis, of collusion between Mr Heseltine and Sir Geoffrey to do down Mrs Thatcher. There was no such sinister co-operation. Mr Heseltine reacted *to* Sir Geoffrey. He could no longer bear to be left out of things. Accordingly he transformed his article into an open letter to his Henley constituency chairman. He wrote of the 'profound loss' of Sir Geoffrey and continued:

> There is only one way to preside over a democratic political party and that is to pay proper regard to the myriad of opinions and, indeed, prejudices that go to make up its support ... In the end we Tories know which side we are on; we know we must reach for the world of tomorrow, which is with our partners in Europe.

Douglas Hurd, in a television interview with Brian Walden, thought the letter 'not particularly wise', though on the next day, in a speech to the CBI conference in Glasgow, he acknowledged the possibility in the end of a single European

[35] Ibid.

currency, and denied that there was any 'dread conspiracy' against Britain in the European Community. John Wakeham described Mr Heseltine's letter as 'an egotistical outburst', while Timothy Raison, who was hardly Mrs Thatcher's most devoted admirer, said that 'she isn't going and she'd be mad to do so'.

Mrs Thatcher was not so sure. She at any rate saw the significance of Mr Heseltine's letter. On 6 November she met Cranley Onslow, the Chairman of the 1922 Committee, and secured his agreement to a shortening by two weeks of the period during which an opponent could stand against her. Nominations had to be in by 15 November – a shameless piece of gerrymandering designed by her and Mr Onslow to safeguard her position. Mr Onslow, unlike his predecessor Sir Edward du Cann at the time of Edward Heath's downfall, saw it as part of his duties to protect the leader of the party.

On the same day the Henley Conservative Association did what the Corinthians on one occasion did to St Paul.[35a] They replied to Mr Heseltine's letter, saying that they supported 'the leadership of the party'. Mr Heseltine sent a message back to the Henleyans: 'I don't know how many times a week I say Mrs Thatcher will lead us into the next election and win it.' It was a little late in the day to be reiterating loyal sentiments of this nature. To this extent, the campaign against Mr Heseltine which took place in the week beginning Monday 5 November was understandable enough. The *Daily Mail* asked: 'Does He Have the Courage?' The *Daily Express* voiced similar doubts with less refinement. Downing Street issued guidance on the lines of 'willing to wound but afraid to strike' and 'he should put up or shut up'. The Taunting of St Michael would have made a suitable subject for a fifteenth-century master, with Sir David English, Sir Nicholas Lloyd and Sir Bernard Ingham, their expressions conveying hatred and malice, piling indignities upon their chained victim.

Should Kenneth Baker be included among these tormentors? He says that he should not, and we must take his word for it. Likewise, he asserts that he had nothing to do with what was called a 'dirty tricks' campaign in Mr Heseltine's constituency.

[35a] I Corinthians 7:1

We need not go into the details of the National Union of Conservative and Unionist Associations. That would be both unnecessary and tedious. It is enough to note that the Henley president supported Mrs Thatcher, while the chairman was sympathetic to Mr Heseltine. And the Henleyans, from his viewpoint, turned up trumps. On Sunday 11 November, after a meeting of nearly two hours in the chairman's house, a statement was put out:

> In view of the widespread misinterpretation of their reply to Michael Heseltine's open letter, regarding the resignation of Sir Geoffrey Howe, the officers of Henley Conservative Constituency Association wish to state that their reply was not intended by them to criticise Mr Heseltine's letter. He retains their full confidence and support as their Member of Parliament.[36]

Mr Heseltine refused to say whether a challenge by him had been discussed at the meeting. He contented himself with: 'I am extremely grateful to my constituency for the excellent statement.' He then got into his car with the speed and agility of a man escaping his creditors, and sped off into the night with his wife Anne.

Mr Heseltine decides to stand

By this time he had already decided to stand. He had just returned from a trip to the Middle East, where the decision had been made with his wife. Looking back, we can see that the crucial event was the dispatch of the open letter. His advisers were divided about the wisdom of this course. Michael Mates was with him when he took it, whereas Keith Hampson was on a train. Dr Hampson considered that, at best, the matter could be argued two ways: on the one hand, Mr Heseltine had continued to keep his name before the public but, on the other, he had restricted his freedom of action. A resignation by Sir Geoffrey had been transformed into a challenge by Mr Heseltine.

But, it may be asked, was this not what he had wanted all

[36] *The Times*, 12 November 1990.

along? Yes indeed: but the challenge was to have been at a moment of his own choosing. Dr Hampson in fact believed that if Mrs Thatcher had staggered on into 1991, Mr Heseltine would have succeeded her in the spring or the summer. Sir Ian Gilmour took much the same view. And Mrs Heseltine was not wholly happy. She thought that her husband would be doing someone else's dirty work for him – and so it turned out.

On 8 November Labour won both the Bradford North and the Bootle by-elections. The Conservatives won 9 per cent of the vote in Bootle and 17 per cent in Bradford North, where they were reduced to third place.

On 12 November Mrs Thatcher spoke at the Lord Mayor's Banquet. She was wearing an Elizabethan cloak, a black velvet dress and pearls. She looked like Mary Queen of Scots on her way to the scaffold. In the course of her observations, which were chiefly about events in the Gulf, she said:

> I'm still at the crease, though the bowling's been pretty hostile of late (*Applause*). And, in case anyone doubted it, can I assure you that there will be no ducking the bouncers, no stonewalling, no playing for time? The bowling's going to get hit all round the ground. That's my style.[37]

These preposterous remarks were reminiscent less of Battling Maggie than of the chatelaine of Toad Hall. Why, some observers wondered, did our politicians turn to cricket for their imagery, when they had never shown the slightest interest in the game, still less any knowledge of it? Bernard Ingham, a Yorkshireman, should at least have been able to tell her that ducking was precisely what one did with bouncers. What was interesting, however, was that at this stage Mrs Thatcher clearly expected a challenge from Mr Heseltine. So did most observers. There was unanimity that Mr Hurd would enter the contest in the second ballot if Mrs Thatcher withdrew, though the consensus was that she would win outright. One hundred and thirty was thought to be the maximum that Mr Heseltine would poll. Sir Geoffrey was also mentioned as a co-runner with

[37] Transcript, *The Thatcher Factor Special*, 103-4; *Independent*, 13 November 1990.

Mr Hurd in the unlikely event of the Prime Minister's failing to win in the first ballot. Mr Major was mentioned occasionally.[38]

The fury of a patient man

Sir Geoffrey did nothing to encourage speculation about his own future. Instead he kept his peace, and wrote, condensed and rewrote his speech. Lady Howe did not write it. Indeed, she had doubts about the whole enterprise, as did David Harris, Sir Geoffrey's PPS. Peter Jenkins of the *Independent* newspaper did not write it either. He never claimed he did. But Mrs Thatcher thought he had written or anyway helped with it, because Geoffrey, she said, would have been incapable of composing such a Philippic unaided. Just before 4.20 on Tuesday 13 November – twelve days after his own resignation – Mr Speaker Weatherill introduced him with:

> I remind the House that a resignation statement is heard in silence and without interruption.[39]

Sir Geoffrey was wearing a grey suit, a white shirt and a grey-blue tie with white spots. Mr Lawson sat on his right, scowling, as was his habit when he considered that a serious expression was required. Mrs Thatcher wore dark blue and a fixed smile, which became more strained as the proceedings developed. She had Mr Major on her right on the front bench and Mr Baker on her left. Sir Geoffrey was by now of course on a back bench, diagonally over Mrs Thatcher's right shoulder. He held his notes as if sheltering them from the rain. He began by rebutting the charge for which Mr Baker had certainly been responsible since his resignation:

> It has been suggested, even, indeed, by some of my Right Honourable and Honourable Friends, that I decided to resign solely because of questions of style and not on matters of substance at all. Indeed, if some of my former colleagues are to be

[38] For example, in *The Times*, 12 November 1990.
[39] 180 H.C. Deb., c.461, 13 November 1990.

believed, I must be the first Minister in history who has resigned because he was in full agreement with government policy (*Loud and prolonged laughter*). The truth is that in many aspects of politics, style and substance complement each other. Very often, they are two sides of the same coin.[40]

Then came the most important part of the speech. He had agreed with Mr Lawson not only a year previously, at the time of the Chancellor's resignation, but five years previously, when entry into the ERM was first mooted. He had concluded that the policy against inflation 'could no longer rest solely on attempts to measure and control the domestic money supply'.[41] The former monetarist Chancellor, author of the 1981 Budget, was rejecting monetarism. It had worked once, maybe: but it was not working in 1985. Mr Lawson had been right not only in 1989 but all along. The delay in entry into the ERM had actually brought about inflation.[42] Accordingly it was not Mr Lawson who was to blame for the recrudescence in inflation, as Mrs Thatcher and her friends alleged. It was Mrs Thatcher herself.

This was powerful stuff. Inevitably it was largely ignored, both at the time and afterwards. So, though to a lesser extent, was Sir Geoffrey's revelation that at the Madrid summit he and Mr Lawson had 'made it clear that he could not continue in office unless a specific commitment to join the ERM was made'.[43] Passion, wit, humour, cheek – these are what politicians and journalists like. Sir Geoffrey quoted the Prime Minister whom Mrs Thatcher referred to familiarly as 'Winston' on the merging of sovereignty:

I have to say that I find Winston Churchill's perception a good deal more convincing, and more encouraging for the interests of the nation, than the nightmare image (*Gasps*) sometimes conjured up by my Right Honourable Friend, who seems sometimes to look out upon a continent that is positively teeming with ill-intentioned people, scheming, in her words, to 'extinguish democracy', to 'disown our national identities' and to lead us

[40] Ibid. The laughter is unrecorded in the Official Report.
[41] Ibid.
[42] Ibid. c.462.
[43] Ibid.

'through the back door into a federal Europe'. What kind of vision is that ...?[44]

Mrs Thatcher had been dismissive of the hard ecu, saying that no one would want to use it.

> How on earth are the Chancellor and the Governor of the Bank of England, commending the hard ecu as they strive to, to be taken as serious participants in the debate against that kind of background noise (*Gasps*)? I believe that both the Chancellor and the Governor are cricketing enthusiasts so I hope there is no monopoly of cricketing metaphors. It is rather like sending your opening batsmen to the crease only for them to find, the moment the first balls are bowled, that their bats have been broken before the game by the team captain (*Laughter*).[45]

He concluded with a call to insurrection:

> The time has come for others to consider their own response to the tragic conflict of loyalties with which I have myself wrestled for perhaps too long.[46]

The Conservatives were stunned. The speech was regarded as more damning than Nigel Birch's against Harold Macmillan in 1963, in which he had quoted Robert Browning, or even than Leo Amery's against Neville Chamberlain in 1940, in which he had quoted Oliver Cromwell. Cromwell and Browning were no match for Churchill and cricket. On the next day Mr Heseltine stood outside his Belgravia house, his wife by his side, and told the assembled press:

> I am persuaded that I now have a better prospect than Mrs Thatcher of leading the Conservatives to a fourth electoral victory and preventing[47] the ultimate calamity of a Labour government ... A significant consequence of my election as a leader would be an immediate and fundamental review of the poll tax, which I believe to be important for the revival of government fortunes.

[44] Ibid. c.463.
[45] Ibid. c.464. The gasps and the laughter are unrecorded in the Official Report.
[46] Ibid. c.465.
[47] Mr Heseltine actually said 'persuading'.

Mr Heseltine now claimed the support of over 100 Members. To one of them, he was to write:

20.11.90

Dear——

You wrote on Nov 7th.
I hold you responsible.
And I thank you for it!
Yrs ever
Michael

But how was Mr Heseltine able to mount a challenge at all to a Prime Minister who was in excellent physical health and possessed a large parliamentary majority? It is to the Conservatives' own electoral system that we must now turn.

7

The Importance of Mr Berkeley

More appropriate for the enstoolment of an African tribal chief.

> Humphry Berkeley, on the old method of choosing a
> Conservative leader, 3 July 1963.

The right of election is the very essence of the constitution. To violate that right, and much more to transfer it to any other set of men, is a step leading immediately to the dissolution of all government.

> 'Junius', Letter to the Duke of Grafton, 24 April 1769

The method of choosing a Conservative leader, by which he 'emerged' following 'the customary processes of consultation' began to be questioned seriously in the 1950s. In 1911 and 1921, Andrew Bonar Law and Austen Chamberlain respectively were confirmed leaders of the party in the House of Commons. Bonar Law was in opposition, whereas Chamberlain was a member of the Coalition government presided over by David Lloyd George. Other leaders were already Prime Ministers when they were confirmed as leader of the party as a whole: A.J. Balfour (1902), Stanley Baldwin (1923), Neville Chamberlain (1937) and Winston Churchill (1940).

The Bonar Law precedent

In 1922 Bonar Law refused to become Prime Minister until he had been elected leader by the party. His biographer, Lord

Blake, uses the word 'elected' rather than 'confirmed'.[1] This personal caution – or constitutional scrupulosity – annoyed George V. His secretary, Lord Stamfordham, recorded that Bonar Law

> explained that he was not the leader of the Conservative Party, that the party was for the moment broken up and, until he knew that he could count on its undivided support, he would not accept office. Therefore it was indispensable that he should be present at a meeting of the representatives of the whole Conservative Party, where he would make the above condition and others including one limiting his holding office to one year.
>
> I ventured to suggest to him that the King sent for him independently of these party considerations into which His Majesty did not enter; that having accepted Mr Lloyd George's resignation, it was the King's duty to form a new government as soon as possible and to send for whoever he considered was the proper person to carry out this great responsibility.[2]

But Bonar Law refused to accept office until the party had elected him leader. Austen Chamberlain was still officially leader but remained loyal to his old Coalition colleagues. There was much telephoning between Buckingham Palace and his home at Onslow Gardens, Kensington. He promised to call a party meeting as soon as possible and to consult with colleagues about their inclusion in the new government. 'It was agreed that the Court Circular should state the bare facts that Lloyd George had resigned and that the King had granted an audience to Bonar Law.'[3] On Monday 23 October 1922 a meeting of Conservative Peers, MPs and parliamentary candidates was held at the Hotel Cecil, and Bonar Law was unanimously elected leader of the party.[4] Despite his insistence on 'election', this procedure was really identical with the mass rally which previous and subsequent Conservative leaders were to attend, including John Major in 1990 following both his election as leader and his appointment as Prime Minister – though there

[1] Robert Blake, *The Unknown Prime Minister* (1955), 460.

[2] Royal Archives, quot. ibid.

[3] Ibid. See also Harold Nicolson, *King George the Fifth* (1952), 370-1; Kenneth Rose, *King George V* (1983, paper edn 1984), 265.

[4] Blake, op. cit. 461.

remain doubts about the validity under the rules of his election.[5] Altogether the Bonar Law precedent casts more light on constitutional practice than on party democracy.

An automatic succession

Anthony Eden felt no need to submit himself to a similar process before he took office in 1955, any more than his three predecessors had done. The argument was about when Churchill should go, rather than about who should succeed him. Though R.A. Butler later persuaded himself that he might have become Prime Minister – and his pre-eminent position in the domestic politics of the early 1950s tends to be overlooked today – there was little doubt about who the successor would be.[6] Eden's most recent biographer states that Butler came to this thought because he had been invited with Eden to see Churchill, whereas the reason for his presence was to co-ordinate the dates of the budget and of Churchill's resignation. The Marquess of Salisbury wrote afterwards to Eden:

> There was no question of who was to succeed Winston. The only problem was the timing.[7]

Yet, whatever hopes he may have entertained retrospectively, in his own memoirs Butler was perfectly clear about the true position, showing no disposition to lament the past or to complain of unfair treatment:

> At the end of March Anthony and I were invited into the Cabinet room. Winston made a slip by asking me to sit on his right, but then corrected himself and beckoned to Anthony. We all gazed out over Horse Guards Parade. Then Winston said very shortly: 'I am going and Anthony will succeed me. We can discuss details later.' The ceremonial was over. We found ourselves in the passage where Anthony and I shook hands.[8]

[5] See below, pp. 173, 207.
[6] On Butler at this time, see Anthony Howard, *RAB* (1987), Ch. 12; R.A. Butler, *The Art of the Possible* (1971, Penguin edn 1973), Ch. 8.
[7] Robert Rhodes James, *Anthony Eden* (1986, paper edn 1987), 397.
[8] Butler, op. cit. 178-9.

Three years previously Butler had complained to Harold Nicolson that his trouble was that Eden was regarded as the heir-apparent. By 1955, from his listening-posts at the Beefsteak and Travellers' Clubs, Nicolson had few doubts:

> At 4.30 Winston handed in his resignation to the Queen, who was graciously pleased to accept it. I suppose she will send for Anthony tomorrow.[9]

Churchill himself had several times threatened to call a party meeting, not so much to choose a successor as to ensure his own continuation in office at the expense of Eden, for whom he had conceived an intermittent hatred, though he was capable of being mollified by what he described as 'Anthony's amiable manner'.[10] Immediately before his resignation he predicted 'with vehemence' to his private secretary: 'I don't believe Anthony can do it.'[11]

Nor did he, though Robert Rhodes James has made a brave attempt to rehabilitate him.[12]

The Macmillan succession

In January 1957 he resigned owing to ill-health. There were two candidates to succeed him, Harold Macmillan and R.A. Butler. The newspapers assumed generally that Butler would get the job. The exception was Randolph Churchill in the *Evening Standard*, whose information, Mr Rhodes James tells us, came from Lord Beaverbrook rather than from Winston Churchill.[13] The more general prediction was not unreasonable. There was a fund of public good will for Butler in which, however, the bulk of the Conservative Party, both in the government and on the back benches, held few shares.

Mr Rhodes James is firm that 'Eden played no part in the

---

[9] Harold Nicolson, *Diaries and Letters 1945-62* (1968, paper edn 1971), 5 April 1955, 257; see also 22 May 1952, 207.

[10] John Colville, *The Fringes of Power* (1985, paper edn 1987), II, Ch. 24.

[11] Ibid. 379.

[12] Rhodes James, op. cit. *passim*. For a contrary view, see the political biography by David Carlton, *Anthony Eden* (1981, paper edn 1986).

[13] Rhodes James, op. cit. 600.

developments that led to the appointment of his successor'.[14] James Stuart, later Lord Stuart of Findhorn, Secretary for Scotland and formerly Chief Whip, asserts that 'contrary to the usual practice, he left without tendering any advice to the Throne as to his successor'.[15] Lord Kilmuir, at that time Lord Chancellor, is less sure but comes down in favour of the view that Eden did not offer any advice and was not asked to do so: 'I do not know for certain, but am fairly sure, that the advice of Sir Anthony Eden concerning his successor was not invited.'[16] Anthony Howard, however, states that Eden was 'certainly' asked, though whether he 'gave any specific recommendations as to his successor is still a matter of some dispute'.[17] Lord Blake is definite that Eden was not only asked to make a recommendation but did so:

> It is untrue, though often alleged, that the Queen did not consult him about his successor. He never revealed his choice, nor was it necessarily decisive, but there is good evidence that he did not recommend Butler.[18]

Keith Kyle asserts the opposite. Having consulted the Avon Papers at Birmingham University, he states that Eden volunteered that Butler had been both helpful and competent when he had deputised as Prime Minister during his periods of indisposition.[19]

Lord Salisbury and Lord Kilmuir then took it upon themselves to handle the succession without, it seems, being specifically asked to do so by anybody.[20] Kilmuir's role has perhaps been underemphasised, partly because, as a somewhat dreary and ill-favoured lawyer, he could not compete in glamour – or in the support he lent to the theory of conspiracy – with the great Marquess of Salisbury, whose family had been involved in

[14] Ibid. 599.

[15] James Stuart, *Within the Fringe* (1967), 179.

[16] Earl of Kilmuir, *Political Adventure* (1964), 286-7.

[17] Howard, op. cit. 247.

[18] Robert Blake, 'Anthony Eden', in *DNB 1971-80*, 262 at 271.

[19] Avon Papers, Birmingham University, 11 January 1957. Cited Keith Kyle, *Suez* (1991), 533.

[20] Kilmuir, op. cit. 285.

political intrigues of one kind or another since the days of Elizabeth I. It may have been depreciated too because it was Salisbury who, on the next day, saw the Queen to give her the Cabinet's (and the party's) advice. She also saw Churchill by her own request, Churchill confiding afterwards to Butler that 'I went for the older man', that is, Macmillan, even though he was by this time personally fonder of Butler.[21] Kilmuir and Salisbury agreed that they would consult all Cabinet Ministers, even though Selwyn Lloyd, the Foreign Secretary, took democratic objection to the Cabinet's being canvassed by a couple of Peers.[22]

> Thereafter Bobbety [Salisbury] and I asked our colleagues to see us one by one in Bobbety's room in the Privy Council Offices, which could be reached without leaving the building. There were two light reliefs. Practically each one began by saying: 'This is like coming to the Headmaster's study.' To each Bobbety said: 'Well, which is it, Wab or Hawold?'[23]

Harold it was, by a large majority. The only certain supporter of Butler was Patrick Buchan-Hepburn, later Lord Hailes;[24] though Butler later claimed the additional support of Walter Monckton and James Stuart.[25] All these were to leave the government when Macmillan became Prime Minister: but in his memoir Stuart says that he left voluntarily:

> It is always a help to an incoming Prime Minister to have a few vacant offices so that he can introduce new blood. Moreover, the new PM, knowing me well, as he had for 30 years, was aware that after nearly six years at the Scottish Office I was looking for something less arduous, or preferably retirement. Certainly at 60 I was not 'new blood' and, worse still, Harold was my brother-in-law by marriage. I suggested to him that if charges of nepotism ever came up he could refute the press by pointing out that at least he had sacked me![26]

---

[21] Butler, op. cit. 197.
[22] Ibid.
[23] Kilmuir, op. cit. 285.
[24] Rhodes James, op. cit. 598 n; Alistair Horne, *Macmillan* (1988-9), I, 460.
[25] Howard, op. cit. 247.
[26] Stuart, op. cit. 179.

It is not altogether correct to describe these events, as Alistair Horne does, as

> in comparison with subsequent procedures, a cosy and domestic way of selecting a new Prime Minister. Whereas in 1963 all Tory MPs would be canvassed by the Whips, the 1957 selection was essentially a straight Cabinet choice.[27]

Oliver, later Lord, Poole, the chairman of the party, was also seen by Salisbury and Kilmuir.[28] The Chairman of the 1922 Committee, John Morrison, later Lord Margadale, 'assessed back bench opinion with surprising confidence from the Isle of Islay'.[29] The Chief Whip, Edward Heath, was also consulted by the two Peers. Mr Heath told an early biographer that

> The outcome was 'highly acceptable' to a 'substantial' majority in the House, a majority to which he himself belonged.[30]

Harold Nicolson recorded:

> It is sad for the left wing of the Tory Party, since Butler was the leader of young Conservatives, but I dare say that in the circumstances it is right.[31]

There was nevertheless a feeling that Butler had been done down by a conspiracy of St James's Street and Hatfield House. Eden's wife wrote to him:

> Dear Rab,
> Just a line to say what a beastly profession I think politics are – and how greatly I admire your dignity and good humour.
> Yours ever,
> Clarissa[32]

The Parliamentary Labour Party then took a hand. A press

[27] Horne, op. cit. I, 459.
[28] Kilmuir, op. cit. 285.
[29] Robert Blake, *The Conservative Party from Peel to Thatcher* (1970, new paper edn 1985), 278.
[30] George Hutchinson, *Edward Heath* (1970), 86.
[31] Nicolson, op. cit. 10 January 1957, 301.
[32] Butler, op. cit. 197.

notice of 21 January 1957 stated that the parliamentary committee, or shadow cabinet, had given careful consideration to the relevant precedents. It had come to the conclusion that the one created by Bonar Law in 1922[33] offered the best guidance. This, in the view of the shadow cabinet, was the precedent 'most in accord with the spirit of the Constitution'. It enabled the Crown to act in a manner 'free of all constitutional ambiguity'. Moreover, this course would be the only one which accorded with 'the democratic organisation of the Parliamentary Labour Party'.[34]

Butler denied again

Harold Macmillan was, in theory, as high for prerogative as any seventeenth-century Anglican – or as Lord St John of Fawsley himself. In 1963 R.A. Butler recorded that, in the course of musing about his departure from 10 Downing Street, his anxiety was 'to retain the discretion of the Crown so that the Crown could choose whomever she wished'.[35]

> He wants to preserve a proper degree of the Queen's choice and does not want a diktat from the 1922 Committee. However we cast our minds back on history, and agreed that almost no PM had chosen his own successor, and that this issue might have to be thrashed out, if he decided to go, without his having the final word. So much for the succession, or as far as we got with it.[36]

Macmillan seemed, illogically, to equate his own conclusive recommendation with the Queen's unfettered discretion. Certainly the burden of Butler's quotation (and, though the two men were hardly the best of friends, there is no suggestion that he misreported Macmillan) is that, while a recommendation or

---

[33] See above, p. 156.

[34] The statement is reproduced in Norman St John-Stevas (ed.), *The Collected Works of Walter Bagehot* (1965-86), V, 91 n. Mr St John-Stevas, later Lord St John of Fawsley, criticised the Labour Party's policy as an unwarranted interference with the exercise of the royal prerogative. He was to do the same when Margaret Thatcher was challenged by Michael Heseltine in 1990.

[35] Butler, op. cit. 238.

[36] Ibid. 23.

'diktat' from the 1922 Committee would be unconstitutional or at any rate undesirable, an identical message from an outgoing Prime Minister would somehow preserve an unsullied prerogative. George V had possessed a choice in 1923 when he preferred Baldwin to Curzon; so had Elizabeth II in 1957 when she chose Macmillan before Butler. In one respect her choice had been more free than she might have expected. For, though there is dispute about whether Eden was either asked for or made any recommendation of a successor, there is agreement that any intervention which he may have made was not decisive.[37] Two years previously, Eden had effectively been presented to the Queen as Churchill's successor. Macmillan resolved to follow this precedent rather than his own. Though there are few who can remain wholly unmoved by the trouble which the outgoing Macmillan, sick and in pain, took in advising his sovereign when she visited him in the Edward VII Hospital for Officers – putting on a white silk shirt under his dressing-gown in her honour[38] – his aim had been to present her with one name only, and not that of Butler.[39]

It is curious that two successive Prime Ministers should have retired on the grounds of ill-health. Yet the first, Eden, lived for another 20 years and died at 79; while the second, Macmillan, lived for another 23 years and died at 92. The difference is that, his physical health notwithstanding, Eden could probably not have carried on, owing to the political climate and his own mental condition. Macmillan could almost certainly have continued as Prime Minister and fought the 1964 election, when he would have been 70. In the couple of years before he resigned his plans had varied, almost, it seemed, from month to month: but before he was struck down by his prostate condition he had decided to carry on. The pain brought about a fit of panic, he was perhaps inadequately advised by his doctors and late on the Thursday afternoon Lord Home read out his resignation statement to a shocked Conservative conference. Several of the journalists present were, however, joyful. 'He's gone at last,' an

[37] See above, pp. 159-60.
[38] Horne, op. cit. II, 565.
[39] See generally ibid. Ch. 18; Howard, op. cit. Ch. 15.

untypically excited Richard West exclaimed unbelievingly.

Macmillan's first choice had been Lord Hailsham. He had fallen out of favour, partly because Macmillan came to consider him unstable. His antics at Blackpool, from his renunciation of his peerage following a Conservative Political Centre lecture, to his fond public fatherhood of his new baby, reinforced this view.[40] Nor did Randolph Churchill help his cause by arriving from the United States and handing out lapel badges marked 'Q' (for Quintin). It soon became clear at Blackpool that Lord Home, who had yet to announce his intention of renouncing his own peerage, was also a candidate. Iain Macleod was nowhere, and took little part in the week's proceedings, except to make his usual fine speech.[41] Reginald Maudling made a less good one, though he was to claim afterwards, as Butler was to claim likewise of his own disappointing effort, that it 'read well'. We tend today to forget that in the 1961-3 period, when Macmillan's position seemed increasingly vulnerable, it was Maudling rather than Butler who was regarded as the natural successor, certainly among Conservative backbenchers.[42] Butler, it was somehow felt, not least by himself, had lost his chance in 1957.[43] As Major Morrison, the Chairman of the 1922 Committee, said rather unhelpfully to him just before he set out for Rhodesia to unravel the Central African Federation: 'The chaps won't have you.'[44]

The important fact in my view [Macmillan wrote to the Queen] is that Lord Home's candidature has not been set forward on his own merits but has been thought of as a last-minute method of keeping out Mr Butler now that Lord Hailsham has (according to the pundits) put himself out of court by his stupid behaviour ... Apart from Home's actual lead, I am impressed by the general good will shown towards him, even by those who give reasons in favour of other candidates, and I cannot fail to come to the opinion

[40] Sir Dennis Walters, who was close to Lord Hailsham in this period, has defended his conduct in his *Not Always with the Pack* (1989), 110 ff; see also Lord Hailsham *A Sparrow's Flight* (1990), 353-4.

[41] See Nigel Fisher, *Iain Macleod* (1973), 238.

[42] Philip Goodhart, *The 1922* (1973), 191.

[43] Howard, op. cit. 304

[44] Goodhart, op. cit. 191.

that he would be the best able to secure united support.[45]

One question was whether Home really had received such firm support. The opinion of many of those whose views had been solicited was that the official canvassers – Lord Dilhorne of the Cabinet, Martin Redmayne and the Whips of MPs, Lord St Aldwyn of Peers and Oliver Poole of the party organisation – had weighted their question in Home's direction, asking: 'What do you think of Alec Home?' or 'Would Alec be your second choice?' Crucially, Butler agreed to serve Home, along with Maudling and Hailsham; Powell and Macleod refused. Home went along to the Palace. The other question now arose: whether the Queen had been rushed into accepting what was in effect Macmillan's nomination of Home, even though it had been propped up by the various canvasses which have just been outlined.[46]

This question was never satisfactorily answered. Mr Horne has tried to show that the various canvasses were not only honest in their conduct but correct in their conclusions. In particular, he has revealed that the first choice of 10 members of the Cabinet, as counted by Dilhorne, was Home – and that Macleod was one of those who had voted for him.[47] Responses have ranged from incredulity (Baroness Macleod of Borve and Mr Powell, who voted for Butler) through accusations of error against Dilhorne (Lord Aldington and Sir Ian Gilmour) to posthumous allegations of deviousness in Macleod (Macmillan and Butler).[48] But this is hardly the point as far as the Palace is concerned. The fact is that Macmillan deprived the Queen, maybe to her relief, of any choice as to her Prime Minister. There is no need to make too much of this. She had been given no choice in 1955. Eden had simply succeeded Churchill.

Macleod perhaps prudently declined to deal with this question of the prerogative in his article in the *Spectator* of 17 January 1964, which was written when he was the editor of the paper (he had been appointed by the proprietor, Ian Gilmour, after

[45] Quoted Horne, op. cit. 556-7.

[46] See Paul Johnson, 'Was the Palace to Blame?', *New Statesman*, 24 January 1964, reprinted in his *Statesmen and Nations* (1971), 88.

[47] Horne, op. cit. 559 ff.

[48] Ibid. 561-2; Ian Gilmour, 'Holding All the Strings', *London Review of Books*, 27 July 1989.

refusing to serve Home). The piece was ostensibly a review of Randolph Churchill's *The Fight for the Tory Leadership*, to which Macmillan had contributed heavily.[49]

> There is a no criticism whatever [Macleod wrote] that can be made of the part played by the Crown. Presented with such a document, it was unthinkable even to consider asking for a second opinion.[50]

In all other respects Macleod could hardly have been more forthright. His case was that Butler was the choice of the majority, that he deserved to be that choice, that he was the best choice and that he was prevented from being recognised as that choice by a 'magic circle' of Etonians, with the exception of the Chief Whip, Redmayne (who had been at Radley). The phrase passed into the language of politics. But was it not a little unfair? Home's succession may or may not have been gerrymandered: but it had manifestly not been fixed in White's Club or Hatfield House. Indeed, by his extensive consultations – by his presentation of one candidate to the Queen – Macmillan laid the foundations for the new system. As Macleod put it:

> The procedure which had been adopted opens up big issues for decision in the future. That everything was done in good faith I do not doubt – indeed, it is the theme of this review to demonstrate it – but the result of the methods used was contradiction and misrepresentation. I do not think it is a precedent which will be followed.[51]

Enter Mr Berkeley

A young Conservative MP, Humphry Berkeley, had anticipated Macleod. On 1 January 1964 he had written to the Prime Minister saying that in March 1963, 'before the leadership of the party was in dispute', he had declared in public that he felt that the party should 'adopt a more formal method of choosing a

---

[49] 1964. Macleod's article is reproduced in George Hutchinson, *The Last Edwardian at No. 10* (1980), at 123.

[50] *Spectator*, 17 January 1964.

[51] Ibid.

leader'. The events of Blackpool and after had 'emphasised this need and would have done so, whoever had emerged as leader of the party'. Since then, he had had

> many talks with our colleagues in the House, including senior members of the Government. I have discovered a widespread view that we should not continue with the present system, which, in any event, as practised a few months ago, bore little resemblance to what has been known as the customary process.[52]

He asked Sir Alec, as leader of the party, to consider setting up a 'small committee' to consider the matter, hear opinions and make recommendations. He added that nothing he had said 'implies any criticism of your leadership of the party' and perhaps presumptuously but, nevertheless typically took 'this opportunity of sending you every good wish for an outstandingly successful year'.[53]

At this time Mr Berkeley was 37 and the Member for Lancaster, which he had represented since 1959. He was the son of Reginald Berkeley, the playwright (author of *French Leave*), and had been educated at Malvern and Pembroke College, Cambridge, where he had been President of the Union. In his last year at Cambridge he had assumed the character of Rochester Sneath, a headmaster, and as such had written to numerous dignitaries asking for their views on various matters of concern. The letters and the replies are much funnier than Henry Root's productions – not least because the joke is maintained with consistency – and almost as funny as *The Diary of a Nobody*.[54]

He had a scornful expression and a superior manner, products of his masterful nose and curling lip, and was not universally popular among his fellow-Members. Once, leaving a Chinese restaurant where he had lunched with Anthony Howard, and noticing that his shoelace was undone, he summoned a waiter to retie it. Mr Howard was so embarrassed by his companion's

---

[52] Humphry Berkeley, *Crossing the Floor* (1972), App. I, 149ff at 149.

[53] Ibid. 149-50.

[54] They are collected in Humphry Berkeley, *The Life and Death of Rochester Sneath* (1974).

demand that he knelt down and retied it himself. This behaviour owed more to Mr Berkeley's imperious nature than to any prejudice against those with differently coloured skins. On the contrary: he was renowned not only for his political and business connections with Africans but also for the affection which he had for them. An elderly fellow-Member once asked him why he was so fond of them. 'I simply love their little woolly heads,' he replied. Afterwards the Member could be heard musing to his friends about whether Berkeley was wholly sane. There could, however, be no doubt about his courage, which had been demonstrated both over Commonwealth affairs and with his campaign to implement the Wolfenden proposals for reform of the law on homosexuality.

Even so, it was perhaps surprising that Sir Alec, as he had now become, replied to him in so friendly and accommodating a manner. He wrote on 14 January 1964 that he was 'not averse' to the idea of a 'private study' which might be used on some future occasion, but did not think it would be wise to initiate this before the election. It would inevitably become known, and would then be taken 'as evidence of dissatisfaction with the present leadership – although I appreciate your assurance that it does not'.[55] Sir Alec ended by inviting Mr Berkeley to get in touch with him later in the year. On 21 January 1964 Mr Berkeley indicated that he and his friends (who included Peter Tapsell) were 'happy to leave the matter in abeyance until after the election'. He added that the prospective study 'should not be so private as to prevent all interested parties from giving their views quite freely'.[56]

Sir Alec's view was that, for the sake of any future holder of his position as leader, the processes of choice must be reviewed, even though 'the "magic circle" of selectors had almost everything to be said for it'.[57] The Whips 'knew the form of every runner in the field'. Some felt, however, that 'candidates favourable to the establishment' had the advantage over 'anyone who might at any time have been rebellious'. There were always

[55] Berkeley, *Crossing the Floor*, 150.
[56] Ibid.
[57] Lord Home, *The Way the Wind Blows* (1976), 218.

those who, 'stirred up by the media', were ready to charge the magic circle with 'rigging the result'. He had not been worried until this accusation 'began to reverberate through the constituencies and to affect party morale outside Parliament'. He then concluded that, 'with all its disadvantages', it was necessary to adopt a system of election, 'where from start to finish everything was seen to be open and above board. I was in the best position to see that business through.'[58]

After the surprisingly narrow Conservative defeat, Sir Alec kept his word. On 5 November 1964 he told the 1922 Committee that he proposed to review the mechanism for choosing a leader. Mr Berkeley at once resumed his correspondence.[59] In December he submitted a memorandum. Sir Alec consulted principally Lord Blakenham, formerly John Hare, and the new Chief Whip, William Whitelaw.[60] On 25 February 1965 he came to the 1922 Committee and announced his decision on the procedure to be followed in future for the selection of the new leader of the party.

The leader would be elected by Conservative (and National Liberal) Members of Parliament, and the machinery presided over by the Chairman of the 1922 Committee. Candidates would be proposed and seconded in writing. If, on the first ballot, a candidate received both an overall majority and 15 per cent more of the total number of votes cast than any other candidate, he would be elected. If no one satisfied those conditions, a second ballot would be held. Nominations made for the first ballot would be void and new nominations, under the same procedure as for the first ballot, would be submitted, if required, for the original and any other candidates.[61] If, as a result of this second ballot, one candidate received an overall majority, he would be elected. If no candidate received an overall majority, the three candidates receiving the highest number of votes would go

---

[58] Ibid.

[59] Berkeley, op. cit. 151 ff.

[60] Hutchinson, *Heath*, 138.

[61] When Margaret Thatcher was challenged by Michael Heseltine in 1990 it was incorrectly stated in several newspapers that the 1965 procedure had restricted the entire election to those candidates who had originally been nominated, and that late entrants – in effect a new election – had been allowed only with the 1975 changes. This was not so.

forward to a third ballot. Each voter had to indicate two preferences, marking his paper '1' and '2'. ('Plumping' – or voting for one candidate only – was not allowed, nor is it today.) The second preference of the bottom candidate would then be redistributed between the top two. The candidate so elected would be 'presented for election as party leader to the party meeting constituted as at present'.[62] There was no provision for annual re-election. George Hutchinson asked Sir Alec about this, who replied that he

> hadn't discussed it much or thought a great deal about it at the time. The thought was that once a party had elected a leader that was that, and it had better stay with him.[63]

Mr Berkeley produces Mr Heath

Sir Alec did well in the 1964 election: but opposition suited him less comfortably than government. Harold Wilson did not treat him with much respect. Though relations between Prime Minister and Leader of the Opposition were nothing like as brutish as they were to become (particularly between Margaret Thatcher and Neil Kinnock), it is probably fair to say that the collapse of civility occurred in this period. It had begun with the elevation of Sir Alec to the Premiership in 1963. And it was Lord Wilson who was primarily responsible for the collapse. In 1965 there were murmurs of dissent concerning Sir Alec, whose 'reaction was boredom with the whole business'. Had he been 10 years younger – he was then 62 – he might have put up a fight, but he had 'no stomach for it'.[64]

There was no coup: the Executive of the 1922 Committee had considered Sir Alec's position several times and concluded, though by a majority, that he should stay. But there were grumbles both on the back benches and in the newspapers. William Rees-Mogg wrote in the *Sunday Times*,[65] in one of the

[62] The full text is reproduced in Hutchinson, *Heath*, App. III, 222 and Goodhart, op. cit. 201.
[63] Hutchinson, *Heath*, 138.
[64] Home, op. cit. 220. See also Goodhart, op.cit. 203 ff; Hutchinson, *Heath*, 138 ff.
[65] 18 July 1965.

few recent political articles which have had a discernible effect on the course of events – another was Iain Macleod's article in the *Spectator*[66] – that Sir Alec had played a 'captain's innings', of the kind to be seen at Weston-super-Mare before the War, when the amateur, usually a 'Blue', would come in at No. 7 or 8 and knock up a small but useful score. It was time, Lord (as he subsequently became) Rees-Mogg wrote, for Sir Alec to surrender the crease.

Though Sir Alec had already made up his mind to go when this piece appeared, it nevertheless concentrated the minds of backbenchers. On 22 July 1965, at a crowded meeting of the 1922 Committee with Sir William Anstruther-Gray in the chair, he announced his intention of resigning. 'We've been bulldozed into this by the press,' exclaimed Greville Howard, the Member for St Ives.[67] What finally made up Sir Alec's mind, however, was not a newspaper but a poll which disclosed that a majority of the British people considered Harold Wilson to be more honest and sincere than he was.[68] Sir Alec said:

> I myself set up the machinery for this change, and I myself have chosen the time to use it.[69]

These words anticipated the fate of Edward Heath in 1975 and of Margaret Thatcher in 1990: all three Conservative leaders since 1963 have played a part in – have, in a sense, almost invited – their own downfall. Unlike his two successors, however, Sir Alec was not an unsuccessful candidate. The candidates were Reginald Maudling, Edward Heath and Enoch Powell. Iain Macleod was nowhere, as he had been in 1963: Humphry Berkeley estimated he might have obtained 40 votes.[70] Mr Heath had impressed with his handling of the Finance Bill: the adjectives applied to him were 'tough', abrasive' and 'gritty', all qualities which Harold Wilson was thought to possess.

66 See above, p.167.
67 Hutchinson, *Heath*, 140.
68 Goodhart, op. cit. 206.
69 Home, op. cit. 221.
70 Berkeley, op. cit. 98.

But Maudling remained the favourite, even though he had fallen back in esteem since 1963. There was an inchoate belief among Conservatives of a certain sort (more common in 1965 than in later years) that violence had been done to the natural succession, which should have been first Butler and then Maudling, with no place for either Macmillan or Home. And yet, even though he was only 48, Reggie's time might have come and gone.

The result was: Heath, 150; Maudling, 133; Powell, 15. To satisfy the 15 per cent rule Mr Heath should have obtained a majority of 45 or more; in fact it was 17. 'That was a turn-up for the book,' Maudling remarked in his usual affable way, and promptly withdrew from the contest.[71] Powell did likewise. At midmorning on the next day the second ballot closed and there was only one nomination, for Mr Heath. Sir William Anstruther-Gray formally declared him the winner. His election was only confirmed at the ceremonial party meeting six days later.[72] Sir William's successor, Cranley Onslow, neglected to follow this punctilious procedure 25 years on, when John Major failed by two votes to satisfy the rules, and Michael Heseltine and Douglas Hurd withdrew.

These rules were not properly understood by many Conservative MPs, either in 1965 or on the three subsequent occasions on which a modified procedure was used. It was not merely that they tended to become glassy-eyed whenever percentages were mentioned: they were also what Anthony Crosland would have called 'frivolous' in their attitude to elections. They failed to understand that elections were a serious business which produced important results. They regarded them much as dissatisfied Conservative voters looked upon by-elections, as an opportunity to register a protest. Thus several Conservatives voted for Mr Heath, not because they wanted — still less because they expected — him to win, but because they wanted to administer a shock to 'the old gang' as represented by Maudling.

---

[71] Alan Watkins, 'Iain Macleod' in *Brief Lives* (1982), 97 at 108.
[72] Hutchinson, *Heath*, 143-4.

Mr Heath digs a pit

Ten years later the same instincts operated against Mr Heath and for Mrs Thatcher.[73] Inevitably there were differences. In 1965 the Executive of the 1922 Committee had maintained a position of benevolent neutrality, a majority favouring Sir Alec's continuation in office, though without any great enthusiasm on their part. In autumn 1974 the Executive wanted Mr Heath to go. This was partly because of the antipathy that existed between the leader and Edward (later Sir Edward) du Cann, Mr Onslow's predecessor as chairman of the committee. In 1967 he had been displaced as party chairman and replaced by Anthony Barber; Mr du Cann and Mr Heath did not like each other. On 14 November 1974 Mr Heath told the 1922 Committee:

> It is perfectly natural that after the election you should want to discuss the leadership. What the party asks is that it should be done reasonably and with restraint and dignity. The Chairman of the 1922 Committee has reported the view of the committee to me. As I understand it, they wish to have a review of procedure. This seems to be perfectly reasonable ... There is no reason why there should be any delay. I would wish to get on with it at once.[74]

In fact the suggestion for a review had come originally from Mr du Cann, and Mr Heath accepted it. To carry out the inquiry he appointed Lord Home, as he once again was (he had been granted a life peerage in 1974 as Lord Home of the Hirsel).

The objections to Mr Heath were not primarily doctrinal, even though the first candidate who was thought of as a possible rival and who rapidly disqualified himself was Sir Keith Joseph. Rather they were that he had mistimed the first election of 1974, had lost both elections of that year and – above all – was rude all the time. 'So *you're* here, are you?' he said to Peter Jenkins, then of the *Guardian*, on espying him about his reporting tasks in a Hampstead committee room during the first 1974 campaign. He

[73] For her accession, see Nicholas Wapshott and George Brock, *Thatcher* (1983), Ch. 7; Patrick Cosgrave, *Margaret Thatcher* (1978), Ch. 2; Morrison Halcrow, *Keith Joseph* (1989), Ch. 12.
[74] Wapshott and Brock, op. cit. 118.

noticed a table of refreshments at the far end of the room, 'So this is where we get the sandwiches, is it?' he said, before moving purposefully in their direction. Stories of his brusqueness, his gaucheness, his lack of small or indeed any talk, his sheer bad manners – omitting to stand up, neglecting to offer a drink, failing to ask about his interlocutor's more pressing concerns – were famous at Westminster. It was one of them which led indirectly to the success of Mrs Thatcher. Airey Neave had suffered a heart attack as a junior Minister in a previous Conservative government. Mr Heath had said to him: 'So that's the end of your political career, then.' He now undertook the leadership of Mrs Thatcher's campaign.

In December 1974 Lord Home's committee reported to Mr Heath. It recommended three changes in the voting arrangements: first, that an annual election should, if requested, take place, so removing the leader's entitlement to stay on at will; second, that the 15 per cent 'surcharge' should be of the whole electoral college, all Conservative MPs, rather than of those actually voting; and, third, that while the electoral college remained unchanged, the arrangements for consulting extra-parliamentary sections of the party should be formalised. The second recommendation, which made it more difficult for Mr Heath (now certain to be challenged) to win on the first ballot, immediately became known as 'Alec's revenge'.

But who was to do the challenging? Sir Keith insisted that he was making way for Mrs Thatcher ('Margaret will stand') rather than for Mr du Cann, whose claims were being advanced by a group led by Peter Tapsell. Mr du Cann declined, partly because he was not certain to win on the first ballot, but mainly because his then wife Sallie did not want him to allow his name to go forward.

The prevailing theory at the time was that Mrs Thatcher would fill the role of that favourite Conservative creature, the stalking horse. She would not beat Mr Heath outright but she would do well enough either to deprive him of victory under the rules or, failing that, to shame him into resignation. The way would then be open for William Whitelaw to enter the contest. He could not stand on the first ballot because he was a loyal old soul. But, Mr Heath out of the way, he would defeat Mrs Thatcher easily on the second ballot. The late Hugh Fraser also announced his intention of entering the contest as the representative of traditional Conservatism, but he did not campaign.

On 25 January 1975 Mr Heath announced that he accepted Lord Home's proposals, that nominations would close on 30 January and that the election would be held on 4 February. The result of the first ballot was: Thatcher, 130; Heath, 119; Fraser, 16. This was a much bigger upset than that of 1965. Sir Geoffrey Howe, John Peyton and Jim Prior now entered the second ballot, in addition to Mr Whitelaw. The result was: Thatcher, 146; Whitelaw, 79; Howe, 19; Prior, 19; Peyton, 11. She had won an absolute majority of 18. It was an even bigger upset than that of the first ballot.

Sir Anthony sets a precedent

Mrs Thatcher was to remain leader for 15 years, 11 of them as Prime Minister. As we have seen, the last years were not very successful for her and were difficult all round. The year 1989 was especially troublesome. She dismissed a Foreign Secretary and lost both a Chancellor of the Exchequer and a by-election. During the summer the talk grew about challenging her in the autumn. Michael Heseltine was adamant that he would not do it. Sir (as he had become) Ian Gilmour was hesitant. In the end Sir Anthony Meyer decided to have – or, rather, was persuaded into having – a go himself.

He was a rich, vague, handsome baronet whose manner was at once diffident and self-assured. He sat for Clwyd in North Wales, which used to be Flintshire West until the Welsh-language-crazed boundary commissioners managed to lay their hands on it. He had previously sat for Eton and Slough. When he was offered Clwyd he thought it was in Scotland. His wife Barbadee accompanied him on all his public engagements.[75] He had been a professional diplomat, serving in

---

[75] Anthony Meyer, *Stand Up and Be Counted* (1990), 56.

Moscow, Paris and London. His instincts were decent and his one political cause was Europe. When he challenged Mrs Thatcher, he was 69. He was persuaded into – some might say, put up to – this course by Chris Moncrieff, the indefatigable political correspondent of the Press Association.[76]

He was treated with much scorn and some abuse by the cheap press, but displayed himself to advantage on television. Not for the first or the last time, BBC and ITV acted as a counterweight to the *Daily Express*, the *Daily Mail* and, above all, the *Sun*. They supported the Prime Minister with a vehemence which was to be exceeded only in the next year.

If Sir Anthony was dignified, Mrs Thatcher was regal. There was no campaign to speak of: its ostensible leader, George Younger, merely let it be known that the Prime Minister expected all good Conservatives to do their duty. This turned out to be an unfortunate precedent, though Tristan Garel-Jones worked for Mrs Thatcher in 1989 as he did not – was not asked to do – in 1990. The result of 5 December 1989 was: Thatcher, 314; Meyer, 33; spoilt, 24; abstentions, 3. Sixty (or 16 per cent) of her parliamentary party had refused to support their Prime Minister. This was certainly damaging enough. What was even more damaging was that Sir Anthony had demonstrated that a Conservative Prime Minister could be challenged constitutionally. In the fall of Mrs Thatcher his part was as important as that of the other backbencher Humphry Berkeley.

[76] Ibid. 159.

8

The Triumph of Mr Major

'Why, damn it all, such a position was never held by any Greek or Roman: and if it only lasts three months, it will be worthwhile to have been Prime Minister of England.'

Tom Young to Lord Melbourne,
quoted in David Cecil, *Lord M*

'It is fitting that we should have buried the Unknown Prime Minister by the side of the Unknown Soldier.'

H.H. Asquith, after Bonar Law's funeral,
quoted in Robert Blake, *The Unknown Prime Minister*

A year after the events, it is still difficult to know whether Margaret Thatcher and her advisers realised they had a fight on their hands. The answer is probably that they did realise this, but misjudged its seriousness, and framed a strategy which was ineffective and annoyed numerous backbenchers. The plan was to emphasise the difference between Margaret Thatcher, Prime Minister and world statesman, and Michael Heseltine, disappointed ex-Minister and flashy demagogue. Essentially, this was the same plan as Harold Wilson had followed in the 1970 general election.

'There's me,' Lord Wilson would say (or words to this effect), 'and there's this other chap. I forget his name just for the moment. Now, who d'you want: me, or the other chap?'

'Thank you very much,' the voters responded, 'but we'll take the other chap, if it's all the same to you.'

And so Edward Heath became Prime Minister.

Mrs Thatcher's campaign

Mr Heath's successor employed Lord Wilson's mistaken strategy. The entire timetable, we should remember, was drawn up by her, in cahoots with the Chairman of the 1922 Committee. Not only did she know about the trip to Paris for the European security summit: she arranged to be away for the final days of the first ballot. Such a visit would, she thought, emphasise her eminence as a world leader and demonstrate her unconcern with the domestic details of the Conservative Party.

The visit to Northern Ireland which preceded the Paris trip was, admittedly, different. Little publicity would come of that, for reasons of security. But Mrs Thatcher felt about the province. She told her staff at No. 10 that she was determined to fulfil the Ulster engagement. Likewise, she had an obligation to attend the Paris meeting. The official ending of the Cold War was, as she said from time to time, the culmination of part of her life's work. But she and Cranley Onslow could still have arranged the ballot for a week or even two weeks later.

In 1989, when Sir Anthony Meyer had challenged her, she had fought an unobtrusive campaign. Tristan Garel-Jones had worked on her behalf. He would have worked for her again had he been asked, but he was not. 'I'd have got the old bat in,' he says disarmingly, and he is probably right. When, on Wednesday 21 November, John Wakeham asked him and Richard Ryder to work for her, they both declined. It was too late. There was also a mystery about the precise composition of Mrs Thatcher's campaign team, and who at any given moment was heading it. Both George Younger, who had organised proceedings in 1989, and Norman Tebbit were nominated at different stages. The first Michael Jopling knew about the job was when he read about it in the newspapers. He did not want it and took no part in the campaign.

Mr Younger, like most Scottish Conservatives of any consequence, sounded more English than the English. As Secretary of State for Scotland he was always threatening to resign over the future of a certain steelworks; as Secretary of State for Defence his opportunities for gestures had been more limited. He was known in some quarters as 'Gentleman George'. No doctrinal devotee of Mrs Thatcher, he had been the object of smart money as her successor in the 1990s.

Unfortunately he was heir to a peerage. In 1989 he had left the government to become Chairman of the Royal Bank of Scotland. This was the trouble. The election, he told people, had come at a most inconvenient time for him. It was the busiest time of year at the bank. There were numerous pressing matters that required his attention. Altogether, he seemed to suggest, securing the re-election of Mrs Thatcher was proving something of a nuisance.

Mr Tebbit was certainly more visible. At one stage he turned up to conduct an early-morning television interview on Mr Heseltine's Belgravia doorstep. 'Even allowing for over-optimism,' he said, 'we have still got a good win in the first ballot.'[1] The Prime Minister did not – because of her travels, could not – turn up in broadcasting studios. No doubt the broadcasters could have come to her instead. But she left most of the talk to Mr Tebbit. He said afterwards:

> I was doing too much but that was partly because not enough of the Prime Minister's colleagues in the Cabinet were willing to make the time to campaign enthusiastically on her part.[2]

Mr Tebbit, however, was an ex-Minister. So also was Sir Norman Fowler – few more 'ex-'. Yet

> Over the next days I appeared for Margaret Thatcher on more television and radio programmes than ever before in my political life.[3]

In addition to Mr Younger, Mr Tebbit and Sir Norman, all ex-Ministers, there were John Moore, ex-Secretary of State for Social Security and Peter Morrison, ex-Minister of State for Energy. Sir Peter was by this time Mrs Thatcher's Parliamentary Private Secretary.[4] Accordingly his position was

---

[1] *Independent on Sunday*, 18 November 1990.
[2] Transcript, *The Thatcher Factor Special*, Brook Productions, Channel 4, 1990, 106.
[3] Norman Fowler, *Ministers Decide* (1991), 350.
[4] On Mrs Thatcher's PPSs, see above, pp. 42-3.

different from that of the others.

Sir Peter has been allocated most of the blame for Mrs Thatcher's failure to win the first ballot outright. It should more properly go to Mr Younger for not really wanting the job of running Mrs Thatcher's campaign, and to Mrs Thatcher for absenting herself. As Sir Norman puts it: 'In truth, it is difficult to run a campaign without the presence of the candidate.'[5]

There is an element of retrospective bullying in the blaming of Sir Peter. His father, Major John Morrison, was a legendary Chairman of the 1922 Committee. He was the richest man in the House of Commons but drove a Morris Minor. He became Lord Margadale. Peter's brother Charles, an MP likewise, was an unashamed Wet who had started his political life sharing an office in Gayfere Street with Ian Gilmour and Peter Walker. Peter Morrison had a political position closer to Mrs Thatcher, though he was by no means one of us.

He spent virtually every Sunday evening when the House was sitting in Pratt's Club. In the 1950s Pratt's, like White's up and across the road, would have been a centre for gossip and a focus for intrigue in any contest for the Conservative leadership. In 1990 it was neither. The only other regular attender was Alan Clark, though he was certainly no mean gossiper or intriguer. On the Sunday before the first ballot Sir Peter said that he thought Mrs Thatcher had the necessary 'surcharge' majority of 15 per cent. Bruce Anderson commented that old Peter probably thought this meant 15 votes.

The days before the first ballot produced two critical events. One was the declaration by Douglas Hurd on Friday 16 November that he would be prepared to stand for the leadership, though not, as he perhaps ungallantly phrased it, 'against her'. The other was the publication of six opinion polls in the Sunday papers of 18 November showing, with a striking measure of agreement, that the Conservatives would not only do better against Labour with Mr Heseltine rather than Mrs Thatcher as their leader: more, they would actually be ahead. The figures were:

[5] Ibid. 351.

	MORI *S. Times*	Harris *Obs.*	NMR *Ind. on S.*	ICM *Corr.*	Cont. *NoW*	NOP *Mail on S.*
Thatcher	−11	−15	−2	−12	−11	−12
Heseltine	+1	+1	+10	+8	+5	+7
swing	6.0	8.0	6.0	10.0	8.0	9.5

True, the figures confirmed no more than was already known. But they came at a useful time for Mr Heseltine.

The leading articles, which counted for less with Mr Heseltine's parliamentary constituency, were more favourable than he could have expected. The *Observer* and the *Correspondent* came out in his favour. There was admittedly no surprise about that. What was more surprising was that both the *Sunday Times* and the *Mail on Sunday* recommended the MPs to vote for him. So, less surprisingly, did the *Independent on Sunday*, though the paper made clear that a vote for Heseltine was intended only to make way for a vote for Hurd in the second ballot. Mrs Thatcher had to be content with the support of the *News of the World*, the *Sunday Express* and the *Sunday Telegraph*, whose editor, Peregrine Worsthorne (as yet unknighted) commented: 'Mrs Thatcher deserves better than to be dismissed in the shoddy and demeaning manner some Tory MPs are minded to have in store for her.'[6]

Two days before, Mr Hurd had called on Mrs Thatcher to allow 'the full Cabinet' to agree a 'united policy' on Europe. He also said of Sir Geoffrey Howe: 'I part company with him over his conclusion that our party's policy cannot be effectively carried through with Margaret Thatcher as our party's leader.' This was praise, of a sort, for Sir Geoffrey, whose place in the demonology of Mrs Thatcher's supporters had only recently been assumed by another Welshman, Mr Heseltine.[7] He nevertheless proclaimed his loyalty to the Prime Minister. At a press conference in Leeds he was asked:

'Under no circumstances then would you stand?'
'Against her.'[8]

[6] *Sunday Telegraph*, 18 November 1990.
[7] *Independent*, 17 November 1990.
[8] *Daily Telegraph*, 17 November 1990.

Sir Nicholas Fairbairn, who lost no opportunity of exalting the Prime Minister and depreciating her challenger, particularly if his views were likely to be publicised, called Mr Hurd's statement 'thoroughly unhelpful. I think he ought to be totally loyal to the Prime Minister.'[9] Mr Hurd had proposed Mrs Thatcher and Mr Major had seconded her. And in a way, Sir Nicholas was right. For all his affectations, he was a perceptive and intelligent man, even if he was not always the most astute of politicians where his own interests were concerned. Mr Hurd had put ideas into people's heads – if they were not there already. He had opened up a box from which all manner of strange creatures, challengers to Mr Heseltine in the second ballot (if there was one), were likely to emerge. He was clearly one of them. He had virtually said so himself.

But what of his fellow-nominator of Mrs Thatcher? Where did Mr Major stand? On television, he declined to rule himself out of any subsequent leadership contest, avoiding all questions of what would happen if Mrs Thatcher failed to win the requisite majority. Speaking on *Channel 4 News*, he conceded that there had been 'very heated discussions' with Mrs Thatcher over European policy. He also disclosed that he disagreed with her view that the hard ecu would not be widely used.[10] By the next day, the Saturday, it was clearly felt that matters were getting out of hand. Mr Hurd and Mr Major were prevailed upon to put out a joint statement:

> As proposer and seconder of the Prime Minister in the leadership election we both want to make it quite clear that what we wish to see is a good victory for Mrs Thatcher in the first and only ballot.[11]

On Monday Mr Major was recuperating at his house in Huntingdon from an operation for an infected wisdom tooth. A certain mystery has been made of this operation. It has been suggested that he so contrived it as to be away from London at the critical time, and accordingly a man with clean hands.

[9] *Independent on Sunday*, 18 November 1990.
[10] *Daily Telegraph*, 17 November 1990.
[11] *Independent on Sunday*, 18 November 1990.

However, Mr Major had been in sometimes distressing pain for months. The operation had been arranged before the Conservatives' election was fixed. Mr Major now wanted company – and political intelligence. He (or, rather, his wife Norma) asked Jeffrey Archer to come and see him from his home in Grantchester outside Cambridge, which was not far away. It was on this occasion that he made his now famous complaint to his wife that he was given jelly only when he was ill; to which she replied that he could have it any time he liked. Mr Archer's recollection of the day is that all the speculation in the papers concerned Mr Hurd and that Mr Major's name was unmentioned. This is correct, to the extent that the Foreign Secretary was considered the most likely candidate to stand against Mr Heseltine should Mrs Thatcher withdraw, or be persuaded to withdraw, after the first ballot. That was certainly the dominant impression. However, Robin Oakley and Philip Webster reported in the lead story of *The Times* that

> although Douglas Hurd remains the leading contender to be the Cabinet's unity candidate in a contest without Mrs Thatcher, John Major, the Chancellor, is attracting increasing support from senior backbenchers.[12]

On page 2 Mr Oakley and Mr Webster wrote, in the course of a roundup of the possible candidates in a second ballot:

> The Chancellor of the Exchequer is the other main 'stop Heseltine' candidate. He has risen so far, becoming Foreign Secretary after only 10 years as an MP and Chancellor soon afterwards, that he might be forgiven for thinking that destiny beckons yet again. His name is being pressed by MPs on the left and right, the right clearly believing that he would take a tougher, closer-to-Thatcher line on Europe than Mr Hurd. Some senior supporters believe that at the age of 47 he can afford to wait until he has more experience.[13]

Mr Major correctly suspected that he might be a candidate. That is why, out of loyalty to Mrs Thatcher, he refused to take any

[12] *The Times*, 19 November 1990.
[13] Ibid.

telephone calls throughout the day at Huntingdon, leaving Mrs Major to say that he was resting after his operation; as, indeed, he was. It is also why Mrs Major said to her husband and Mr Archer that they were discussing his becoming Prime Minister. At this stage, however, Mr Major did not want to stand against Mr Hurd, whom he liked and respected.

Meanwhile Mrs Thatcher was giving interviews: not, as Mr Heseltine was doing, on television, but to the newspapers or, rather, to three newspapers, the *Sunday Telegraph*, the *Sunday Times* and *The Times*. To the *Daily Telegraph* she contributed an article. It was hardly saturation coverage. It also contradicted Sir Gordon Reece's maxim that only the cheap press was important politically. But then, her electorate of Conservative MPs was narrower than the one that Sir Gordon had in mind. In the *Sunday Telegraph* she was interviewed by Charles Moore, deputy editor of the *Daily Telegraph*. She made clear that she would refuse to resign as Prime Minister even if she won the first ballot only narrowly.

> If we win according to the rules, we win. The rules were not made by me. I abide by the rules. I expect others to abide by the rules.[14]

The other notable feature of the interview was her espousal of a referendum on the question of a single European currency. It – or her support for it – had been speculated on before, but this was the first occasion on which she had committed herself to it so firmly.

> I would not rule out a referendum. My views on referendums are really quite simple. I think you should hold them only on constitutional issues. I think they are right for constitutional issues because otherwise you cannot separate out a particular issue in an election ... It is a mechanism which enables you to put a single question to the people.[15]

Some of her supporters were not so keen. Mr Wakeham

---

[14] *Sunday Telegraph*, 18 November 1990.
[15] Ibid.

expressed doubts.[16] Mr Parkinson said on London Weekend Television that this was 'precisely the sort of issue' that Members were sent to Parliament 'to take decisions about'.[17] While Mr Heseltine's supporters claimed that this provided another example of Mrs Thatcher's disposition to make up policy as she went along.[18] They also unearthed a quotation of Mrs Thatcher herself, speaking in the House of Commons on 11 March 1975 in opposition to the Labour government's referendum on Europe: 'Perhaps the late Lord Attlee was right when he said that a referendum was a device of dictators and demagogues.'[19] The referendum idea was not, on the whole, a success.

In her article in the *Daily Telegraph*, she allowed herself to become more personal about Mr Heseltine, though she did not name him: 'Too often in recent months personal ambitions and private rancour have been all too much in evidence.'[20] And:

> All the history of this nation shows that it is when you try to fudge …, when you try to apologise for what you have done rather than defend it, when you prefer gloss to substance, that people turn aside in disgust. The Conservative Party which I lead will never cynically put appearances first.[21]

But it was in her interview in *The Times* that Mrs Thatcher was thought by MPs to have gone, in the popular phrase of the day, over the top, sometimes abbreviated to OTT. The interview was with the paper's new editor, Simon Jenkins, who was more of a political animal than his immediate predecessor (it would have been difficult to be less of one). In it she made the mistake of accusing Mr Heseltine of being little better than a socialist. She said he would 'jeopardise all I have struggled to achieve'.[22] She referred to 1974:

---

[16] Ibid.
[17] *Daily Telegraph*, 19 November 1990.
[18] *Sunday Telegraph*, 18 November 1990.
[19] Quot. *Independent*, 20 November 1990.
[20] *Daily Telegraph*, 19 November 1990.
[21] Ibid.
[22] *The Times*, 19 November 1990.

We lost because we had gone too far to the left. We had strayed from every single thing we believed in. If you read Michael Heseltine's book, you will find it more akin to some of the Labour Party policies: intervention, corporatism, everthing that pulled us down. There is a fundamental difference on economics and there's no point in trying to hide it. Those of us who sat with Michael on economic discussions remember full well.[23]

There was undoubtedly some justice in this criticism. An interventionist Mr Heseltine manifestly was. In books, articles, speeches and private conversation, the themes of European public investment and even protectionism would recur. He might have proved more persuasive with Mrs Thatcher if he had drawn his examples from the United States. At any rate, he responded with some style:

As long as I was a member of the government I was regarded as really rather a good egg … Nobody ever said I was interventionist or corporatist.[24]

Mr Heseltine's first campaign

There was some justice in this as well. Mr Heseltine was a supporter of privatisation and had, through the sale of council houses, done more than anyone (with the exception of Jim Prior and his union reforms) to put his mark on Mrs Thatcher's first term. Nevertheless his touch was not always as light as this. When Jonathan Dimbleby referred to Mrs Thatcher's promise not to put a single European currency to this Parliament, he responded:

She won't put it to this Parliament? Is Parliament not to be allowed to consider these matters? Has the Cabinet got no role in these things? That is the essence of the problem. That is why Sir Geoffrey Howe resigned; that is why Nigel Lawson resigned; that is why I resigned – because the Prime Minister feels so strongly on these matters that collective Cabinet responsibility on this issue is not acceptable to her.[25]

[23] Ibid.
[24] *Guardian*, 20 November 1990.
[25] Transcript, *On the Record*, BBC1, 18 November 1990.

Later in the interview he returned to the same subject in relation to the Westland affair:

> I can remember very clearly the Cabinet at which she decided that the matter had to be end ... *(gulp)* ... It's the only time I can ever remember the Prime Minister reading out the conclusions of the meeting of a discussion which didn't take place. They were already written before the meeting started. Mrs Thatcher was not prepared to allow my case to be put to Cabinet and perhaps that's understandable because, when it was put to the Economic Affairs Committee of the Cabinet, I actually won and she didn't.[26]

Mr Heseltine's proposer was Sir Neil Macfarlane, his seconder Sir Peter Tapsell. Sir Neil had been Minister of Sport until 1985. Some people regarded him as having been unjustly dismissed. He was certainly disillusioned with Mrs Thatcher.

Sir Peter, on the other hand, had never had any illusions about her. He had held shadow jobs under Mrs Thatcher in opposition, resigning as a Treasury spokesman in 1978. He was a Keynesian who, like Mr Heseltine, had made a lot of money, though not as much as Mr Heseltine. He was perhaps the most intelligent of all the auxiliaries involved in the election but was certainly not the most tactful.

He disapproved of Mr Heseltine's being constantly photographed at, or in front of the monogrammed wrought-iron gates of, his country house on the Oxfordshire-Northamptonshire border. It was always a mistake, Sir Peter thought, for politicians to be photographed at their country houses. On the whole, he was surprised at how perfunctory and lacking in resource the Heseltine campaign was: the more so as Mr Heseltine had enjoyed four years in which to think about it. Sir Peter had come late to the campaign. Indeed, he had said to Mr Heseltine that he would be better off with a former Minister as his seconder. Mr Heseltine replied that he had known him for 30 years, and that was good enough.

Sir Peter's task was to accept every single invitation offered by radio or television. When he hazarded that this constant exposure might convey the impression that Mr Heseltine had

[26] Ibid.

only one active supporter, namely himself, he was told that resources did not permit any other arrangement. Accordingly Sir Peter accepted every broadcasting invitation that came his way, relinquished strong drink, subsisted on cornflakes and lost half a stone in weight.

At the core of the campaign were Michael Mates and Keith Hampson. Dr Hampson was a former lecturer in history who was married to Sue Cameron, the television political journalist. He came from Durham, though many took him for a Yorkshireman of the less aggressive variety, for he had represented Ripon and Leeds seats since 1974. Partly through his wife, but more on his own account, he had a wide acquaintance with journalists of one sort and another.

The chief of staff was Michael Mates, known as 'The Colonel'. For once, the appellation was not fictitious, even though it may have been jocular. He had been a regular soldier, ending up as a Lieutenant-Colonel in the Queen's Dragoon Guards. He had previously been a choral scholar at King's College, Cambridge. He was a heavy, dark, handsome man, whose prominent black eyebrows contributed to the impression that he had just been made up – contrasts emphasised, features accentuated – with a view to his appearing on the stage, perhaps as the Demon King in a pantomime. Despite a certain brutality of aspect, he was a sensitive, musical man. He had been one of William Whitelaw's principal organisers during his abortive election campaign of 1975, even though he had been in Parliament for only a year at the time. And yet he had never been given office, as his role in this event, or as his subsequent prominence in the party (notably over defence matters), might have indicated. His want of preferment could be viewed as a sign of either the injustice of politics or the distrust which the Colonel somehow aroused in some sections of his party.

The Colonel had the names of all Conservative MPs displayed, and then stuck blue or red pins into them according as they were supporters or non-supporters. Those who came into neither category were then talked to. Sir Dennis Walters and Quentin Davies were also droppers-into the Heseltine headquarters. In the evenings the campaigners would meet in a room downstairs, underneath the Chamber on the Committee Floor (which is to be distinguished from the Committee Corridor on the first floor). Mr Heseltine would sit at the head of a large teak table flanked by Mr Davies, Sir Dennis, Dr Hampson or Sir Neil and, almost always, Colonel Mates. The last forecast 150 votes.

From the begining, the Colonel's troops were in a dialectical difficulty about Mr Hurd. On the one hand, they had to maintain that Mr Hurd, should he choose to enter the contest on the second ballot, was a loser, certainly a loser of general elections. Though there was a perceptible swell of support for Mr Major even before the first ballot took place, Mr Hurd was still seen as the candidate of Cabinet unity. One the other hand, however, the Colonel's troops had to say that if the honest voter wanted to see Mr Hurd – or, for that matter, anyone else – as leader of the party, the best, the only course was to cast a vote for Mr Heseltine on 20 November.

Some Ministers outside the Cabinet certainly followed this prescription. For instance, David Mellor voted for Mr Heseltine in the first ballot, having urged him to stand, only to become one of Mr Major's principal campaigners in the second ballot. With one possible exception, the Cabinet voted for Mrs Thatcher, some making the reservation that they would not vote for her in any second ballot. Thus Kenneth Clarke voted for her, as also, from outside the Cabinet, did Tristan Garel-Jones.

There has been some misunderstanding about the position of the Welsh Secretary, David Hunt. He was in Japan during and before the first ballot. After the result he sent Mrs Thatcher a telegram urging her to fight on 'with no holds barred'. He claims that, owing to his absence in Japan, he did not know that there was in effect a Cabinet agreement to vote either for Mr Hurd or for Mr Major on the second ballot. A Merseysider, he voted for Mr Heseltine because he admired his actions in Liverpool in the early 1980s. Mrs Thatcher did not reproach Mr Hunt for voting for Mr Heseltine. On the contrary: she thanked him for his 'loyal support'.

On Saturday 17 November there was a dinner-party at Chequers. Those present included Kenneth Baker, Tim Bell, Gordon Reece, Alistair McAlpine, Peter Morrison, Michael

Neubert and Gerry Neale. They were all, apart from Mr Baker, recipients of either past or future honours from Mrs Thatcher. Certainly the campaign that was fought on her behalf did not justify any medals.

The Whips Office under Tim Renton preserved a scrupulous neutrality, which Mrs Thatcher considered to be a form of disloyalty. It was Mrs Thatcher's own fault for appointing him, or allowing him to be appointed, in the first place. Dry in economics though he might be, he was not and had never purported to be one of us. Nor was Sir George Young, a recent and even more surprising addition to the Whips Office, likely to prove more sympathetic to the Prime Minister. And yet, information about the state of party opinion did get through to Mrs Thatcher, whereas it did not reach Mr Heseltine. Whatever the lines of nice constitutional demarcation, she was Prime Minister and First Lord of the Treasury as well as Leader of the Conservative Party; and the Patronage Secretary was her strong arm in the Lower House. Clearly, either the intelligence was faulty, which it probably was not, or Mrs Thatcher's managers neglected to pay proper attention to it, which was more likely.

On the morning of Tuesday 20 November a meeting was held in the Commons that included Mr Wakeham, Mr Baker, Mr Younger, Sir Gerry and Mr Onslow. They expected Mrs Thatcher to win outright and composed an uplifting message on party unity for her to read out in Paris later that day. They composed another message which was to be used in the unlikely event of Mrs Thatcher's winning, though not by the requisite majority. Mr Baker, for one, was not wholly happy with what was agreed. He would have preferred: 'I shall return to London tomorrow for consultations and make my position known.' Mr Wakeham was in favour of a stronger approach, though he did not want her to sound as firm about her plans as some of her extra-parliamentary entourage did. The gathering, led by Mr Wakeham, settled on her saying that it was her 'intention' to allow her name to go forward to the second ballot.[27] As we have seen, what had been

[27] Private information; Robert Shepherd, *The Power Brokers* (1991), 24.

thought about carefully, and had been meant to sound statesmanlike, sounded brash when Mrs Thatcher uttered the words.[28] They did her considerable damage on the Tuesday evening and the following day. Sir Peter Morrison then cast his vote and a proxy for Mrs Thatcher, and travelled to Paris by air. On the aeroplane he said, in answer to a question from a television reporter:

> It certainly looks as if a handy number, let's put it no higher than that, are going to be supporting the Prime Minister today.[29]

Sir Peter carried with him a piece of paper giving his forecast: Thatcher, 238; Heseltine, 80; abstentions, 70.[30] He had overestimated Mrs Thatcher's vote by 34 and underestimated Mr Heseltine's by 72. The present writer won the *Observer*'s sweepstake on Mr Heseltine's vote (there was no sweep on Mrs Thatcher's vote) by predicting 151. He had a luck which was denied to Sir Peter.

Mr Heseltine's second campaign

Colonel Mates said afterwards that he would have liked to know the origin and circumstances of the Cabinet agreement that there should be two candidates rather than one opposing Mr Heseltine. With only one candidate – Mr Hurd or Mr Major – he was convinced that Mr Heseltine would have won. Almost certainly he would have beaten Mr Hurd. Whether he would have beaten Mr Major is more doubtful. In fact there was no Cabinet agreement as such, a possibility which the Colonel, a fair man, was prepared to recognise.

Mr Major had first thought of becoming leader of the party four years previously, on a canal-boat holiday with Robert Atkins and their wives.[31] Mr Lamont had thought of Mr Major as leader of the party for about two years. Mr Lilley had thought of him similarly for the same length of time. Despite Mr Major's

---

[28] See above, p. 4.
[29] Transcript, *The Thatcher Factor Special*, 106.
[30] 'The Fall of Thatcher', *Economist*, 9 March 1991.
[31] Shepherd, op. cit. 55.

refusal to take telephone calls during Mr Archer's visit to Huntingdon, Mr Lamont admitted that he had been in touch with Mr Major before the first ballot.[32] During and after Tuesday evening's meeting at Mr Garel-Jones's house, Mr Lamont refused to acknowledge that Mr Hurd was the only or the best candidate to stop Mr Heseltine. Mr Hurd did not see the contest in this light. There is no reason to believe that Mr Major differed from him. Mr Hurd said:

> We decided it was sensible to let Conservative MPs decide which of us was better able to unite the party. Divisions of the kind we have had are disastrous.[33]

The contemporary opinion poll evidence was that they were nothing of the sort. On the contrary: the polls recorded an extraordinary rise in the Conservative Party's standing after Mrs Thatcher's departure, irrespective of who was to succeed her. Thus, on the same day as *The Times* reported Mr Hurd's opinion that divisions were 'disastrous', it also reported the findings of On-Line, a telephone-polling subsidiary of MORI, about the parties' electoral prospects with Mr Heseltine, Mr Major or Mr Hurd as Conservative leader:

	Heseltine	Major	Hurd
Conservative	47	45	44
Labour	42	44	45

These findings were to be confirmed two days later, on the Sunday, after a more comprehensive survey but, in one respect, one with more surprising results:[34]

	Heseltine	Major	Hurd
Conservative	47	48	43
Labour	42	40	44

Poor Mr Hurd was shown to be a 'loser': the aspect of the contest which Mr Heseltine's connections had correctly anticipated and

[32] Private information.

[33] *The Times*, 23 November 1990.

[34] *Independent on Sunday*, 25 November 1990, NMR poll. Other newspapers produced similar polls.

about which they had hoped to make much. But Mr Major was also shown to be a winner, an even more comprehensive winner that Mr Heseltine, if the polls were to be believed. It was in this respect that the polls were surprising. Mr Heseltine's principal asset, which had impelled probably a majority of the 152 to vote for him – that he would retain their seats for them, whereas Mrs Thatcher no longer could – was now, it was clear, shared by another. Not only that: the other had, it appeared, the bigger share. In Mr Lamont's view, the opinion polls showing the favourable way in which Mr Major was regarded by the national electorate was the single most important factor in the second ballot.

Mr Heseltine's campaign was constructed for fighting Mrs Thatcher and no one else. In this regard, his difficulties were the same in principle as, though they differed in detail from, those of the Labour Party after Thursday 22 November 1990. The enemy was no longer plain in view: quite suddenly, she had disappeared through a trap door. There was a different set of characters displaying themselves before our eyes.

Mr Heseltine was understandably elated when he thought Mrs Thatcher was going on with the contest. He was asked by Brian Redhead on *Today*, on the Wednesday morning, whether he ought not to withdraw, 'because by any normal method of counting' he had lost. This was a point which Mrs Thatcher herself was to make, in slighty different form, in the succeeding months. Mr Heseltine replied that he did not mind what the rules were but, whatever they were, he would stick to them. The basis of his belief that he should now stand in the second round was that just over a week previously 100 colleagues asked him to stand 'and I was much impressed with that and decided to do so'.[35]

Mr Heseltine was either being disingenuous in claiming that the rules required him to go on into the second ballot or, alternatively, did not know what they were. Perhaps it was the latter, as Mr Heseltine prided – still prides – himself on being a man of action, with little patience for juridical minutiae. What

[35] Transcript, *Today*, BBC Radio 4, 21 November 1990.

the rules say is that 'nominations made for the first ballot will be void. New nominations will be submitted by the Thursday ...'[36]

If Mr Heseltine had indeed withdrawn on the Wednesday, it is inconceivable that Mr Major, Mr Hurd or anyone else would have stood against Mrs Thatcher. To this extent, Mr Hurd was being disingenuous in thinking that he and Mr Major were not 'stop Heseltine' candidates. If Mr Heseltine had not been standing, they would not have been standing either. True, the officers of the 1922 Committee believed that the party ought to have a 'wider choice'. This was what Mr Onslow perhaps tactlessly said to Mrs Thatcher at the 'greybeards' meeting', as Mr Hurd called it, on the Wednesday, when she was still talking of carrying on. Even so, without Mr Heseltine there would have been no further contest.

At least one of Mr Heseltine's close connections thought in retrospect that he ought to have withdrawn, though he did not press this course upon him at the time. He also believed that the Epistle to the Henleyans would have been better left unsent. No matter that Mr Heseltine toppled a Prime Minister: he also sunk himself, or anyway confined himself to the weed-infested shallows of the Department of the Environment. A withdrawal after the first ballot could still have kept him afloat – to challenge Mrs Thatcher in spring 1992. Instead Mr Heseltine went on.

He heard about Mrs Thatcher's resignation when he was on his way to London Zoo to plant a tree. Trees had become his hobby – even his obsession – in the autumn of his days. When, shortly before the election, he was asked whether he had read a recent political biography, he replied that he devoted such spare time as he had to his trees. On Mr Heseltine's way to plant this tree, his aide

phoned him on the car radio and said: 'Christ, have you heard she's gone?' He said: 'Yes, I just have.' I think he probably heard it on the radio. I don't think anyone phoned him before I did on the car phone, because I think that most people didn't know he

36 Procedure for the Selection of the Leader of the Conservative Party, H. of C. Library, 24 October 1989, r. 18.

actually was in the car. He said he was going to go on to the Zoo and then back to the office and that I had to meet him in the office.[37]

His response to the news of Mrs Thatcher's withdrawal was

I think rather typically Heseltine. No reaction really. He was all very matter-of-fact. I don't think he made any other comment than 'Yes' and then I said: 'What are you going to do?' And he said: 'I'm going to go on to the Zoo and then come back as quickly as I can and meet you at Victoria Street.'[38]

Mr Heseltine's office was in Victoria Street. In fact he went straight to the House, where he met Dame Jill Knight, and successfully solicited her support. Mr Heseltine had wanted Tom King as a proposer or seconder or anyway as a prominent supporter. Within 45 minutes of Mrs Thatcher's departure he heard that Mr King, with Chris Patten, was to nominate Douglas Hurd. He did not reproach Mr King, saying that a Defence Secretary was placed in an impossible position if the Foreign Secretary asked for his nomination.

In the event Mr Heseltine persisted with his loyal knights, Neil Macfarlane and Peter Tapsell. This demonstrated an admirable loyalty on his own part, but whether it was the most profitable course open to him is more doubtful. Former Ministers who were still in the Commons and were by now supporting him included Sir Geoffrey Howe, Nigel Lawson, Peter Walker, Sir Ian Gilmour, Paul Channon and David Howell. Current Ministers who were supporting him publicly – an important qualification – were David Trippier, who was regarded as an important acquisition (even though the North-Western MPs to whom he was close were natural Heseltine supporters anyway on account of the poll tax), and the Welsh contingent of David Hunt accompanied by his junior Ministers, Sir Wyn Roberts and Ian Grist. Neither Sir Neil nor Sir Peter (a conceited but not a vain man) would have objected if he had been replaced for the second ballot, an entirely new election.

[37] Transcript, interview with aide.
[38] Ibid.

For these and the other supporters

> it was a matter of going through the list to see who we thought
> would survive from the 152 now that there was a new ball game.
> Like the Chalker [Lynda Chalker] and others who we knew would
> be sympathetic to Douglas.[39]

The 'others' included Steven Norris.[40]

> We felt that the most important feature was to persuade
> Margaret's right wing to come to us. So an enormous amount of
> effort was concentrated upon the Oppenheims and the Browns
> and the David Evanses to get them to come over. With some
> success, but actually not bulk numbers. I think that Major's
> people knew that they had the bulk of members of that group and
> they, I think, concentrated primarily on going for the right-wing
> ballast of Douglas's team.[41]

Mr Hurd's campaign

Sir Giles Shaw, Mr Hurd's principal organiser, categorised his
supporters afterwards as '56 gents of the House of Commons'.[42]
Ann Widdecombe and Virginia Bottomley were clearly honorary
gentlemen. Miss Widdecombe was often described as 'much-
respected', a phrase that was formerly used of such figures as
Jim Griffiths, and she was only 43. Mrs Bottomley was the most
popular girl in the school. She and her husband Peter (a Hurd
supporter likewise) had voted for Mrs Thatcher in the first
round. Contrary to reports at the time, they made clear to the
Whips soon afterwards that they would vote for her if she stood
in the second ballot.

But why were there only 56 of them? After all, Mr Hurd's
supporters included, in addition to his nominators, Kenneth
Clarke, William Waldegrave, Malcolm Rifkind and John Patten.
He had the backing of the Party's two senior greybeards, Lords
Whitelaw and Home. Not that his campaign was Toffs-for-Hurd

---

[39] Ibid.
[40] Lists of the candidates' supporters are given in an Appendix.
[41] Transcript cit.
[42] Personal knowledge.

exactly. Indeed, Mr Waldegrave deplored what he regarded as
the desertion of their class by Lord Carrington, Sir Ian Gilmour
and Sir Charles Morrison, Heseltine supporters all. It might,
however, have been even worse for Mr Hurd if there had been
solidarity among the toffs. His alleged membership of the upper
classes played a prominent part in the campaign.

Everyone joined in merrily, while simultaneously deploring
that the subject had been raised at all – rather as the *People*
newspaper of old would run lengthy stories about prostitutes
(which, alas, always promised more than they produced) as a
warning to young girls. Mr Hurd was cross. He did not blame Mr
Major himself but his team. They had broken an agreement
between Mr Major and Mr Hurd that they would not attack each
other personally. A scholarly man, Mr Hurd was distressed at
the inaccuracy of the cheap press. By the end of the campaign he
was being described as a product of Eton, Oxford and the
Guards, whereas in fact it was Eton, Cambridge and the
Diplomatic Service. Even Jonathan Dimbleby was not immune.
He asked Mr Hurd about the 'rarefied' atmosphere of his old
occupation. Mr Hurd replied:

> Do you think? – I was brought up on a farm. I don't know how we
> get into all this. This is inverted snobbery. I thought I was
> running for Leader of the Conservative Party, not some demented
> Marxist – Since we are into that –.[43]

On another television programme Mr Hurd played the game
of Lowlier than Thou even more strenuously. 'There would have
been no question of him sending me to Eton if I hadn't won a
scholarship,' he said of his father, Sir Anthony, later Lord, Hurd
(Marlborough and Pembroke, Cambridge). 'That is what social
mobility is all about, I understand.' He said that his father had
been 'a tenant farmer' of 500 'not particularly good acres' on the
Marlborough Downs.[44] This claim to a boyhood of rural
privation was oddly reminiscent of Michael Meacher contesting
the deputy leadership of the Labour Party seven years

[43] Transcript, *On the Record*, BBC1, 25 November 1990.
[44] Quoted *Independent*, 26 November 1990.

previously. Mr Hurd, however, was provoked as Mr Meacher had not been on that earlier occasion. As the monetarist Member for Wolverhampton South-West, who voted for Mr Hurd, recorded with evident enjoyment:

> Major's campaign was superbly run. David Mellor's advocacy for the boy from Brixton was highly effective and forced Hurd to apologise for Eton and Cambridge.[45]

Mr Garel-Jones voted for Mr Hurd as well. There is the story that, when a participant suddenly died at a diplomatic conference, Count Talleyrand remarked: 'Now, I wonder what he can have meant by that?' Likewise with Mr Garel-Jones: his actions or inactions provoked the same question. There were some who said that Mr Garel-Jones did not vote for Mr Hurd at all but, rather, for Mr Major. There were others who claimed that, though he may have voted for Mr Hurd, the earlier operation – the candidature of Mr Hurd – was intended to make Mr Major Prime Minister. This was Colonel Mates's theory of the split vote all over again. It was echoed, from a different perspective, by Alan Clark, who hated Mr Heseltine. Indeed, he tried to persuade Chris Patten to stand, confessing frankly that the object was to 'stop Heseltine'.

In fact Mr Garel-Jones campaigned for Mr Hurd but, for once, his diabolic powers proved ineffective. He calculated 60 votes but refrained from telling the candidate because this would have depressed him and been unfair. He knew Mr Major better than he did Mr Hurd. Mr Major had stayed several times at his house in Spain. He was the last to speak to him before he went into hospital for his tooth operation and the first to speak to him after he came out. Nevertheless he worked for Mr Hurd because he was his senior Foreign Office Minister and because, some months previously, he had promised him his support. It was as simple as that. Or perhaps it was not quite so simple. Mr Garel-Jones wanted his friend Chris Patten to lead the Conservative Party in the end. Mr Hurd was 60, the oldest of the candidates; Mr Patten was 46. Mr Garel-Jones's Spanish wife wanted him to support Mr Major but he stuck to Mr Hurd.

[45] Nicholas Budgen in the *Guardian*, 10 December 1990.

Mr Major's campaign

Mrs Thatcher was disposed of by means of a coup. Mr Major became Prime Minister through a conspiracy, which operated from Tuesday 20 November, when the result of the first ballot was announced, to Wednesday 28 November, when Mr Major became Prime Minister. A conspiracy has been defined as 'the agreement of two or more persons to effect any unlawful purpose'.[46] Mrs Thatcher would certainly regard the removal of herself as an unlawful purpose. On that Tuesday night, Mr Lamont, Mr Lilley and numerous others concluded, first, that she could no longer remain Prime Minister and, second, that they wanted Mr Major to succeed her.

Mr Major would have liked to attend the Cabinet meeting at which Mrs Thatcher announced her resignation, but was dissuaded by Mr Lamont, who advised that he would create a better impression if he appeared to be above the battle. Mr Major arrived shortly afterwards: but it would be wrong to suggest that all he had to do at this stage was to step into the driving seat of a fully furnished vehicle. He had only a short time to get his nomination in. John Gummer and Norman Lamont were selected as his proposers because Mr Gummer was considered more ecumenical in his appeal than the other possibility, Michael Howard. On 23 November they sent forth a letter:

Dear Colleague,

As John Major's proposers we thought you might like to see the statement which we have put out with the nomination.

John Major has always made himself very available as a Minister; but if you would like to speak to him at this time you have only to get in touch with us and it will be arranged.

Since nominating John we have been very heartened by the response. Support for him is coming in from all parts of the party and the country. Strong support is coming from the constituency associations.

As a former chairman of the party, John Gummer has kept in close touch with the constituencies. They are saying John Major

[46] J.W.C. Turner (ed.), *Kenny on Crime* (new edn 1952), 339.

with his personal background and experience of running the economy relates best, by far, to the voters.

John Gummer

Norman Lamont

Their statement went:

Statement by Proposer John Gummer and Seconder Norman Lamont

John Major would make the best Prime Minister for our country. We are proposing him to be the Leader of the Conservative Party.

John is the candidate most likely to unite the party, representing the next generation of Conservative leadership. He has experience of taking tough decisions in the crucial area of economic policy as well as in social and international affairs. He will lead a united party to a general election victory. We are enormously encouraged by the spontaneous groundswell of support he has received in all parts of the party.

We call on our colleagues to support John Major in the ballot next Tuesday.

The groundswell to which Mr Gummer and Mr Lamont referred was indeed apparent on the Friday, the day on which they dispatched their letter and statement. They were not making it up. It had, however, taken everyone slightly by surprise. Twenty-four hours previously the opinion of the wise had been that Mr Heseltine had performed so unexpectedly well in the first ballot that, owing to his momentum – comparable to Mrs Thatcher's in 1975 – he would be carried on to a narrow lead over Mr Major in the second ballot, with Mr Hurd in third place. The near-universal assumption was that a third ballot was inevitable, to be decided by means of a simplified version of the Alternative Vote (not, as some newspapers reported, the Single Transferable Vote), and that, as the football managers said, there was everything to play for. This was the opinion of those who prided themselves on their astuteness.

In 1975, however, Mrs Thatcher had defeated Mr Heath in the first ballot, though not by the requisite majority. Mr Heseltine had not defeated Mrs Thatcher in the same way. Oddly enough, Mrs Thatcher found herself, in relation to the rules, in the same position as she had occupied 15 years previously, with Mr Heseltine filling Mr Heath's place.

There were more important factors. The first was fear. The mood in the constituencies during the weekend of 23-5 November has been described as ugly, horrible and frightening. The villain was Mr Heseltine. However, several MPs have reported that anger about Mrs Thatcher's treatment was strongest among officers and bigwigs generally.[47] Ordinary members tended to take a more temperate line, some of them saying that 'she should have gone' on her tenth anniversary as Prime Minister. Members who were old enough to remember recalled a similar division in 1975, when the local officers supported Mr Heath, whereas the local members thought it might be time for a change. It may be significant that, despite all the fury of the weekend, not one MP was deselected. Cyril Townsend at Bexleyheath, a former personal assistant to Mr Heath, had the narrowest escape. Yet Nicholas Budgen recorded that

My constituency association was strongly in favour of Mrs Thatcher. They supported her out of personal loyalty and because they agreed with her views.[48]

The second factor was guilt. Members of Parliament echoed the *Daily Express* headline and asked themselves: What have we done? The overwhelming mood of the Tory back benches was: 'We assassinated the leader. The only act of atonement is to vote for her choice. The details of why she chose between Major and Hurd are unimportant.'[49]

It is inconceivable that she could have chosen Mr Hurd. She might have chosen Mr Tebbit if she had not cast him into darkness shortly after the Westland crisis.[50] Mr Tebbit, however, might still have chosen himself. Indeed, he had promised earlier in the year that, if no one else would stop Mr

[47] Cf Mr Heseltine's experiences at Henley, above, pp. 148-50.
[48] Budgen, art. cit.
[49] Ibid.
[50] See above, pp. 45-6.

Heseltine, he would. When it came to the issue, he worked first for Mrs Thatcher and then for Mr Major. Clearly, his standing would have split Mr Major's vote, with possibly catastrophic consequences in the third ballot.[51] Mr Major's camp were grateful for Mr Tebbit's support but tried to keep him as far as possible out of sight in case he frightened off those of more sensitive dispositions.

Mrs Thatcher's instructions were that, as Mr Lamont later put it, 'they must all go out and stop Heseltine'. In pursuance of this object, Mr Major was turned into an honorary Cantabridgian, whose election was to be arranged by former officers of the Conservative Association and the Union Society, exactly as in the old days.

Thus Mr Major's campaign manager was Norman Lamont (Fitzwilliam; President, 1964). His proposer was John Gummer (Selwyn; President, 1962). Other Cabinet members who were campaigning for him were Peter Lilley (Clare) and Michael Howard (Peterhouse; President, 1962). In charge of canvassing on his behalf was Francis Maude (Corpus Christi), while Richard Ryder (Magdalene) handled the press, one of whose ornaments, Bruce Anderson (Emmanuel), joined Mr Major's team for the campaign; though Mr Anderson had been far from a Conservative in his own undergraduate days. His most distinguished acquisition from the back benches was perhaps Terence Higgins (Caius; President, 1958), now chairman of the Treasury Committee, whose principal task was to talk to Ministers. Another of Mr Higgins's functions was to convince doubters that Mr Major had not been party to a conspiracy to remove the Prime Minister.

In this endeavour he was overwhelmingly successful, though it is difficult to know where else those who thought Mrs Thatcher had been shockingly treated could have found a resting-place. Clearly not with the proximate cause of her fall, Mr Heseltine. This left only Mr Hurd, who was considered by

---

[51] If there were four or more candidates in the second ballot, and none of them obtained an absolute majority, MPs were restricted to marking their choices 1 and 2 in the third ballot, rather than 1, 2 and 3. To this extent the third ballot was not a true application of the Alternative Vote.

some to have made matters worse for Mrs Thatcher by hinting that he would be prepared to stand in the second ballot, and was seen by Members like Anthony Beaumont-Dark (a Heseltine man) as inconceivable as a leader. And yet, all those who were at the front of Mr Major's campaign – Mr Lamont, Mr Gummer, Mr Lilley, Mr Howard, Mr Maude, above all Mr Wakeham – were the same Ministers who had crushed the Prime Minister's spirit only 24 hours previously. If this was not a conspiracy, it was certainly a coincidence.

What made everything more or less all right – anyway, less awful than it might otherwise have been – was that Mr Major was Mrs Thatcher's preferred candidate and her acknowledged heir. He had inherited rather too soon: that was the trouble. To make the fearful symmetry complete, Mr Lamont *et al.* had broken Mrs Thatcher's spirit precisely because they were the Ministers, now in their forties, whom she had preferred and regarded as on the correct doctrinal lines. Mr Major was the chief example, though he had stayed at home in Huntingdon while the others were closeted by Mrs Thatcher's room in the House.

There is no doubt that Mrs Thatcher broke her word. Mr Wakeham confirmed on *The World This Weekend* on the Sunday: 'The Prime Minister has said that she is not going to endorse any of the candidates.'[52] In fact she endorsed Mr Major. She more than endorsed him: she worked on his behalf. In this labour, hatred of Mr Heseltine and devotion to Mr Major were mingled in roughly equal portions, the former probably predominating. She telephoned Ministers:

> Now, just remember what *you* owe *me*. If it wasn't for me, you wouldn't have got into Parliament. If it wasn't for me, you wouldn't have become a Minister. If it wasn't for me, you wouldn't have stayed as a Minister. Now, all you need to do to repay me is to vote for John.[53]

It was perhaps a pity, from her own point of view, that she had

[52] Transcript, *The World This Weekend*, BBC Radio 1, 25 November 1990.
[53] Quoted in 'The Fall of Thatcher', *Economist*, 9 March 1991.

not used identical language to her Ministers on the Wednesday, except that the last sentence would have been: 'Now, all you need to do to repay me is to vote for me *and to persuade others to vote for me.*'[54]

All this is not to say that Mr Major's campaign had been planned beforehand, for it had not. Mr Lamont was not even appointed his campaign manager until half-way through Thursday morning. There was discussion about his most appropriate proposer and seconder. His campaign was run partly from 11 Downing Street, partly from 18 Gayfere Street, Westminister. This house was owned by Alan Duncan, who had contested Barnsley West in 1987 and was described as an oil trader. He was a friend of William Hague, Member for Richmond (Yorkshire), a supporter of Mr Major's, who had once caused a sensation at a Conservative conference in Blackpool by appearing on the rostrum at the age of 16 and delivering an attack on Labour in tones reminiscent of Harold Wilson. Mr Hague occasionally occupied a room in Mr Duncan's house and had keys to the premises.

The Major forces proceeded to occupy them, not altogether pleasing Mr Duncan, for it is never pleasant to have one's house invaded by strange people. He possessed 12 telephone lines, a priceless advantage in running a campaign conducted chiefly by telephone. These were there before Mr Hague's invasion, owing to Mr Duncan's occupation, but they were not connected up. This was done after the start of Mr Major's campaign on the Thursday. Mr Lamont and others are keen to emphasise this sequence. Mr Lamont and Mr Ryder proceeded to write three speeches for Mr Major to use if he won outright victory, was just ahead or was just behind. Three hours before the declaration of the result he was seen wandering around 11 Downing Street in his pyjamas. He was told that he could not go to sleep now because he was about to become Prime Minister. He replied that, in that case, he would need all the sleep he could get.[55]

---

[54] See above, p. 15ff.
[55] Art. cit. *Economist.*

The unknown Prime Minister

The result was two votes short of an outright victory for Mr Major: Major 185; Heseltine 131; Hurd, 56. Dr Hampson was in the Commons and telephoned Colonel Mates at Mr Heseltine's house. This was within a minute of the result's being announced on television, which enabled Mr Heseltine and his wife to appear immediately after the announcement and gracefully to concede defeat before the viewers' eyes. He looked windswept and noble, whereas Mrs Heseltine looked miserable and cross. When he stepped back into the house, he noticed that his children had left a book open for him to see, at A.H. Clough's poem 'Say Not the Struggle Naught Availeth'. Mr Hurd conceded defeat almost immediately afterwards, with similar grace.

With Mrs Thatcher in No. 10 were her son Mark; John Wakeham and his wife; Gordon Reece and Tim Bell; Charles Powell and Andrew Turnbull; her husband's secretary, Joy Robillard; and her dresser, Miss Crawford, inevitably known as 'Crawfie'. Someone said it was an awful thing that her colleagues had done to her. She replied: 'We're in politics, my dear.' This attitude – that politics was a rough old trade – the Prime Minister had maintained throughout the campaign. When she heard the result on television she rose and, instead of going out into Downing Street (as her companions had feared she might be about to do), she entered No. 11 by the connecting door, located Mr Major in the hall (he was telephoning Mr Hurd) and hugged him.

Mr Major went out into Downing Street to address the nation. She still wished to accompany him. Her advisers explained why she should not. At a party at Central Office on the day before she had said she was a 'good backseat driver'. She had been referring not to Mr Major in this country but to President Bush in the Gulf. The misquotation had been taken up, however. If she went outside with Mr Major, she might be seen to be confirming it. Instead, she watched Mr Major from behind a net curtain on the first floor of No. 11.[56] Mr Major, Mrs Major by his

---

[56] Stephen Fay in the *Independent on Sunday*, 2 December 1990; Frank Johnson in the *Sunday Telegraph*, 2 December 1990.

side, said:

> It's been a very clean election … I'd like to offer my very grateful thanks to Douglas Hurd and to Michael Heseltine both for the way they conducted the election and also for the very gracious way they have conceded that they will not stand on the third ballot. It is a very exciting thing to become Leader of the Conservative Party and particularly exciting, I think, to follow one of the most remarkable leaders the party has ever had.[57]

Mrs Thatcher was still Prime Minister. She remained so until the next day, when Mr Major went to the Palace, where, oddly some may think, he did not kiss hands. The Wilson-Callaghan precedent of 1976 was followed: Mrs Thatcher did not resign but informed the Queen of her intention to resign after her party had elected a new leader.[58] This could have happened after Tuesday 27 November if the contest had gone to a third ballot, as it might have done and was expected to do.

Though Mr Major was duly made Prime Minister, he was never properly elected party leader as the rules required. Cranley Onslow said it would be silly to have the colleagues back for a formal third ballot.[59] Instead, next week, Mr Major was confirmed as leader at the traditional mass meeting, held this time at the Queen Elizabeth Conference Centre, and everyone was happy.

[57] Transcript, *The Thatcher Factor Special*, Brook Productions, Channel 4, 1991,114.
[58] Private information.
[59] See above, p. 173.

9

Epilogue

He who believes that new benefits will cause great personages to forget old injuries is deceived.

Nicolo Machiavelli, *The Prince*

I have always thought complaints of ill-usage contemptible, whether from a seduced, disappointed girl or a turned-out Prime Minister.

Lord Melbourne, after his dismissal
by William IV, 1834

Mrs Thatcher resolutely followed Dylan Thomas's somewhat impertinent advice to his dying father, and declined to go gentle into that good night. She began with a few weeks of quiet, in which there were regular reports about her fluctuating mood. She quickly jettisoned the house in Dulwich which she and her husband Denis had bought for their retirement. Instead she occupied a house in Belgravia lent to her by a political admirer. Her friend Alistair McAlpine lent her one of the company's houses in Westminster for use as an office. After he retired from being joint Treasurer of the party, she was to miss him more than anyone, with the exception of Ian Gow.

The undefeated Prime Minister

Moves were made towards the setting up of a Thatcher Foundation, for the propagation of her gospel: but, owing to its inevitably political character, doubts were cast on its charitable status. Her son Mark (who would in due course inherit his father's newly-acquired baronetcy) was appointed, or appointed himself, literary agent for her forthcoming volumes of memoirs. He was said to be asking too much money. It was decided that the work should be one not of autobiography but of political biography covering her years of office 1979-90, written by two former aides, Robin Harris and John O'Sullivan, and entitled *Undefeated*.

Mrs Thatcher (who made it known that she did not wish to be called 'Lady Thatcher') was to place increasing emphasis on the absence of defeats at general elections or in the House of Commons. She was even to suggest sometimes that she had not been properly defeated as leader of the Conservative Party, having gained 204 votes to her successor's 185. In a technical sense, as we have seen, this was true.[1]

In Moscow she raised a constitutional point with the citizens, who no doubt had enough constitutional problems of their own. She claimed that, though she may have been defeated as leader of the Conservative Party, she had not been defeated as Prime Minister. She could, if she had chosen, have continued in that office until beaten by a vote in the Commons. This was heady stuff, of which Lord St John of Fawsley had been doling out measures, on television and in the newspapers, since Michael Heseltine had made his initial challenge. Lord St John's view was that party elections to choose leaders were inherently destructive of the Queen's prerogative to choose a Prime Minister, at any rate when the party concerned held a majority in the Commons.[2] It is enough to note that this view did not prevail either with the Queen or (until it was too late for any damage to be done) with Mrs Thatcher.

The disappointing Prime Minister

After some weeks she made it known that she was disappointed in her successor. He did not, it appeared, believe in anything; or, if he did, it was not what she believed in. What was surprising

[1] See above, p. 173.
[2] See Norman St John-Stevas, 'The Political Genius of Walter Bagehot' in St

was that Mrs Thatcher and some of her advisers should have thought John Major a politically kindred spirit in the first place. But they undoubtedly did. It was not merely that Mr Major was believed to be the candidate who could best defeat Mr Heseltine. He was also considered doctrinally sound.

That he was not so, as he was not, had less to do with his belief in a 'classless society', first proclaimed at the Bournemouth Conference 1990, than with his enthusiasm for the Welfare State, in particular for a free, comprehensive National Health Service. His naming of Iain Macleod as his political hero in 1989 gave or, rather, should have given the game away. Indeed, in the early 1990s mention of Macleod was political code – what, in the 1980s, had also been called 'sending out a signal' – much as mention of Disraeli had been a decade earlier.

Mrs Thatcher maintained through her friends that she had been misunderstood; as perhaps she had been. But the party managers took alarm. They had before them the awful example, or what they thought was the awful example, of Edward Heath. In fact there was little evidence that Mr Heath's disobligingness had harmed either Mrs Thatcher or the party, which had won three consecutive elections during his period in Winston Churchill's old seat on the front bench below the gangway. Still, the cry went up that Mrs Thatcher ought to go to the Lords.

Off to the Lords

It was resisted by only a few political writers, such as Paul Johnson in the *Spectator*. It was even suggested by some that Mrs Thatcher should be elevated straightaway, without remaining as Member for Finchley until the general election, which would have to take place in July 1992 at the latest. It was certainly made clear by Conservative newspapers and former colleagues that she ought to make clear her intention to resign the seat, so that the machinery for selecting a successor could be set in motion. Even old friends took a hand. Though Alistair McAlpine would say that it was no use telling her to do

John-Stevas (ed.), *The Collected Works of Walter Bagehot* (1965–86), V, 35 at 90ff.

anything, Cecil Parkinson was clear. 'Margaret,' he would advise (or words to this effect), 'it's all over. You must go to the Lords.' After some weeks of being badgered in this way, by Mr Parkinson and others, Mrs Thatcher gave in, and in so doing probably refused to let her instincts prevail. She announced that she would not be contesting Finchley at the next election. And yet, few recent former Prime Ministers had both relinquished the Commons and accepted the Lords as rapidly as she, as the following table demonstrates:

Prime Minister	Ceased being P.M.	Left the Commons	Entered the Lords
C. Attlee	1951	1955	1955
W. Churchill	1955	1964	–
A. Eden	1957	1957	1961
H. Macmillan	1963	1964	1984
A. Douglas-Home	1964	1974	1974
E. Heath	1974	–	–
H. Wilson	1976	1983	1983
J. Callaghan	1979	1987	1987

Of these, James Callaghan had enjoyed a distinguished eight years as a backbencher; whereas Lord Home, having given up his hereditary title in 1963, had emulated A.J. Balfour half-a-century earlier and served as Foreign Secretary after being Prime Minister, accepting a life peerage as Lord Home of the Hirsel.[3] Mr Heath, however, had been sulking on the back benches for 15 years. Though he had perked up with the advent of Mr Major, there could be little doubt that his change of mood owed more to the discomfiture of his successor than to the accession of a new Prime Minister.

It was suggested in some quarters that Mrs Thatcher could be Mr Major's Lord Home and serve him as Foreign Secretary, even if necessary from the Lords, as Lord Carrington had originally served Mrs Thatcher.[4] But Mr Major had made it clear when he took over that he would not welcome such an arrangement. As far as Ministers were concerned (backbenchers and the party in the country were a different matter), foreign policy had been as

---

[3] Lord Hailsham followed the same path, relinquishing his hereditary peerage for the same reason as Lord Home in 1963, and becoming Lord Hailsham of St Marylebone in 1970 to assume the office of Lord Chancellor.

[4] See e.g. *Independent on Sunday*, 1 September 1990.

powerful a cause of Mrs Thatcher's fall as the poll tax. Rather, it was Mr Heath that the fearful Conservatives had in their minds. Mrs Thatcher might well say that she had been right all along, as Mr Heath had been saying about himself.

A false rhetoric

And, indeed, there were signs of almost as severe a break between Mr Major and Mrs Thatcher as there had earlier been between her and Mr Heath. It was less a question of policies – though policies were involved too – as of what Maurice Cowling and the Cambridge Conservative historians like to call *rhetoric*. Mrs Thatcher's rhetoric of the 1987-90 period had come to sound increasingly false.

Two of her achievements remained unchallengeable, except by the very silly: the sale of council houses and the reform of the trade unions. It was perhaps significant that these changes were made in her first term, by Ministers, respectively Michael Heseltine and Jim Prior, who were ideologically antipathetic to her. But through the rest of the city the mist swirled, the rainwater dripped and the noise of buildings cracking in the night could be discerned. The economic miracle was undoubtedly over. But had it ever really taken place at all? Those who had doubted the claim all along – Ian Aitken, Ian Gilmour, Wynne Godley, Roy Jenkins and, perhaps above all, William Keegan – began to look increasingly justified in their opinions. In retrospect, it can be seen that there were two crucial events.

One was economic or, rather, financial: the City crash of autumn 1987. Not only did it start the great inflation, because the Government, wholly understandably (and with the support of the Opposition), wished to avoid any repetition of 1929-31.[5] It also symbolised the end of that period of greed, ostentation and conceit with which the name of Margaret Thatcher will always be linked, as will that of Ronald Reagan. In a way this will be unfair: for she herself was always kindly, frugal and, in her

[5] See above, p. 111.

fashion, modest. But there was a moment, in the mid-1980s, when British society became quite horrible. It took a recession to restore a modicum of decency and responsibility.

The other crucial event was political or, rather, personal: the tenth anniversary of Mrs Thatcher's premiership in 1989. She did not care for the celebrations surrounding this occasion; shunned the newspapers and avoided the television (that is, avoided watching television) with even more determination than usual; instead gave interviews proclaiming her intention to carry on. Her instinct told her that the time had come to say good-bye. But she neglected to follow it.

The connections lit up

Her departure confounded the professors of politics. They had long maintained, certainly since the publication of John Mackintosh's *The British Cabinet* in 1962, that the position of a Prime Minister in good health and with an adequate parliamentary majority was impregnable. To be fair to the academic observers, the circumstances of November 1990 may never be repeated. Nevertheless there is a lesson. It is imprudent to go around stating rules about prime ministerial power as if they must be true at all times and in all places. John Wakeham said to the present writer: 'She will to her dying day think it was a plot.' John Biffen said: 'You know those maps on the Paris Metro that light up when you press a button to go from A to B? Well, it was like that. Someone pressed a button, and all the connections lit up.'

Appendix

Declared Supporters of the Candidates

for Michael Heseltine

Julian Amery
Spencer Batiste
Anthony Beaumont-Dark
William Benyon
Sir Antony Buck
John Carlise
Lord Carrington
Paul Channon
Derek Conway
Patrick Cormack
Julian Critchley
Quentin Davies
Tim Devlin
Den Dover
Sir Peter Emery
David Evans
Keith Hampson
Alan Haselhurst
Christopher Hawkins
Jerry Hayes
Sir Barney Hayhoe
Kenneth Hind
Sir Geoffrey Howe

David Howell
David Hunt
Sir Ian Gilmour
Sir Philip Goodhart
Ian Grist
Dame Jill Knight
Michael Knowles
David Knox
Michael Latham
Nigel Lawson
John Lee
Edward Leigh
Sir Neil Macfarlane
Tony Marlow
Michael Mates
Michael Morris
Sir Charles Morrison
Anthony Nelson
David Nicholson
Emma Nicholson
James Pawsey
Elizabeth Peacock
Barry Porter

William Powell
Sir David Price
Lord Prior
Keith Raffan
Robert Rhodes James
Lord Rippon
Sir Wyn Roberts
Peter Rost
Lord St John of Fawsley
Nicholas Soames
Robin Squire
Ivor Stanbrook
Sir Peter Tapsell
Peter Temple-Morris
Patrick Thompson
Malcolm Thornton
David Trippier
Peter Walker
Sir Dennis Walters
Charles Wardle
Kenneth Warren
Bowen Wells
Jerry Wiggin

for Douglas Hurd

Tony Baldry
Henry Bellingham
Peter Bottomley
Virginia Bottomley
Julian Brazier
Peter Brooke
Nicholas Budgen
Kenneth Carlisle
Matthew Carrington
Lynda Chalker
Kenneth Clarke
Michael Fallon
Tristan Garel-Jones

Jeremy Hanley
David Heathcoat-Amory
Douglas Hogg
Lord Home
Sir Peter Hordern
Alan Howarth
Andrew Hunter
Robert Key
Tom King
Andrew Mackay
Richard Needham
Steven Norris
Chris Patten

John Patten
Timothy Raison
Malcolm Rifkind
Nicholas Scott
Sir Giles Shaw
Ian Taylor
Peter Viggers
William Waldegrave
Sir John Wheeler
Lord Whitelaw
Ann Widdecombe
Tim Yeo

for John Major

Jonathan Aitken
James Arbuthnot
Jeffrey Archer
Jacques Arnold
Robert Atkins
Nicholas Bennett
Andrew Bowden
Graham Bright
Alan Clark
Anthony Coombs
David Davis
Lord James Douglas-Hamilton
Tony Favell
Barry Field
Michael Forsyth
Eric Forth
Cecil Franks
Roger Freeman
John Gummer

William Hague
Archie Hamilton
Robert Hayward
Terence Higgins
Michael Howard
Robert Hughes
Michael Jack
Robert Jackson
Roger King
Norman Lamont
Ian Lang
Peter Lilley
Sir Nicholas Lyell
John MacGregor
David Maclean
John Maples
David Martin
Francis Maude
David Mellor

Andrew Mitchell
John Moore
Malcolm Moss
Gerry Neale
Michael Nenbert
Tony Newton
Michael Portillo
Angela Rumbold
Richard Ryder
Gillian Shephard
Andrew Stewart
Norman Tebbit
Margaret Thatcher
Peter Thurnham
David Waddington
John Wakeham
Bill Walker
John Watts
Ann Winterton
Nicholas Winterton

Select Bibliography

Bruce Anderson: *John Major* (1991)
Humphry Berkeley: *The Power of the Prime Minister* (1968)
  Crossing the Floor (1972)
Robert Blake: *The Unknown Prime Minister* (1955)
  The Conservative Party from Peel to Thatcher (new edn 1985)
Samuel Brittan: *The Price of Economic Freedom* (1970)
R.A. Butler: *The Art of the Possible* (1971)
  The Art of Memory (1982)
Ronald Butt: *The Power of Parliament* (2nd edn 1969)
David Carlton: *Anthony Eden* (1981)
Peter Catterall (ed.): *Contemporary Britain* (1990)
  Contemporary Britain (1991)
John Colville: *The Fringes of Power* (1985)
Tim Congdon: *Monetarism Lost* (CPS, 1989)
  EMU Now? (CPS, 1990)
Patrick Cosgrave: *Margaret Thatcher* (1978)
  Thatcher: the First Term (1985)
David Cox (ed.): *The Walden Interviews* (1990)
Julian Critchley: *Heseltine: the Unauthorised Biography* (1987)
Susan Crosland: *Looking Out, Looking In* (1987)
R.H.S. Crossman: Introduction to Walter Bagehot: *The English Constitution*
  (Fontana edn 1963)
Macdonald Daly and Alexander George (eds): *Margaret Thatcher in Her Own
  Words* (1987)
S.A. de Smith: *Constitutional and Administrative Law* (5th edn 1985)
K.D. Ewing and C.A. Gearty: *Freedom Under Thatcher* (1990)
Henry Fairlie: *The Life of Politics* (1968)
'The Fall of Thatcher', *Economist*, 9 March 1991
Nigel Fisher: *Iain Macleod* (1973)
Michael Forsyth: *The Case for a Poll Tax* (CPC, 1985)
Norman Fowler: *Ministers Decide* (1991)
Ian Gilmour: *The Body Politic* (1969)
  Inside Right (1977)
  Britain Can Work (1983)
  'Holding All the Strings', *London Review of Books*, 27 July 1989
Philip Goodhart: *The 1922* (1973)
J.A.G. Griffith: *The Politics of the Judiciary* (4th edn 1991)

Lord Hailsham: *A Sparrow's Flight* (1990)

Morrison Halcrow: *Keith Joseph* (1989)

Kenneth Harris: Interview with Margaret Thatcher, *Observer*, 25 February 1979

Robert Harris: *Good and Faithful Servant* (1990)

Michael Heseltine: *Where There's a Will* (1987)

    The Challenge of Europe (1989)

Lord Home: *The Way the Wind Blows* (1976)

Alistair Horne: *Macmillan* (2 vols 1988-9)

Anthony Howard: *RAB: the Life of R.A. Butler* (1987)

Geoffrey Howe: 'Sovereignty and Interdependence,' 66 *International Affairs* (1990)

Douglas Hurd: *An End to Promises* (1979)

George Hutchinson: *Edward Heath* (1970)

    The Last Edwardian at No. 10 (1980)

Bernard Ingham: *Kill the Messenger* (1991)

Robert Rhodes James: *Anthony Eden* (1986)

Peter Jenkins: *Mrs Thatcher's Revolution* (1987)

Christopher Johnson: *The Economy Under Mrs Thatcher 1979-1990* (1991)

Paul Johnson: 'Was the Palace to Blame?' *New Statesman*, 24 January 1964

William Keegan: *Mr Lawson's Gamble* (1989)

Earl of Kilmuir: *Political Adventure* (1964)

Keith Kyle: *Suez* (1991)

Nigel Lawson: 'Riddled with Errors, Reeking of Bile', *Spectator*, 13 July 1991

Layfield Committee Report, Cmnd 6453 (1976)

Magnus Linklater and David Leigh: *Not With Honour* (1986)

John P. Mackintosh: *The British Cabinet* (2nd edn 1967)

Iain Macleod: 'The Tory Leadership,' *Spectator*, 17 January 1964

Anthony Meyer: *Stand Up and Be Counted* (1990)

Harold Nicolson: *King George the Fifth* (1952)

    Diaries and Letters 1945-62 (1968)

Paying for Local Government, Cmnd 1794 (1986)

Edward Pearce: *The Quiet Rise of John Major* (1991)

Jim Prior: *A Balance of Power* (1986)

Francis Pym: *The Politics of Consent* (1984)

Redcliffe-Maude Commission Report, Cmnd 4040 (1969)

Peter G. Richards: *The Reformed Local Government System* (1973)

Peter Riddell: *The Thatcher Era* (new edn 1991)

Nicholas Ridley: *My Style of Government* (1991)

Kenneth Rose: *King George V* (1983)

Norman St John-Stevas: 'The Political Genius of Walter Bagehot' in Norman St John-Stevas (ed.): *The Collected Works of Walter Bagehot*, V (1974)

Robert Shepherd: *The Power Brokers* (1991)

Adam Smith Institute: *Omega File* (1985)

John Stewart and Gerry Stoker (eds): *The Future of Local Government* (1989)

James Stuart: *Within the Fringe* (1967)

Margaret Thatcher: *Let Our Children Grow Tall: Selected Speeches 1975-7* (CPS, 1977)

Norman Tebbit: *Upwardly Mobile* (1988)

Treasury and Civil Service Committee: International Monetary Co-ordination, HC 304 of 1988-9 (1989)
Alan Walters: *Sterling in Danger* (1990)
Dennis Walters: *Not Always with the Pack* (1989)
Nicholas Wapshott and George Brock: *Thatcher* (1983)
Hugo Young: *One of Us* (new edn 1991)
    and Anne Sloman: *The Thatcher Phenomenon* (1986)

Index